Other Titles by *Langaa* RPCIG

Francis B. Nyamnjoh
Stories from Abakwa
Mind Searching
The Disillusioned African
The Convert
Souls Forgotten
Married But Available

Dibussi Tande
No Turning Back. Poems of Freedom 1990-1993
Scribbles from the Den: Essays on Politics and Collective Memory in Cameroon

Kangsen Feka Wakai
Fragmented Melodies

Ntemfac Ofege
Namondo. Child of the Water Spirits
Hot Water for the Famous Seven

Emmanuel Fru Doh
Not Yet Damascus
The Fire Within
Africa's Political Wastelands: The Bastardization of Cameroon
Oriki'badan
Wading the Tide

Thomas Jing
Tale of an African Woman

Peter Wuteh Vakunta
Grassfields Stories from Cameroon
Green Rape: Poetry for the Environment
Majunga Tok: Poems in Pidgin English
Cry, My Beloved Africa
No Love Lost
Straddling The Mungo: A Book of Poems in English & French

Ba'bila Mutia
Coils of Mortal Flesh

Kehbuma Langmia
Titabet and the Takumbeng
An Evil Meal of Evil

Victor Elame Musinga
The Barn
The Tragedy of Mr. No Balance

Ngessimo Mathe Mutaka
Building Capacity: Using TEFL and African Languages as Development-oriented Literacy Tools

Milton Krieger
Cameroon's Social Democratic Front: Its History and Prospects as an Opposition Political Party, 1990-2011

Sammy Oke Akombi
The Raped Amulet
The Woman Who Ate Python
Beware the Drives: Book of Verse

Susan Nkwentie Nde
Precipice
Second Engagement

Francis B. Nyamnjoh & Richard Fonteh Akum
The Cameroon GCE Crisis: A Test of Anglophone Solidarity

Joyce Ashuntantang & Dibussi Tande
Their Champagne Party Will End! Poems in Honor of Bate Besong

Emmanuel Achu
Disturbing the Peace

Rosemary Ekosso
The House of Falling Women

Peterkins Manyong
God the Politician

George Ngwane
The Power in the Writer: Collected Essays on Culture, Democracy & Development in Africa

John Percival
The 1961 Cameroon Plebiscite: Choice or Betrayal

Albert Azeyeh
Réussite scolaire, faillite sociale : généalogie mentale de la crise de l'Afrique noire francophone

Aloysius Ajab Amin & Jean-Luc Dubois
Croissance et développement au Cameroun : d'une croissance équilibrée à un développement équitable

Carlson Anyangwe
Imperialistic Politics in Cameroun:
Resistance & the Inception of the Restoration of the Statehood of Southern Cameroons

Bill F. Ndi
K'Cracy, Trees in the Storm and Other Poems
Map: Musings On Ars Poetica

Kathryn Toure, Therese Mungah Shalo Tchombe & Thierry Karsenti
ICT and Changing Mindsets in Education

Charles Alobwed'Epie
The Day God Blinked

G.D. Nyamndi
Babi Yar Symphony
Whether losing, Whether winning
Tussles: Collected Plays

Samuel Ebelle Kingue
Si Dieu était tout un chacun de nous?

Ignasio Malizani Jimu
Urban Appropriation and Transformation : bicycle, taxi and handcart operators in Mzuzu, Malawi

Justice Nyo' Wakai:
Under the Broken Scale of Justice: The Law and My Times

John Eyong Mengot
A Pact of Ages

Ignasio Malizani Jimu
Urban Appropriation and Transformation: Bicycle Taxi and Handcart Operators

Joyce B. Ashuntantang
Landscaping and Coloniality: The Dissemination of Cameroon Anglophone Literature

Jude Fokwang
Mediating Legitimacy: Chieftaincy and Democratisation in Two African Chiefdoms

Michael A. Yanou
Dispossession and Access to Land in South Africa: an African Perspevctive

Tikum Mbah Azonga
Cup Man and Other Stories

John Nkemngong Nkengasong
Letters to Marions (And the Coming Generations)

Amady Aly Dieng
Les étudiants africains et la littérature négro-africaine d'expression française

Tah Asongwed
Born to Rule: Autobiography of a life President

Frida Menkan Mbunda
Shadows From The Abyss

Bongasu Tanla Kishani
A Basket of Kola Nuts

Fo Angwafo III S.A.N of Mankon
Royalty and Politics: The Story of My Life

Basil Diki
The Lord of Anomy

Scribbles from the Den

Essays on Politics and Collective Memory in Cameroon

By
Dibussi Tande

Langaa Research & Publishing CIG
Mankon, Bamenda

Publisher:
Langaa RPCIG
Langaa Research & Publishing Common Initiative Group
P.O. Box 902 Mankon
Bamenda
North West Region
Cameroon
Langaagrp@gmail.com
www.langaa-rpcig.net

Distributed outside N. America by African Books Collective
orders@africanbookscollective.com
www.africanbookscollective.com

Distributed in N. America by Michigan State University Press
msupress@msu.edu
www.msupress.msu.edu

ISBN: 9956-558-91-5

© Dibussi Tande 2009

DISCLAIMER

All views expressed in this publication are those of the author and do not necessarily reflect the views of Langaa RPCIG.

Content

Dedication ix
Preface xi
Foreword xv

Part One: The Anglophone File
1. Language as a Tool for Exclusion: Reflections on Cameroon's National Bilingualism Day 3
2. Culture and Political Statehood: Another Perspective on Southern Cameroons Nationalism 7
3. The Politics of Pidgin English in Cameroon 11
4. Cameroon Literature in English – Vibrant but Invisible 16
5. A Baobab Fell in the Forest But Did They Notice? Bate Besong or the Symbol of the Cameroon Divide 19
6. Cameroon Unification: Were Southern Cameroons Leaders Inexperienced and Illiterate? 24
7. Revisiting The Legacy of Dr. EML Endeley 28

Part Two: Citenzenship in the Global Village
8. Brain Drain: Why are Cameroonian Medical Doctors Leaving? 35
9. Dual Citizenship (I): Time for a Long Overdue National Debate ... 40
10. Dual Citizenship (II): A Win-Win Situation 44
11. Citizenship in the Age of Globalization 49

Part Three: Collective Memory
12. Individual Memory and Collective Amnesia: Where are the Political Memoirs? 53
13. The Cultural Alienation and Historical Amnesia of Public Spaces in Cameroon 57
14. France's Dirty War in Cameroon: The Assassination of Félix-Roland Moumié 60
15. Once Upon a Time… Osende Afana 65
16. Repaid in his Own Coins: Ahmadou Ahidjo and the Politics of Ostracism 76

Part Four: The University in Crisis

17. When History Repeats Itself: The Government Spin Machine and the UB Crisis 83
18. Deconstructing Regional Balance and Higher Education in Cameroon 88
19. University of Buea: What is the Cost of Quality Education? 92
20. Regional Balance, Educational Quotas and (Under)development in Northern Cameroon 96
21. Stuck on the Fringes of the Knowledge Economy 100

Part Five: Presidential Politics

22. President Paul Biya: 25 Years and Counting 107
23. How to Eliminate Presidential Term Limits (Notes from the Biya Playbook) 112
24. Biyaism Without Biya? The Battle for Regime Change in Cameroon 115
25. «La Politique de Pourrissement»: Why Biya Remains Defiant 117

Part Six: Political Pluralism

26. Indigenous Minorities and Political Pluralism in Cameroon 123
27. Cameroon: Why So Many Political Parties? 126
28. State Funding of Political Parties: A Democratic Imperative or Hush Money for the Opposition? 130
29. Social Democratic Front (SDF): A Dream Derailed? 134

Part Seven: Profiles of Courage

30. A Dream Deferred: Emmanuel Njela Nfor 139
31. Isaac Menyoli: Living Up to the Olympic Creed 141
32. Sita Bella: The Final Journey of a Renaissance Woman 143
33. Joe la Conscience: Cameroon's Forgotten Prisoner of Conscience ... 144
34. Jean-Marc Ela – Remembering Africa's "Liberation Theologian" ... 147

Part Eight: Law, Justice & Corruption

35. Trail of Death: Maintaining Law and Order in Cameroon 153
36. Can Cameroon's New Criminal Procedure Code Deliver "Justice with a Human Face"? 156
37. The Untouchables (Politically Mediated Loans and Political Impunity in Cameroon) 160
38. 100 Ways to Pilfer a Public Corporation: Notes from the Trial of Gerard Ondo Ndong 163
39. How Cameroon Auctioned Its Internet Namespace 169

Part Nine: Random Notes

40. Gerontocracy in Cameroon – These Old Men Who Govern Us 175
41. Football and the "Burden of Patriotism" in Africa 179
42. When Private and Public Spaces Collide: Power, Sex and Politics in Cameroon 181
43. Political Rumor in Cameroon: The "Weapon of Mass Destruction" of the Masses 184
44. Mystery and Intrigue in a Tropical Paradise – Revisiting the Speedboat Attack on Limbe 187
45. The Government of Cameroon on a PR Offensive in the United States 192
46. The Lake Nyos Disaster 20 Years After: Revisiting the Israeli Connection 196
47. Zimbabwe at 27: When a Fairy Tale Becomes a Gory Nightmare 200
48. Obama and Africa: Change and Changelessness in US Foreign Policy 204
49. In Search of the Elusive "Big Foot": Where are the Cameroonian Bloggers? 208

Dedication

To Mokali and Terese
for the unconditional support

Preface

The last decade has witnessed a dramatic surge in "citizen journalism" which has effectively asserted itself as a legitimate alternative voice to the mainstream media. Bowman and Willis describe citizen journalism as:

> The act of a citizen, or group of citizens, playing an active role in the process of collecting, reporting, analyzing and disseminating news and information. The intent of this participation is to provide independent, reliable, accurate, wide-ranging and relevant information that a democracy requires.

According to Dan Gillmor, a leading advocate of citizen journalism,

> What became known as citizen journalism is the result of the digital era's democratization of media – wide access to powerful, inexpensive tools of media creation; and wide access to what people created, via digital networks – after a long stretch when manufacturing-like mass media prevailed. Blogging was one of the first major tools in this genre....

Without doubt, weblogs or blogs have been the driving force behind the exponential growth of citizen-generated media in recent years. According to Technorati's *State of the Blogosphere / 2008* report, there were an estimated 184 million blogs worldwide as of August 2008. Today, thousands of Africans at home and in the Diaspora have joined the blogosphere to create vibrant cyber-communities that provide alternative analyses and fresh perspectives on events taking place in the continent. As Zimbabwean blogger *Zimbabwean Pundit* explained in an August 15, 2005 post titled "The State of the African Blogosphere":

> This miracle of cyberspace – that it allows for cheap communication unfettered by geopolitical boundaries – has made it possible for the African odyssey to share center stage alongside the big issues in the west, thanks in part to Africa's bloggers... African bloggers are retelling the African story from their authentic perspective with an avid passion for their countries and continent to boot. It is impossible to read the posts on any of the blogs in the African blogosphere and come away without a sense of the writer's deep connection to the country and continent.

And all over Africa, regimes which once had absolute control over the flow of information are taking note of, and trying to adapt to, this new phenomenon.

In January 2006, I joined the fast growing and vibrant African blogosphere when I launched my blog, *Scribbles from the Den* (http://www.dibussi.com/) – a platform where I could provide that alternative perspective on events and issues, particularly Cameroonian issues, and which would also serve as an unfettered space for readers to freely comment on these issues without fear or favor. For half a century, Cameroonians have been systematically deprived of the appropriate *repères historiques* or historical reference points that would enable them to analyze political and other events in the country in an informed manner, and place these events in their appropriate historical and geo-political context. Over the last three years, *Scribbles from the Den* has, from its little corner in the blogosphere, tried to recreate those reference points by taking a fresh look at events of the past and going beyond the official narrative when interpreting today's events. The growing popularity of the blog seems to indicate that it is playing a role, albeit a small one, in shaping national discourse on key issues of our time.

Today, *Scribbles from the Den* is one of the most consulted alternative/non-traditional media sources of news analysis on Cameroon. At the beginning of April 2009, it had 400 posts (including podcasts and videos), 2,463 reader comments, over 300,000 individual page hits and over 168,000 unique visitors from a record 195 countries. *Scribbles from the Den* has consistently ranked as the number one Cameroonian blog on *Afrigator*, Africa's largest social media aggregator and blog directory. It also won the Judges' Vote for the *Best International Blog* during the *2008 Black Weblog Award*.

This volume consists of 49 selected essays which appeared on *Scribbles from the Den* between 2006 and 2009. They cover a variety of key issues such as Cameroon's stalled democratic transition, the country's never-ending higher education crisis, the "Anglophone problem," and the brain drain, among others. It also includes a couple of non-Cameroonian articles on the political crisis in Zimbabwe and the impact of the Obama presidency on Africa. Hopefully, the general public, from the casual observer of the Cameroonian political scene to researchers and students of African/Cameroonian affairs, will find this collection of essays useful.

While editing this text, I tried as much as possible to remain faithful to the look and feel of the original blog postings, many of which were interactive articles with hyperlinks and/or embedded videos and podcasts. This is why there are no footnotes and endnotes in the text. This omission is also explained by the fact that a good number of the hyperlinks in the original postings are now broken due to "the ephemeral and transient nature of Web pages" – a growing problem for digital libraries and academic citations. I have, however, included a reference section at the end of each chapter whenever possible.

This collection of essays would not have been possible without the dedicated readers of *Scribbles from the Den*, whose regular visits and comments have made the blog a very dynamic, interactive and entertaining one, and encouraged me to keep on blogging, in spite of an increasingly busy schedule. Special thanks go to Kangsen Wakai who meticulously proofread the manuscript. I am, however, most indebted to my wife Terese and son Mokali who have selflessly and lovingly given me the necessary time and space to pursue my interest in blogging and writing at the expense of more quality family time. This collection is especially dedicated to them.

Chicago, April 14, 2009

References

Bowman, S. & Willis, C. (2003). *We Media: How audiences are shaping the future of news and information*. Reston, Va.: The Media Center at the American Press Institute.

Gillmor, D. (2008). *Where Did "Citizen Journalist" Come From?* Retrieved March 15, 2009 from *The Center for Citizen Media* Blog: http://citmedia.org/blog/2008/07/14/where-did-citizen-journalist-come-from/

Heavens, A. (December, 20 2005). *African bloggers find their voice. BBC Focus on Africa magazine*. Retrieved March 15, 2009 from: http://news.bbc.co.uk/2/hi/africa/4512290.stm

Jewels in the Jungle. (2005). *African bloggers find their voice: My reflections*. Retrieved March 15, 2009 from: http://jewelsnthejungle.blogspot.com/2005/12/african-bloggers-find-their-voice-my.html

Sellitto, C. (2004). *Web Cit(ation)es in scholarly articles*. Retrieved March 15, 2009 from: Melbourne.http://ausweb.scu.edu.au/aw04/papers/refereed/sellitto/paper.html

Technorati. (2008). *State of the Blogosphere / 2008*. Retrieved March 15, 2009 from: http://technorati.com/blogging/state-of-the-blogosphere/

Foreword

Creative Appropriation of New Technologies: Dibussi Tande at the Forefront of Cameroonian and African Blogging

When Dibussi Tande sent me an email requesting a preface to this collection of essays on politics and collective memory scribbled from his blogging den since 2006, I readily agreed in recognition of the outstanding contributions he has made in promoting the creative appropriation of ICTs by Cameroonian journalists, intellectuals and the blogging public. In three years Dibussi Tande has established himself not only as a leading and award-winning blogger, but also as a critical reviewer of African blogging in a weekly *Pambazuka News* column titled "Blogging Africa". As I write this afternoon of March 20th 2009, his blog, *Scribbles from the Den*, has registered 305,045 page hits.

In collaboration with Emil Mondoa, Dibussi Tande established *JimbiMedia* in 2004 with the primary objective of using affordable blogging technology to give a solid online presence to powerful African voices – creative people, trendsetters, academics, journalists, etc. – through personal blogs that could easily be updated from any place that had internet connectivity. The simplicity of the platform entails that one does not need more than basic computer skills to be relevant, an aspect critical in contexts where many newsrooms still do not afford computers and the necessary technical sophistication to maximize their use.

In Cameroon where repressive laws and censorship have contributed to stifling freedom of expression and drying out vital sources of meaningful news and information, the press has been reduced to a level of underdevelopment that makes print runs perpetually difficult to predict, and yields little profits beyond what it takes to barely subsist. The result of repression has been a dearth in cultural creativity and production. The *JimbiMedia* initiative has thus been generally welcomed, particularly by the Anglophone community who have felt politically, economically and culturally marginalized since independence and reunification with their Francophone counterparts.

JimbiMedia has so far created blogs for 4 Cameroonian newspapers,[1] 3 online and print magazines,[2] about 25 intellectuals, and 5 cultural groups and non-profit organizations. It has also created one activist blog, *France Watch*[3] and a collective blog, *Imhotep*.[4] *JimbiMedia*'s main achievement – apart from giving African intellectuals, groups and newspapers a larger audience than they would have ever imagined – is its introduction of the concept of personal websites and blogging to

---

1. http://www.postnewsline.com; http://www.leffortcamerounais.info;
   http://www.leffortcamerounais.com; http://www.entrepreneurnewsonline.com

2. http://www.successstorymagazine.info; http://www.palapalamagazine;
   http://www.summitmagazine.net/.com

3. http://www.francewatcher.org/

4. http://www.greatimhotep.com/

Cameroonians, particularly the Cameroonian Diaspora. *JimbiMedia* blogs serve as forums for heated and informative discussions about key cultural and socio-political issues of the day. In his blog, Dibussi Tande has focused on social commentary bearing on politics, collective memory and socio-economic developments within Cameroon and of relevance to Anglophone Cameroonians in particular.

If one takes *The Post* newspaper for example, one sees how a skills inadequacy in the newsroom together with weak telecommunications infrastructure, prompted the paper in 2004 to launch its online version (http://www.postnewsline.com/) in collaboration with *JimbiMedia*. This version, which primarily targeted a diasporic audience, at the same time as it relied on the expertise and resources in the development and administration of its website, lasted till March 2009 when it was replaced by a more conventional website, after clocking well over 8 million visits. Writing on this experiment in 2005, Lilian Ndangam argued that this model of online publishing illustrates the nature and significance of transnational relationships in the diffusion and adoption of online publishing. It simultaneously reflects an alternative transnational practice through which African migrants engage with their home of origin from which they draw culturally to recreate identities in their host cultures.[5] Dibussi Tande has been quite instrumental in this symbiosis, as *The Post* has regularly fed his Den, just has the Den has fed from *The Post*.

Both Dibussi's Den and the other blogs within the *JimbiMedia* staple are very democratic in their design. Blog owners do not have to rely on a webmaster to update the blog as is the case with standard websites, the reader is not just a passive consumer but an interactive participant who is free to comment any story – usually anonymously – with little or no restriction.[6] The challenges of connectivity posed by low bandwidth and high costs notwithstanding, Anglophone Cameroonians, big and small, at home and in the Diaspora, have over the past five years harnessed the ICTs (digital video, digital photography, interneting, cell-phoning, reporting, SMSing and blogging) in ways indicative of what has been termed 'citizen journalism'.

Indeed, thanks to innovations in ICT, the structure and content of the conventional state and private media in Cameroon are being challenged and compelled to be more sensitive to cultural diversity and minority interests. The very same innovations facilitate new media cultures and practices through the possibilities they offer radical, alternative, small independent, local, community media and blogs. This is evidenced in the Anglophone Cameroonian journalist's embrace of the blogging phenomenon as a means of circumventing in-house media gatekeepers and their appropriation of pseudonyms which protect their identity as they challenge hegemonic structures. Through their capacity for flexibility and accessibility, the ICTs that make possible new media, cultural communities hitherto marginalised are better catered for even within the framework of dominance by the global

---

5. See Ndangam, L. (2008). "Free lunch? Cameroon's diaspora and online news publishing." *New Media and Society*. 10 (4), 585-604.

6. See Chapter Forty-nine of this collection for a discussion of how far Cameroonian blogging has come since *JimbiMedia* introduced its initiative in 2004.

cultural industries. The current advantage being taken of ICTs by cultural communities the world over seeking recognition and representation should be seen in this light, and above all, as an example from which conventional journalism draw.

What is exciting about the *JimbiMedia* initiatives are the opportunities it provides for "citizen journalism." I've had occasion in the past to criticize mainstream journalism in Africa for being so neatly detached from what is really going on in the ordinary lives of people and how they make news, how they gather news and how they communicate. It is because our journalists, by sticking to Western canons of journalism miss the point of African value added in terms of how people communicate and how they share communication with one another. And Africa has a much richer landscape in this regard that can inform journalism. Before citizen journalism came to the West, you had citizen journalism all over Africa. So, how did the excluded succeed in making news about their experiences and sharing this news among themselves? Today, with ICTs this seems like something new, but if we look at Africa, people have been using ways like 'radio trottoir' to obtain information, share it and create possibilities where normal channels were beyond their reach. So citizen journalism through blogging such as Dibussi's and others promoted by *JimbiMedia* is something that helps readers overcome an old problem, that of devising and investing in popular forms of communication and blending these with conventional media for the best of society.

Journalism, to be relevant to social consolidation and renewal in Cameroon, must embrace professional and social responsibilities in tune with the collective aspirations of Cameroonians. In a context where economic and political constraints have often hindered the fulfillment of this expectation, the advent and increasing adoption of information and communication technologies (ICTs) offer fascinating new possibilities. While journalists are usually open to new technologies in their work, their practice of journalism has not always capitalized upon the creative ways in which the public they target for and with information adopt, adapt and use the very same technologies. The future for democracy and the relevance of journalism therein would have much to learn from the creative ways in which Cameroonians are currently relating to innovations in ICTs. The same popular creativity that has been largely ignored by conventional journalism in the past is remarkable today all over Cameroon and amongst Cameroonians in the Diaspora. There is abundant evidence that individual Cameroonians and the cultural communities they represent have mostly refused to celebrate victimhood. As we note from the essays in this volume, they seek to harness, within the limits of the structural constraints facing them, whatever possibilities are available to contest and seek inclusion. Hence the need to highlight the importance of blending conventional and citizen journalism through the myriad possibilities offered by ICTs to harness both democracy and its nemesis. The current context of globalization facilitated by the ICTs offers exciting new prospects not only for Cameroonians citizens and journalists to compete and complement one another, but also an opportunity for new solidarities to challenge undemocratic forces, ideologies and practices that stand in the way of social progress in Cameroon and globally.

The lessons for Cameroonian journalism of such creative appropriation processes underway are obvious. Comprehending the overall development, usage and application of ICTs within African social spaces would take the fusion of keen observation and complex analysis to capture structural, gendered, class, generational, racial and spatial dimensions of the phenomenon. A dialectical interrogation of the processes involved promises a more accurate grasp of the linkages than would impressionistic, linear and prescriptive narratives of technological determinism. Technologies are always shaped by the socio-economic, political and cultural forces at play in society. Power relations mean that access and content are often determined by forces independent of a given technology. For journalists therefore to effectively play a central role, there is need to understand the structural constraints to the empowerment of ordinary Cameroonians and their various communities, and to bringing about an enabling environment for ICT driven-journalism and development in the country.

If Cameroon journalism pays closer attention to the creative usages of ICTs by ordinary Cameroonians, Cameroon journalists could begin to think less of professional journalism in the conventional sense, and more of seeking ways to blend the information and communication cultures of the general public with their conventional canon and practices, to give birth to a conventional-cum-citizen journalism that is of greater relevance to Cameroon and its predicaments. Dibussi Tande, in this collection, shares with us a bumper harvest of essays that are instructive on how we could begin to go about the process of harnessing blogging and the ICTs in the interest of positive social change in Cameroon.

Francis B. Nyamnjoh
Professor of Anthropology, University of Cape Town, South Africa

Part One

The Anglophone File

1

Language as a Tool for Exclusion: Reflections on Cameroon's National Bilingualism Day

February 03, 2006: Today is National Bilingualism Day in Cameroon. I didn't even know that such a day existed until I read about it in the Monday, January 30, 2006 online edition of the Government-owned daily, *Cameroon Tribune*. According to an article in the newspaper titled "Bilingualism is still a Challenge," this day was instituted because,

> Bilingualism is enshrined in the Constitution of Cameroon since September 1st, 1961, when English and French were recognised as official languages, with equal status in every sphere of national life. Bilingualism was chosen, not only as an instrument to ensure equity, but also as a pivot of socio-economic integration for the two entities, Francophone and Anglophones, who opted for unification.

Now, that it is the political theory, the national fairy tale.

Here is the reality as reported by the Buea-based *The Post* newspaper: "French Frustrates ASMAC Anglophone Students," screams the headlines in an article about the plight of English-speaking students at the Advanced School of Mass Communications in the University of Yaoundé. According to *The Post*:

> Only 3 of the 42 permanent lecturers in the Advanced School of Mass Communication, ASMAC, are of English expression. Over the years, English-speaking students in ASMAC, just like other higher education institutions in Yaoundé, receive lectures almost exclusively in French. Some English-speaking students have described this situation as 'deplorable'.

Yes, that is the real Cameroon where the English language and English Speaking Cameroonians are treated like inconvenient step-children who are barely tolerated.

Institutional and Systemic Marginalization

The simple truth is that in as much as Cameroonians obsess about national unity and nationhood, those in charge rarely go out of their way to ensure that these political clichés become reality, not even through largely symbolic gestures such as having a fully bilingual website for the Presidency of the Republic, arguably the official gateway of the Cameroon government.

Such acts of omission go to reinforce the feelings of institutional and systemic marginalization that run rampant in the ex-British Southern Cameroons; feelings that have largely contributed in creating the combustible socio-political climate that now exists in the region. Cameroon may be officially bilingual, but there is ample evidence that English and English-speaking Cameroonians are generally an afterthought to the movers and shakers of its predominantly Francophone socio-political system.

This is a serious problem which has absolutely nothing to do with English-speaking Cameroonians stupidly aping the "Anglo-Saxons" or "always whining" about their lot in Cameroon, as some have argued. It is a question of the government failing to use all the means at its disposal to create a climate of inclusion indispensable in building that mythical "Cameroon nation" that government officials always talk about.

A few years ago, I had a discussion with a Cameroonian translator who revealed that even though he was head of a translation department made up of three Francophones and two Anglophone translators, officials in the ministry in question either simply ignored the translation bureau and put out official documents solely in French, or generally went ahead and did the English translations themselves, with monstrous results. He stated that whenever confronted by the translators (since this reflected poorly on the translation department), the standard response from ministry officials was *le message passe quand même* (the message is at least getting through)... a clarion call for mediocrity which has, ironically, never been used as the standard for official government documents published in French...

Le message passe quand même was the same response given by Yaoundé Urban Council officials back in the early 1990s when they launched a multimillion clean-up campaign but did not bother to have the campaign posters translated into English by someone with even a rudimentary mastery of the English language. The result? The French campaign slogan *"Balayer, nettoyer, ramasser la saleté c'est bien. Ne pas salir c'est mieux"* was translated as follows: "Sweep, clean away, to gather dirtiness is good, not to make dirty is better." When questioned about this linguistic massacre, the response was that Anglophones should at least be happy that an attempt was made to have posters in both English and French. Yes, the Yaoundé urban council had just done Anglophones a huge favor, and these ungrateful *Anglos* were complaining as usual!!!! As CRTV journalist Sam Nuvalla Fonkem later pointed out in an article in *Cameroon Life* magazine, there could not have been a more insidious way of making Anglophone Cameroonians and the official language of Anglophone Cameroon seem inconsequential, if not an outright nuisance within the bilingual Cameroon Republic.

National Unity in Perspective

Sometimes, "national unity" or national inclusion is not just about the distribution of the "national cake" or about the attribution of cabinet positions to different regions. In many cases, it is about largely symbolic but emotionally laden issues such as language matters. As Rothchild and Foley have rightly noted:

> Not all group actors will be mobilized around distributive issues. Inevitably,

those issues with a symbolic dimension in a pluralist society – group status, identity or territory – are likely to become the basis for more inelastic or non-negotiable communal claims, setting the stage for intense conflicts of a political nature.

The rise of "Anglophone extremism" or "Southern Cameroons Nationalism" in recent years is largely the result of Cameroonian leaders ignoring these inelastic communal claims.

The irony is that it is the country as whole that loses in the long run as a result of the lack of political will to establish truly bilingual institutions. A case in point: In 2000, The Cameroon Tourism Board came up with the idea of selling the country via the Internet, and to set up a website for that purpose (http://www.camerouninfotourisme.com/). Unlike the website of the Presidency whose English section has been "under construction" since 1996, this one does not even pretend to have an English section. A website aimed at marketing a bilingual country to the world is entirely in French!!! Without doubt, this oversight is deeply rooted in a Cameroonian political culture whose hallmark is systemic or institutional monolingualism. No wonder veteran Cameroonian journalist, Abel Mbengue, once described Cameroon as *un pays francophone bilingue…*

The Tourism Board officials are totally oblivious to the fact that advertising a country's socio-economic and touristy potential in more than one language increases that country's marketability, and brings in more revenue from tourism. In Cameroon, where language has become a tool for exclusion, this obvious fact is lost to its ruling class.

Facing the Democratic Challenge

The democratic challenge in a plural society, Author Lewis once argued,

> is to create political institutions which give all the various groups the opportunity to participate in decision-making, since only thus can they feel that they are full members of a nation, respected by their more numerous brethren, and owing equal respect to the national bond which holds them together.

This is a challenge that the predominantly Francophone Cameroonian ruling elite – who have largely excluded one official language from state institutions – have failed to live up to, in spite of their repeated references to those bonds that allegedly bind English and French-speaking Cameroonians together as a people.

Language is a vehicle for identity and participation, and by institutionalizing the marginalization of one official language, the Cameroon government is in effect preventing citizens who use this language from fully participating in national life. And, even when these citizens do master "the language of gods," they still feel alienated from these institutions, from government, and from the rest of the nation. Yes, Cameroon's "language problem" is neither pedagogic nor individual, it is political. And, it is at the core of Cameroon's unending crisis of identity.

References

Lewis, A. (1965). *Politics in West Africa*, London: Allen and Unwin.

Rothchild & Foley. (1988). "African States and the Politics of Inclusive Coalitions." In D. Rothchild and N. Chazan. (eds.) *The Precarious Balance: State and Society in Africa*, Boulder: Westview Press.

The Post (2006). *French frustrates ASMAC Anglophone students.* Retrieved March 15, 2009 from: http://www.postnewsline.com/2006/01/french_frustrat.html

2

Culture and Political Statehood: Another Perspective on Southern Cameroons Nationalism

> Cultural heritage is important to the identity of a society. In times of need, songs, texts and works of art can be a beacon of hope and comfort. Cultural heritage reinforces the cultural and historical self awareness – *Power of Culture*.

April 30, 2006: In a recent posting on his blog, Cameroonian political analyst George Ngwane analyzes what he perceives as the exclusively political mindset of activists of the former British Southern Cameroons who are seeking to reassert the region's identity and "political statehood." According to Ngwane,

> The Anglophone struggle in Cameroon has, in the main, been a political manifesto aimed at reasserting the statehood of Southern Cameroon, West Cameroon or Anglophone Cameroon, appellations that depend on the generational shift or liberation mind-set of the advocates.

He goes on to point out that the cultural dimension has been completely absent in the struggle even though culture is a vital and indispensable weapon in the search for a new political dispensation in the former United Nations Trust Territory. As he puts it,

> for if the constitutional rape of the geo-political territory has had both political and economic toll, part of its redemption can be situated within the building block of a dynamic and potent creative industry within that same geo-political territory.
>
> That geo-political territory has lost the Tiko, Besongabang, Bali and Weh airports but so is it losing a vibrant media landscape. It has lost its road infrastructure but so is it losing its Art and Culture industry...Today's national political rainbow threatens by omission or commission to eclipse the distinct Anglophone cultural colours needed to radiate the geo-political territory.

Ngwane therefore concludes that "cultural entrepreneurship" is the missing piece in the political search for constitutional redress because "every cultural tonic carries along a Mao Tse-Tungian revolution and a Meiji restoration needed for the renaissance of any Kwame Nkrumahian political kingdom."

Ngwane's analysis is very relevant and timely and begs the question whether a nation can be established on and through politics alone. In this posting, I will take Ngwane's analysis a step further by asking whether (1) groups fighting for political statehood can be successful if they ignore the socio-cultural angle of their fight, and (2) whether nationalist movements can be truly relevant to the key segments of their target communities if they define and articulate their nationalist struggles only in purely political terms.

Referring specifically to the case of nationalist movements in Southern Cameroon, can these movements effectively mobilize their geographical and political base without a clear strategy for reaching out to those Southern Cameroonians who are not politically-inclined and who are most likely to be mobilized through social causes and civil society organizations?

To better understand the context of Ngwane's analysis and my follow-up questions, it is necessary to briefly compare the "Anglophone struggle" of the 1990s and the "Southern Cameroons Campaign" of the 21st millennium.

The Rainbow Coalition of the 1990s

When the "Anglophone renaissance" began with the wave of political liberalism that swept through Cameroon the 1990s, it was a broad-based movement that went way beyond the mere articulation of political demands or the proposal of constitutional redress to the Anglophone problem. It also included a vibrant cultural component that promoted artistic and literary works (paintings, poetry, theater, fiction, song, etc) highlighting the plight of Anglophone Cameroonians – many of which were publicly patronized, if not subsidized by the leadership in the budding Anglophone movement. In fact, these cultural activities were considered an integral part of that renaissance.

Another prominent aspect of the Anglophone renaissance was the establishment of vibrant Anglophone civil society organizations and pressure groups with issue-specific goals that were not necessarily political – or at least not overtly so. This was the case, for example, of the Teachers Association of Cameroon (TAC) and the Confederation of Anglophone Parents-Teachers Associations of Cameroon (CAPTAC) which mobilized a large segment of the Anglophone community around issues of equitable access to quality education and the protection of the Anglophone educational system. It is thanks to these issue-oriented groups that many individuals who would not have otherwise been involved in "Anglophone Activism" became torchbearers of the movement – Not every Anglophone activist was a member of the Cameroon Anglophone Movement (CAM) nor necessarily shared CAM's federalist political vision for the bilingual Cameroon Republic…

What resulted was mass mobilization across the board, which united the Anglophone community around broad issues of constitutional redress, political equality, access to quality "Anglo-Saxon" education, and a shared socio-cultural and political heritage. This rainbow coalition created "a thousand points of pressure" on the system. This pressure was manifested in landmark events such as the memorable workshops on Anglophone literature which resulted in the first major work on that often ignored literature in decades; an endless series of book launching ceremonies organized across the length and breadth of the territory, which served as platforms for political activism and for the promotion of works of art that told the Anglophone story in all its complexity; the famous *Post* Night organized by *Cameroon Post* publications, which rewarded the best political, literary and cultural icons in the Anglophone community, thus reinforcing the notion of a uniquely

"Anglophone way of life" in Cameroon; the *All Anglophone Conference* in Buea, the largest and most diverse political gathering of Anglophone Cameroonians since unification to discuss their status within the bilingual Cameroon republic; the creation of the General Certificate of Education (GCE) Board after a fierce and unrelenting campaign spearheaded by CAPTAC and TAC., etc.

Radicalization and Politicization

Today the socio-political landscape in Southern Cameroons is totally different due to a series of events that began in the mid nineties and continued until the end of that decade. The rainbow coalition of the 1990s has faded into oblivion, and replaced by a more radical and largely monolithic front defined in purely political terms with the sole focus of establishing an independent Southern Cameroons state. Protest literature still pops up occasionally in bookstores in Buea or Bamenda. And, occasionally, it is possible to stumble across a work of art narrating the journey of Southern Cameroonians in the union. However, unlike in the 1990s, these are largely, if not exclusively, solitary efforts with little or no institutional or nationalist backing. Cultural and social issues seem have become a burden rather than assets, and the much-touted "Southern Cameroons Heritage" is defined strictly in political terms. The "struggle" is now a purely political campaign meant primarily, if not exclusively, for the lion-hearted political activists at home and abroad. The "million man army" of the 1990s made up of farmers, civil servants, teachers, street vendors, taxi drivers, illiterate rural dwellers, etc., has been demobilized. The rainbow coalition, which actively contributed in placing the Anglophone problem on the national and international map has been dismantled.

Some might argue that this is exactly where the struggle should be today, and they probably have a point. But one can't help but wonder whether a revolution can truly remain relevant to its base and eventually succeed in its mission by being totally political... From another perspective, could Anti-Apartheid movement in South Africa have kept the flame of resistance burning for decades (with the oppressed masses constantly being roused out of apathy and complacency) without a deliberate policy by the movement to promote a protest culture (through song, photography, painting, fiction, theater, etc.) that resonated not just among the intelligentsia, but also among the masses in the Shanty towns and rural areas? The answer is an emphatic No!

Hence, in order for the Southern Cameroons revolution (however it is defined) to fully fire up the imagination of Southern Cameroonians and recreate the formidable rainbow coalition of the 1990s, it must imperatively seek to mobilize its base not just around tales of unimplemented United Nations Resolutions, of legal and political victories in Abuja, Banjul and the Hague, etc, but also around those real and imagined cultural and social values that supposedly make the people of the region unique.

For the movement to truly come of age, it must be able to make a clear distinction between (1) the political struggle carried out be a highly focused "lean and mean" ideological machinery with a precise goal and (2) the broader struggle for socio-cultural independence which supports any endeavor (be it from a federalist, provincialist, etc.) that shines the light on the plight of Southern Cameroonians, serves as a tool for mobilization, or increases the relevance of the movement to the daily lives of the people of Southern Cameroons.

References

"Cultural Heritage." Retrieved March 15, 2009 from: http://kvc.minbuza.nl/en/theme/heritage.html

Ngwane, G. *Creative industries, Cultural entrepreneurship and Political statehood: (An Invitation to Anglophone Cameroon Diasporans)*. Retrieved March 15, 2009 from: http://www.gngwane.com/2006/03/creative_indust.html#more

3

The Politics of Pidgin English in Cameroon

August 14, 2006: Although Pidgin English is the most widely spoken language in English-speaking Cameroon, and rivals French as the language of choice in some parts of French-speaking Cameroon (particularly in the Littoral and Western Provinces), it is still treated with scorn and disdain by the elite who consider it a language for the illiterate masses. The origins of this disdain go back to the pre-colonial and colonial eras when Pidgin was the lingua franca used by Cameroonians to communicate with Europeans, hence the tagging of Pidgin as bad, bush, or broken English. "It is interesting that even today Cameroonians popularly associate Standard English, commonly known as 'grammar,' with the elite; Pidgin English is perceived as the language of the common man, " says Augustin Bobda.

Today, critics of Pidgin English claim that it is polluting Cameroonian English, and preventing English-speaking Cameroonians from speaking Standard English correctly. According to a survey carried out by Jean-Paul Kouega on the attitude of educated Cameroonians towards Pidgin, "the respondents commented that the use of Pidgin by pupils interferes with their acquisition of English, the language that guarantees upward social mobility."

English in Cameroon: Is Pidgin the Culprit?

Nowhere is the disdain for Pidgin more glaring than at the University of Buea, Cameroon's lone English language university, where anti-Pidgin English signboards have been placed all over campus:

- "Succeed at university by avoiding Pidgin on campus"
- "Pidgin is like AIDS – Shun it"
- "English is the Password, not Pidgin"
- "Speak English and More English"
- "Pidgin is taking a heavy toll on your English – Shun it"
- "Commonwealth speak English not Pidgin"
- "If you speak Pidgin you will write Pidgin"
- *"l'Anglais un passeport pour le monde, le Pidgin, un ticket pour nulle part"*

("English, a Passport to the World, Pidgin, a Ticket to Nowhere" – Yes, this one is in French....)

The perennial critics of Pidgin cannot even fathom that the decline of language standards in Cameroon may be due to ineffective teaching methods in Primary and Secondary Schools. Neither does it even cross their minds that the dramatic encroachment of the French language into the English sphere has resulted in a new form of Cameroonian English which is usually a word-for-word translation of French sentences – and which is regularly on display in the English section of the state-owned *Cameroon Tribune*. Pidgin, they insist, is the sole culprit for declining English standards in Cameroon.

In a recent interview with Martin Jumbam, Prof. Abioseh Porter of Drexel University attributed attitudes towards Pidgin, particularly at the University of Buea, to intellectual snobbery:

> I find such notices senseless. In fact, the people who seemed to have understood the import of Pidgin as a language of mass communication are the missionaries. They quickly realized that language is a great cultural binder and they knew how to exploit it to reach the greater masses of the people. To me, this opposition to the use of Pidgin is nothing short of intellectual snobbery, period. You and I are now communicating in English, but if we were either in Cameroon or in Sierra Leone, Pidgin or Krio would be the most appropriate means of communication. But where you're warning people against using the language they master best, that doesn't make sense to me.

The fate of Cameroon Pidgin English is similar to that of other "Creoles" around the world, which also carry the stigma of illiteracy and "bushness." For example, "Despite their rich cultural heritage," says Morgan Dalphinis, "Creoles have been devalued of prestige, in the same way that their speakers have been, for at least five hundred years."

Today, the attacks on Cameroonian Pidgin English stand out because of their ferociousness and the quasi-criminalization of Pidgin in certain quarters, as in the University of Buea where it is banned.

So, is Cameroon's "Pidgin Problem" simply a pedagogic issue (even if it is a misplaced one), or is the "problem" fueled by broader societal conflicts about class, linguistic and communal identity, and political marginalization? In other words, are we dealing here with the *Pedagogy* of Pidgin or with the *Politics* of Pidgin in Cameroon?

Pidgin and the Politics of Identity and Power

In order to understand the position of Pidgin English in Cameroon, and the fury with which its critics go after it, one has to first contextualize the unequal relationship between Cameroon's English-speaking minority (20% of the population) and the French-speaking majority, and also decipher the assimilationist tendencies that underlie that relationship. As Lyombe Eko points out,

> In the 40 years since the reunification of English-speaking Southern Cameroons and French-speaking Republique du Cameroun, the resulting over-centralized government, run mostly by the French-speaking majority, and operating under what is essentially an Africanized version of the Napoleonic code, has attempted to eliminate the British-inspired educational, legal, agricultural, and administrative institutions which the Anglophones brought to the union. This has been accompanied by a concerted attempt to assimilate the English-speakers into the French-dominated system.

A key aspect in this assimilationist policy has been a systematic attempt to devalue anything of Southern Cameroons origin, including its people. As Lyombe points out, "To this day, when speaking of English-speaking Cameroonians, many French-speaking Cameroonians use the word 'Anglo' as an epithet to mean 'uncouth,' 'backward,' 'uncivilized,' 'inconsequential,' and so on."

This view of the backward "Anglo" extends to the English that they speak and its byproduct, Pidgin English. It is quite common for barely literate Francophone Cameroonians to insist that the majority of Anglophone Cameroonians are incapable of speaking standard English, and that even the most educated among them speak only *"l'anglais de Bamenda"* – by this they mean a dumbed-down and "Pidginized" English which is supposedly as barbaric as Pidgin itself. Of course, there is no truth to this claim, but it serves the purpose of transforming Cameroon English and Cameroon Pidgin English into symbols of Anglophone inferiority, and of Anglophone inability to fit into the mainstream. So instead of Pidgin being seen as a symbol of Anglophone creativity and resilience, it has become a stigma and an anathema, which supposedly reinforces the perception that English-speaking Cameroonians are unable to excel even in their own English or Anglophone sphere.

The underlying message is a fairly simple one: In order to fit in, English-speaking Cameroonians must shun their inferior culture and language(s) which are obstacles to their integration into the national (read Francophone) mainstream, and gravitate towards French which is the language of access, success and power. Pidgin in particular is therefore portrayed as a language of confinement (in the "Anglophone Ghetto"), of exclusion (from "national mainstream") and of inferiority (vis-à-vis the French language).

Buying into the Myth of Inferiority

It was Manuel Castells who noted that:

> If nationalism is, most often, a reaction against a threatened autonomous identity, then, in a world submitted to culture homogenization by the ideology of modernization and the power of global media, **language, the direct expression of culture, becomes the trench of cultural resistance, the last bastion of self-control, the refuge of identifiable meaning**. [My emphasis]

Cameroon's Anglophone elite have failed to appreciate the role of Pidgin as a tool for identity formation and protection in the former British Southern Cameroons. Instead, they see it as a threat that must be eradicated. The result, among other things, says Ngefac & Sala, is a steady "depidginization" of Cameroon Pidgin English:

> It is demonstrated that the feeling that Pidgin is an inferior language has caused Cameroon Pidgin speakers to opt for the "modernization" of the language using English language canons, instead of preserving the state of

the language as it was in the yesteryears.

This again is in line with the traditional relationship of domination and submission which Creole languages have had to deal with all over the world. As Dalphinis has pointed out in the case of Caribbean Creoles,

> Creole languages... have, therefore, traditionally been devalued by their own speakers who may point to these languages and at times their own African features and say that these are the cumulative reasons for their poverty and underdevelopment. They mistakenly equate cause with effect.

The persistent attack on Pidgin English in Cameroon cannot be taken at face value because it points to a more insidious phenomenon, i.e., the steady destruction (deliberate or inadvertent) of Anglophone culture and identity – something which Juliana Nfah-Abbenyi recognized so well in her keynote address at a conference organized by the University of Albany's *Consortium on Africa*. According to a blog about the event,

> Pidgin English competes with English proper, French and the more than 200 native languages in polyglot Cameroon, and is being singled out at this Anglophone University as a special threat. Using Gloria Anzaldua, Homi Bhabha and other theorists as a framework, Dr. Abbenyi showed how these signs reveal "a deep anxiety and malaise" about linguistic and national identity in Cameroon. **Pidgin, she said, drawing on her personal experience as a native speaker of this vernacular, is "the language of playfulness, informality, vulgarity, transgression, trade, celebration, and family." To ask students to "shun it" is to ask them to enter the English-speaking public sphere – which is already fraught in majority-Francophone Cameroon – and not look back.**" [My emphasis]

In an earlier article on my blog about the second class status of English in Cameroon, I argued that "Cameroon's 'language problem' is neither pedagogic nor individual, it is political. And, it is at the core of Cameroon's unending crisis of identity." Today's national hand-wringing over Pidgin English is also not a pedagogic problem as its critics would like us to believe, but part and parcel of that unending struggle between competing and conflicting visions about Cameroonian identity.

I will like to emphasize that my conclusion in no way ignores the real issue of falling English standards in Cameroon. However, rather than blaming Pidgin or any other language for these declining standards, we should turn to the educational system itself with its poorly-trained teachers and outdated language teaching methods which have barely changed since the 1960s. Once we factor in the nefarious influence of the dominant Francophone culture and its ubiquitous French language, then it becomes obvious why English standards are going down the drain...

References

Bobda, A. S. *Varying Statuses and Perceptions of English in Cameroon.* Retrieved March 15, 2009 from: http://www.inst.at/trans/11Nr/bobda11.htm

Castells, M. (2004). *The power of identity. The information age : economy, society, and culture*, v. 2. Malden, Mass: Blackwell.

Dalphinis, M. (1985). *Caribbean & African languages: Social history, language, literature, and education.* London, U.K.: Karia Press.

Eko, L. (2003). "The English-Language Press and the 'Anglophone Problem' in Cameroon: Group Identity, Culture, and the Politics of Nostalgia." *Journal of Third World Studies.* 20, 79-102.

Jumbam, M. (2006). *Interview with Professor Abioseh Michael Porter (Part One): Give Pidgin a chance.* Retrieved March 15, 2009 from: http://www.martinjumbam.net/2006/07/interview_with_.html#more

Kouega, J. (2001). "Pidgin Facing Death in Cameroon." *Terralingua Discussion Paper #17.* Retrieved March 15, 2009 from: http://www.terralingua.org/2/DiscPapers/DiscPaper17.html

Ngefac, A., & Sala, B. M. (2006). "Cameroon Pidgin and Cameroon English at a confluence: A real-time investigation." *English World-Wide.* 27 (2), 217.

Women's Crossroads. *Speaking Pidgin at the University at Albany.* Retrieved March 15, 2009 from: http://womenscrossroads.blogspot.com/2006/03/speaking-pidgin-at-university-at.html

4

Cameroon Literature in English – Vibrant but Invisible

> Anglophone Cameroon writing... is too little known and much underrated... consequently, much that has been written in English in Cameroon and what has been written about writing in English in Cameroon must have the character of a first encounter with the unseen, a getting to know and shedding of light on a dark spot in the literary development of Africa - *Ekhard Breitinger*

March 26, 2009: In 1978, Patrick Sam-Kubam published an article in *Abbia* (31/33, February 1978, 205-208) in which he lamented about "The paucity of literary creativity in Anglophone Cameroon". In 1997, Juliana Nfah-Abbenyi picked up on the same theme in her seminal book on gender when she also commented about "the paucity of Cameroonian Anglophone writing." To a certain extent, these two statements, made some two decades apart, reflected and still reflect a reality on the ground. Literature in English speaking Cameroon has not developed at the same pace as other "national" African literatures.

Hemmed in to the east by the more established literature of Francophone Cameroon which produced the Mongo Betis, Ferdinand Oyonos, Patrice Nganangs and Calixthe Beyalas, and to the west by Nigerian literature and its plethora of award winning and world famous writers – Achebe, Soyinka, Osundare, etc. – Cameroon Anglophone literature has been small fish in the pond trying very hard to establish its own unique identity.

The plight of this literature is made worse by the fact that it defies any clear classification; is it an extension of Nigerian literature of which it was an integral part until 1961? Is it simply a sub-set of Cameroonian (read Francophone Cameroon) literature? Does it even deserve a category of its own? Even among English-speaking Cameroonians, there is no unanimity on how to describe their literature; Cameroon literature in English? Cameroon Anglophone literature? There are those who argue that both of these terms are incorrect because they define that literature through a foreign prism – English language – rather than through a territory, the Southern Cameroons which just happened to have been a UN Trusteeship territory controlled by Britain.

The result of this identity crisis (for lack of a better term) is that literature west of the river Mungo has become invisible. In fact, even when it is mentioned in "respectable circles," it is done with reluctance and usually as a guilty afterthought. As Ashuntantang points out in,

> When Albert Gerard was editing *European Language Writing in Sub-Saharan Africa*, Anglophone Cameroon was omitted. In a last ditch effort to save the situation, Stephen Arnold wrote a basic account of Anglophone Cameroon literature titled "Emergent English Writing in Cameroon" and it

was included in the collection as an appendix to Nigerian Literature! In the same vein, Richard Bjornson's seminal work on Cameroon, *The African Quest for Freedom and Identity: Cameroonian Writing and the National Experience* barely makes mention of writers from Anglophone Cameroon. Although the book is 528 pages and Bjornson's research references are up to 1988, Bjornson only devotes less than twenty pages to Anglophone Cameroon Literature as a whole.

The obstacles to the emergence of a well-established Cameroon Anglophone literature are legion; the dearth of publishing opportunities for Anglophone writers that have incidentally always been available to their Francophone counterparts through state-funded publishers such as *Editions Cle*; the legacy of being the neglected "colony of a colony" (Nigeria) during the British colonial enterprise; the systemic neglect and marginalization of anything "Anglophone" within the bilingual Cameroon republic; the close to 40-year exclusion from the commonwealth which deprived Anglophone Cameroon writers of those publishing/sponsorship and recognition opportunities which helped propel writers from other Anglophone African countries to fame, etc.

This then is the fate of what Buma Kor aptly described as the literature of the "hunchback," i.e., that burden which the Republic of Cameroon grudgingly carries on its "back" while pretending that it doesn't exist, and making sure that no one else notices it...

The Shadow and the Reality

So is there really a dearth of literary creativity in Anglophone Cameroon as critics claim or have been claiming since the 1970s? Is Anglophone Cameroon literature truly an underperforming literature that is unable to hold its own against Francophone Cameroon literature and even more so against other "African literatures"? The answer is a resounding NO! The lack of international recognition and the existence of publishing difficulties do not automatically translate into a dearth of literary creativity – the critics are still reading from an outdated script. Beneath the veil of literary darkness, beyond the "resounding silence" that the literary world hears East of Bakassi is a third generation literature that is thriving against all odds.

Among these emerging writers are amazing talents such as Rosemary Ekosso, whose debut novel, *House of Falling Women*, has received critical acclaim; the award-winning novelist *Dipita Kwa* who honed his craft under the guidance of another Cameroonian literary giant, Mbella Sonne Dipoko; poet/playwright, Lloney Monono, author of *Dance of Scorpions*, whose poetry has been described as being among the finest to come out of Anglophone Cameroon in decades; the passionate Bernice Angoh who shows us that good African poetry can be non-militant and non-political; Francis Nyamnjoh, arguably the most prolific Anglophone novelist in the past decade, whose novel *Souls Forgotten* can hold its own against any African classic, etc.

This is merely the tip of the iceberg of the ongoing Anglophone Cameroon literary renaissance at home and in the Diaspora.

Yes indeed, behind the wall of silence is a buoyant and thriving literature impatiently waiting for the world to discover its depth, diversity and beauty. The time has come to lift that veil take a quick peek at what lies beneath. Here then is a toast to "Cameroon Anglophone literature," "Cameroon literature in English," "Southern Cameroons literature" or whatever you wish to call the literature of the marginalized but resilient people who live to the West of the Rever Mungo, or East of Bakassi as *Palapala Magazine* puts it.

References

Ashuntantang, J. (2009). *Landscaping Postcoloniality: The Dissemination of Anglophone Cameroon Literature*. Mankon [Cameroon]: Langaa Research & Publishing CIG.

Kor, B. (1993). "The literature of the hunchback." In Lyonga, N., Breitinger, E., & Butake, B. *Anglophone Cameroon writing*. Bayreuth African studies series, 30. Bayreuth, Germany: Eckhard Breitinger.

Nfah-Abbenyi, J. M. (1997). *Gender in African women's writing: Identity, sexuality, and difference*. Bloomington [u.a.]: Indiana Univ. Press.

5

A Baobab Fell in the Forest But Did They Notice? Bate Besong or the Symbol of the Cameroon Divide

> And yet, there was a time when people had faith, implicit faith - in this Union – without making any investigations. But I ask you, where is that faith now? It has vanished. So utterly! The bonds have snapped. We carry the scars of 'brotherhood' in a country so unaccustomed to candour" – *Bate Besong, 1993*

March 21, 2007: A common (in fact the most prevalent) theme in Bate Besong's writings (fiction and non-fiction) is the fate of Cameroon's English-speaking minority whom he referred to in his famous *Beasts of No Nation* as 'nightsoilmen" locked up in the antechamber of the bilingual Cameroon republic; a people whose culture, history and even existence was an afterthought to the French-speaking majority of Cameroon.

BB strongly believed that the unification of the British Southern Cameroons and the French Cameroons in 1961 was an unmitigated disaster for the Southern Cameroonians; that rather than giving birth to a new rainbow nation that took great pride in its diversity, the union had created a state built on deceit and the exploitation and marginalization of Southern Cameroons. As BB lamented in his legendary keynote address at the Goethe Institute in 1993:

> ...after the lunatic route we took from Foumban, as in a Dantean Inferno, the Anglophone Cameroonian occupies the center of Hell. The surrounding concentric rings of this smouldering infernal canyon may embrace a multitude of other victims in the present Cameroonian reality, but there is no doubt that our people, subjected to perpetual mental and psychological servitude, are the story book victims of a cultural holocaust. History has since the biblical Cain and Abel – carved no grimmer monuments to its own propensity for unfathomable cynicism and evil.

In many quarters BB was described as unpatriotic and radical because of his uncompromising stance on the Anglophone problem in Cameroon. But that did not bother him one bit. As he responded tongue-in-cheek to a question about his patriotism and nationalism in 1992: "I can sell Cameroon for less than Asoumou's whisky. So I will not say I am a nationalist as such, for, I am definitely a patriot of Southern Cameroons, not La Republique."

But being a Southern Cameroons 'patriot" did not mean blindly following or uncritically embracing the sometimes suspect leadership and dogma of the plethora of Southern Cameroons "liberation movements" that sprang up in the past decade. In this regard, his merciless flaying of the SCNC leadership back in 2000 (*The Post*, No. 155, Monday, January 24, 2000) which according to him "gave no leadership, clarified nothing, and confused everything" was one for the history books:

> We, Southern Cameroonians, have always had leaders that are archetypal mediocres: tribalistic, deceitful and fraudulent – since Foumban. Our daily lives are, therefore, viewed by the neo-colonial askari, through a distorted Quai d'Orsay prism, where the sum total of a person's character, merit, and worth is defined by De Gaulle's language. We have always been frog-marched in the limbo of marginality, alienated and directionless. In the depths of ignominy.

As far as BB was concerned, the bilingual Cameroon republic was a state made up of two distinct nations, and that the country's curse was its continued refusal to come to terms with this reality that no amount of state-decreed "national integration" could ever erase.

Even in his death, Bate Besong – that vocal symbol of Anglophone alienation – was still able to prove his point that national integration was a sham whose ultimate goal was to make English speaking Cameroonians invisible and irrelevant. Today, March 21, 2007, some two weeks after the three prominent Cameroonian men of arts – BB, Hilarous Ambe and Kwansen Gwangwa'a – perished in that horrific accident in Misole II, not one leading French language newspaper (at least not their online editions) has devoted a single line to their death. Even the fact that with their death, the University of Buea has lost a record 8 lecturers within a year and the country, and Cameroon one of its leading TV and Film directors, was not enough to interest the French language tabloids – even as a purely human interest story...

That Bate Besong, the award-winning literary colossus whom critics labeled the "Cameroonian Soyinka" or the "Anglophone Mongo Beti" died and folks "on the other side of the bridge" –– as he euphemistically referred to Francophones –– did not notice, would surprise many non-Cameroonians, especially those in African literature Circles. However, this would not come as a surprise to BB at all. In fact, I can see him in my mind's eye laughing sarcastically with an I-told-you-so look on his face. As he pointed out in numerous articles, post independent Cameroonian literature is characterized by a systemic disdain, marginalization, neglect, and non-recognition of the works by English-speaking Cameroonians – a point that Edward Ako grudgingly conceded in "Nationalism in Recent Cameroon Anglophone Literature":

> If it is true that there can be no meaningful discussion of African literature without reference to such Cameroonian authors as Mongo Beti, Ferdinand Oyono, Rene Philombe, Calixte Beyala and Guillaume Oyono Mbia, it is also true that such discussions never include authors writing in English. (Page 57)

In *New Engagements in Cameroonian Literature: The other Side of the Bridge*, BB reminded Francophone literary critics that the "literature of the Hunchback" from West of the River Mungo had nothing to envy qualitatively from the literature from the other side of the bridge:

> On the Cameroonian muses' crowded pantheon therefore, we too have been firm of feet as your own Fabien Eboussi Boulaga, Guillaume Oyono Mbia, Charly Gabriel Mbock, Gaston Paul Effa, Jacques Fame Ndongo, Hubert Mono Ndjana, Ferdinand Leopold Oyono, the immortal Mongo Beti. (But, Ignorance, as Plato remarked, is at the root of most misfortunes).

The official discourse in Cameroon may propagate the myth of "oneness"; the fairytale of one people and one nation under God living happily ever after, but BB knew better and said it loud and clear: There are TWO Cameroons, with two very different and sometime diametrically opposed histories and cultures; two Cameroons with two different sets of socio-political and literary icons – strangers in the night walking past each other and barely saying Hello.

This explains why in 1990, for example, a special edition of the French language *Le Messager* newspaper which profiled dozens of "real heroes" of Cameroonian independence and reunification, did not mention a single citizen of the former British Southern Cameroons – not even those who helped keep the flame of the nationalist UPC burning after it was banned in the French Cameroons. Or those Southern Cameroonians who in 1961 rejected the Nigerian option against all odds to throw in their lot with the alien and French-speaking *La Republique du Cameroun* in the name of the *Kamerun Idea*.

In an October 1998 discussion on the CAMNET internet forum about the systemic disdain for everything Anglophone particularly its history, Steve Andoseh wrote that:

> What is clear is that the propensity for Francophones to ignore Anglophone Cameroon history reflects the systemic marginalization of Anglophone Cameroon by the majority. The fact that it goes almost unperceived by them only proves how endemic the problem is.
>
> This exercise in the appropriation of history – replete with complete discretion over its revision upon the authority of the narrator being of or from whence such history emanates – is what passes for education of our people on our history. Even the events currently unfolding under our very eyes are distorted unscrupulously by those who think they have the moral authority to do so – who think they have some right to determine what is truth.

It is as a result of a similar appropriation of Cameroonian literature by those on the other side of the bridge that the Bate Besongs, the Hansel Ndumbe Eyos or the Kenjo Jumbams can be considered – oh sacrilege! – literary nonentities in Cameroon. And, it is this appropriation, which has given birth to that lopsided "narrative" in which Bate Besong the literary giant never existed and therefore never died – hence the silence of the Francophone media. BB can feature prominently in the *Encyclopedia of African Literature* along greats such as Soyinka, Achebe, Ngugi, Coetzee, etc. but he definitely has no place in an *Encyclopédie de la littérature Camerounaise* alongside Calixte Beyala and others from the other side of the bridge.

Again, BB would be totally unfazed by the preceding observation. Which is why he did not believe that the writer West of the Mungo should waste time, resources and energy trying to gain access into a mythical Francophone-controlled Cameroonian literary pantheon. Instead, he saw the writer as a revolutionary activist busy documenting and echoing the plight of his people. As he argued ferociously back in 1993:

> The Anglophone Cameroonian Writer must never forget his origins. His writing must depict the conditions of his people, expressing their spontaneous feeling of betrayal, protest and anger.
>
> It must challenge. It must indict head on. His writing must open up the Chinese Wall of Opportunity, closed to his people for over three decades.
>
> Our literature must convey with remarkable force the moods of the Anglophone Cameroonian caught in the assimilation-nightmare of Sisyphean existence. That literature must be inspired by an historical myth-informed consciousness. It must embody in bold relief the specific historical features of the entire Cameroonian reality.
>
> We must not evade the issues raised by economic, social and political change. We will be criticized for presenting the frustration and agony of a people held as a hostage minority. But we must insist on the truth of what we write. The Anglophone Cameroonian writer at home and in the Diaspora must tell the outside world the story of his tragic land from the point of view of its hostage minority.

That determination to tell the story of his people no matter the personal and professional cost; to empower the people of the former British Southern Cameroons with the facts of their history and instill in them an unshakable pride in their own identity, is what simultaneously made BB "The symbol of Anglophone hope" and the "symbol of the Cameroon Divide." Bate Besong was a visionary who clearly understood the role of reconstituted memory in awakening the collective consciousness of his people being crushed under the weight of "feudal oppression, mountains of suspicions and hate, retrogression, post-Foumban pauperization [and] resentment." As he opined in one of his pieces, "Memory will remain an important talking drum to the present on how the historical journey of a people is perceived, against the backdrop of an oppressive, neo-colonial culture."

> In that landmark address at the Goethe Institute in 1993, Bate Besong hammered home the fact that:
> No one can speak for us. Only those who daily live through the humiliations, the third class citizenship, in the abattoir of servitude, only we

can fully comprehend and explore these contradictions in a society undergoing such rapid and confusing transition.

That is BB's ultimate message to the children of the former British Southern Cameroons: They may despise and ignore us on the other side of the Mungo bridge; they may trample on our history, our literature, our culture, our people and our heroes; but as long as we never stop singing "King Alpha's song in a strange land" the day of reckoning will eventually come to pass...

So a baobab fell in the forest and they refused to notice? We don't give a damn!!!!

Farewell BB. See you on the other side.

References

Ako, Edward. "Nationalism in Recent Cameroon Anglophone Literature" In Marsden, P. H., & Davis, G. V. (2004). *Towards a transcultural future: Literature and human rights in a 'post'-colonial world.* ASNEL-papers, 8. Amsterdam: Rodopi.

Besong, Bate. (2004). *New Engagements in Cameroonian Literature: the Other Side of the Bridge.* Retrieved March 15, 2009 from: http://www.batebesong.com/2004/08/new_engagements.html#more

_____ (1993). "Literature in the season of the Diaspora: Notes to the Anglophone Cameroon Writer". In Lyonga, N. & Breitinger, E., & Butake, B. *Anglophone Cameroon writing.* Bayreuth African studies series, 30. Bayreuth, Germany: Eckhard Breitinger.

Gikandi, S. (2003). *Encyclopedia of African literature.* London: Routledge.

6

Cameroon Unification: Were Southern Cameroons Leaders Inexperienced and Illiterate?

September 03, 2007: Cameroon's history is a history replete with half-truths, myths, fallacies, and outright distortions. The Foumban Conference of July 1961, which sealed the fate of the British Southern Cameroons in its stormy marriage to French-speaking *La Republique du Cameroun*, is no exception to that rule. It has always been the position of even the most seasoned experts on Cameroon that the Southern Cameroons delegation was routed by their French Cameroons counterparts at Foumban because that delegation was composed of a bunch of politically inexperienced and intellectually inferior politicians who were no match for the politically savvy Ahmadou Ahidjo and his French advisers.

This was a view that Dr. Nfor Susungi articulated in a series of articles on the now defunct *SCNC Forum* back in 1997. Back then, he argued that the British abandoned "...the inexperienced Southern Cameroonian team of Foncha, Endeley, etc." to their own devices at the conference. To hammer this point home, he emphasized that "Foncha [was] a Grade Two teacher who had been a Prime Minister for only two years." Definitely not a person who could logically be expected to negotiate the future of an entire nation! Most recently, the issue of the "illiteracy and inexperience" of Southern Cameroons political and administrative class in the late 1950s and early 1960s has resurfaced on *Camnetwork*, the leading Cameroonian internet forum, with some insisting that this is the reason behind the inferior status that Southern Cameroons ultimately had within the bilingual Cameroon republic.

My Contention

This school of thought completely ignores the fact that the fate of Southern Cameroons was sealed long before the June 1961 Foumban conference, or even before the Plebiscite, and that by the time this conference took place, Southern Cameroons was doomed – not even the most astute negotiators from Her Majesty's Government could not have saved her from the clutches of Ahidjo's *La Republique du Cameroun* – and this had little or nothing to do with President Ahidjo's "superior political skills" as some claim today.

My contention, therefore, is that Southern Cameroonian politicians were neither naive nor inexperienced negotiators, and that even if they were, they benefited immensely from the expertise of Southern Cameroons intellectuals who played a key role in the movement toward unification. The resolutions of the Bamenda Conference, for example, which the Southern Cameroons delegation presented at Foumban tend to confirm this claim. My claim therefore is threefold;

> 1. That Southern Cameroons politicians were political veterans who knew what the stakes were at Foumban;

2. That the pro-unification positions of these politicians had been defined and refined over the years by various pro-unification lobbies in Southern Cameroons whose members were products of the some of the best universities in Nigeria and Britain, and;

3. That other Cameroonian and British administrators, legal and constitutional experts also helped these politicians at both informal and formal levels.

1) Southern Cameroons Politicians, Country Bumpkins?

What is generally ignored is that while Southern Cameroons politicians may not have been Ph.D. holders, they were nonetheless veteran politicians who had been groomed in the tough and very dynamic pre-independence Nigerian political scene. The Kales and Endeleys, etc., had fought alongside leading Nigerian nationalists in the *National Council of Nigeria and the Cameroons* (NCNC) such as Nnamdi Azikiwe, and later, they successfully wrested major political concessions from the British on the negotiating table – ranging from the granting of quasi-federal status for Southern Cameroons, to the granting of full regional autonomy and a ministerial government. Many, like Muna, Shang, Mukete, etc., had occupied top legislative and ministerial positions in the Eastern Nigerian House of Assembly and in the Federal government in Lagos. Others like Mbile [and Endeley] were not just seasoned politicians, but also reputable Trade Unionists who had successfully launched the CDC trade union, which became a perpetual thorn in the British colonial flesh.

Practically all of these politicians were veterans in political negotiations; skills that had been developed and sharpened not just through their involvement in Nigerian politics, but also at various constitutional conferences from Enugu in Nigeria, Lancaster in Britain, to Mamfe in the Cameroons, etc. – conferences which were no different from that which took place in Foumban . To put it bluntly, these guys were not illiterates and neophytes from the backwoods, but political pros. The reasons for their "failure" at Foumban should therefore be found elsewhere.

2) The Pro-Unification Lobby

It should be noted that the fight for unification was not merely a concern of politicians. In fact, the essence and ideology behind the Pan-Kamerunist idea were primarily articulated by the various pro-unification lobbies that existed at the time. The most influential of these was the *Kamerun Society*, the brain trust of Foncha's *Kamerun National Democratic Party* (KNDP), whose members are considered by many to be the real architects of unification. Its members were among the *crème de la crème* of Southern Cameroons intelligentsia trained in the most prestigious British and Nigerian universities.

Prominent among them were; Dr. G.G. Dibue, who later worked with WHO in East Africa; British-trained lawyer E.T. Egbe; Dr. Victor Anomah Ngu, Prof. of Surgery at the University of Ibadan from 1965 and winner of the prestigious Albert Lasker award Medical Research Award in Clinical Cancer Chemotherapy in 1972; Oxford-trained economist, S.J. Epale, who in 1956 helped S. A. George to formulate his famous "Kamerun Unification : Being a discussion of a 7-point Solution of the Unification problem"; famed West Cameroon educationist A.D.Mengot; PEN Malafa; REG Burnley; S. Lyonga; O.S. Ebanja, J. Pefok; Tamanjong Ndumu; S.C. Tamanjong; N. Ekeng, J.A. Kisob, F. N. Ndang, E.D. Quan, N.A. Ngwa, I.N. Malafa, J.B. Etame, N.A. Ngwa and S. E. Abangwa, etc.

Members of this KNDP think-thank, who helped to articulate most of that party's positions on unification, can certainly not be described as uneducated, even if a good number of them were at the beginning of their careers in 1961. Their leader may have been a Grade Two teacher but they were intellectuals in every sense of the word.

Also prominent in the Pro-Kamerun camp were the various branches of the *National Union of Kamerun Students* (NUKS), whose members like Albert Mukong (Nigeria), Fon Gorji Dinka and Anomah Ngu (Great Britain), etc., were active participants in most of the conferences and discussions leading to unification. For example, the Secretary General of the Ibadan Cameroon Students' Union which championed secession from Nigeria, was a certain J.N. EKANG, who later became Deputy Foreign Minister of the Federal Republic of Cameroon and Secretary General of the Organization of African Unity (OAU) under the name of Nzo Ekhah-Nghaky.

3) Contributions of Administrators and Legal Practitioners

The formal and informal contributions of British and Cameroonian administrators and legal practitioners, and constitutional experts should not be overlooked. Some like retired Ghanaian Supreme Court judge and former Attorney General for West Cameroon, Emmanuel Kofi Mensah, a British-trained constitutional expert, was a legal adviser at Foumban. Retired Justice Inglis, originally from the British West Indies, was also a prominent player in the unification process and eventually occupied a ministerial seat in the first post-unification West Cameroon government as the Attorney General.

Southern Cameroonian politicians, therefore, had more than enough "intellectual backup" in their frenzied quest for the Pan-Kamerun chimera, and their failure to achieve unification on their terms can be traced to factors that existed well before Foumban. To blame the so-called rout at Foumban on naiveté and illiteracy is a cop out. It is sometimes quite hilarious to watch both the supporters and critics of the Southern Cameroonian leadership use this particular argument to defend their contradictory positions; the former to absolve these leaders of any blame for the Anglophone predicament in the bilingual Cameroon republic, and the latter to simply denigrate the intellectual abilities of Anglophone Cameroon's pre-unification leadership.

The Real Culprits

The truth is that while the United Nations and Britain may be blamed to a certain extent for the bungled decolonization of Southern Cameroons, the bulk of that blame lies with the Southern Cameroons political class, which allowed ethnicity, personality conflicts, and inter-party rivalry to interfere with the adoption of a truly pro-Southern Cameroonian agenda.

The widespread belief that Ahidjo outsmarted the Southern Cameroonians at Foumban is one of those myths that take a life of their own over time and substitute themselves for reality. Ahidjo was never the smart, cunning and calculating politician that history has made him to be. He was just another brutal African dictator who, thanks to an accident of history (i.e., the early independence of *La Republique du Cameroun* and the political myopia of Southern Cameroons pro-unificationists), found himself in total control of the process leading to the unification of the two Cameroons. And like a true tropical dictator, he simply imposed his will on everybody else.

7

Revisiting The Legacy of Dr. EML Endeley

> Had he not by accident of birth come from a minority tribe, monuments would have been raised to his honour in the Cameroons, for his thirty-seven years of counsel and vision to his people – *N.N Mbile*

June 28, 2008: Twenty years have gone by since Dr. Emmanuel Mbella Lifafe (EML) Endeley, the first Premier of the British Southern Cameroons, passed away on June 29, 1988. Over the years, much has been said about and against him, particularly by a younger generation of Anglophone Cameroonians who still do not understand his naive romanticizing of the Nigerian option during the 1961 plebiscite, and his lukewarm attitude towards the so-called Third Option (i.e., the school of thought defended by P.M. Kale that called for the complete independence of Southern Cameroons from both the Nigerian federation and *La Republique du Cameroun*).

What interests us in this article, however, is his vision on the possible fate of the English-speaking minority of the then British Southern Cameroons in a unified and predominantly French-speaking bilingual Cameroon republic; a vision which, more than ever before, is of supreme relevance at a time when Anglophones are constantly taking stock of their stormy marriage with *La Republique du Cameroun*, and are trying, for better or for worse, to chart a new course for themselves.

According to Mr. N.N. Mbile (*Cameroon Post*, July 29, 1988), Dr. E.M.L. Endeley was:

> a descendant of the great Kuva, a giant war leader of the upper Bakweris who is reputed to have led the Bakweri armed resistance to the German occupation of Buea... Moved by the irresistible force of the blood of his ancestors, Dr. Endeley soon found himself... at grips with the mighty CDC over the need for improved working conditions and better amenities for its 25,000-man work force... [the] preliminary to the much bigger anti-colonial struggle...

This struggle was to take Endeley through the corridors of power both in Southern Cameroons and Nigeria, before propelling him to the enviable position of first Prime Minister of Southern Cameroons in 1958.

By the time Endeley became Premier, the struggle for independence – or to be more precise, for integration with Nigeria or unification with the French Cameroons – had become the key political issue in the British Cameroons. After initially flirting with the unification idea, Endeley became one of the staunchest opponents of the "Kamerun Idea" championed by the Pan Kamerunists who advocated for the reconstitution of the Cameroon "nation" within its pre-1916 borders. According to him, unification was not a priority, but an issue that had to be tackled from an evolutionary perspective, that is, if it had to be tackled at all... As he pointed out in a speech on May 25 1958,

> The advocates of immediate unification...still have to show the world how they propose in the interest and peace of all the sections concerned to achieve their aim. We of this government ... are convinced that far from being a priority issue, unification should only be achieved through evolutionary means...

And in his most apocalyptic and probably most prophetic statement against unification on the eve of the plebiscite, he warned Southern Cameroonians that,

> If you vote for Cameroun Republic, you will invite a new system under which everyone lives in fear of the police and army. You will not be free to move about; you cannot lecture freely or discuss your political views in public; ...and you can be arrested and flogged by the police and even imprisoned without a fair trial .

"Who amongst you," he asked,

> would like to live in French Cameroun, a country red with the blood of thousands of innocent victims killed by terrorists and the Ahidjo regime...who amongst you will like to live in a country which lacks complete respect for human dignity and where you cannot speak out your mind freely or pursue your business in peace... Who amongst you will like your children to grow up in servitude?... That will be our lot if we join French Cameroun.

The majority of Southern Cameroonians refused to heed to his warnings and voted for the Cameroun option on February 11, 1961. Once again in history, a visionary had been rejected by his people who refused to come to terms with his sense of foresight. Like a true democrat, however, E.M.L. Endeley accepted the people's verdict, and went on to contribute his own quota to the molding of the new Federal Republic. "The greatest legacy which Dr. Endeley left, " according to Julius Ngoh (*Cameroon Tribune*, August 5, 1988),

> was, I think, the fact that he graciously accepted the decision of the electorate on February 11, 1961 and unleashed all his energies to achieve what voters had asked, without hesitating to counsel his colleagues to have in mind the interests and wishes of the Cameroonian people.

As Endeley himself pointed out at the end of the Foumban Constitutional Conference of July 1961,

> I have come here to set an example - that by working together, we can

make a better country. If by this example, which I have set with my colleagues we cannot produce a peaceful Cameroon, then we will be a laughing stock to the rest of the continent.

E.M.L. might have been "brash, scornful, supercilious and downright contemptuous of other politicians"; he might have been characterized by "intellectual arrogance combined with princely haughtiness," but he was one who, according to Elive Peterkins (*Cameroon Post*, July 29 1988), "was cleverly aware that where two cultures meet, the bigger one is apt to eclipse the smaller one."

Today, a majority of Cameroonians west of the Mungo have finally come to terms with EML's pre-unification prophecy. The most glaring manifestation of this change occurred on April 2 - 3 1993, when over five thousand Anglophone delegates from all over the country gathered at the Mount Mary Hill in Buea for the first ever "All Anglophone Conference" – a conference that was supposed to analyze the state of the union between the former British Southern Cameroons and the former French Cameroun, and also map out a future course of action for Anglophone Cameroon(ians). In what amounted to a posthumous vindication of the E.M.L. Endeley prophesy, the participants, among them some of Endeley's most strident pre-unification critics, condemned the "numerous indignities (and) humiliations" suffered by the Anglophone community in Cameroon since 1961;

> Our problem... springs from a breach of trust on the part of the Francophone leadership and from a lack of openness in matters of public interest. Within these thirty-two years our union accord has been violated. We have been disenfranchised, marginalized, treated with suspicion. Our interests have been disregarded. Our participation in national life has been limited to nonessential functions ... The opponents of reunification had warned against these forms of repression which even then were already being practised in La Republique du Cameroun. Today, thirty-two years later, Anglophones regret that they had not heeded to those warnings.

In a unanimous pang of nostalgia, the delegates recalled that:

> Before our territory attained independence in 1961, we had been practising parliamentary democracy in a politically pluralistic society, which was far more developed than what obtains in Cameroon today, three decades later. We regarded democracy as a way of life, and as an ideal towards which to strive. We were neither saints nor angels; far from it. But we believed then, as we do now, that whenever a government becomes fraudulent and repressive, it is the democratic right of the people to change that government and vote in another.

In spite of his shortcomings, therefore, history will remember E.M.L. as one of the few Southern Cameroons leaders who lucidly analyzed the practical consequences of unification with *La Republique du Cameroun* at a time when collective myopia seemed to have gripped his people; one who foresaw that Southern Cameroons would become, to quote George Ngwane, "the biblical Jonah swallowed in the belly of the annexationist whale"; and whose dire predictions about the Anglophones' second class status within the bilingual Cameroon Republic ultimately came true in the most spectacular manner less than five years into the union (see, for example, the KNDP memorandum of August 1, 1964).

Close to five decades after his prophesy of Anglophone marginalization within the bilingual Cameroon republic and two decades after his death, the Anglophone journey in the wilderness continues unabated. As the late Professor Obenson, pointed out after EML's death, "There is no doubt that if we had had many West Cameroonians with the additional educational clout of Dr. E.M.L. Endeley, we would have been singing a different song today."

Part Two

Citenzenship in the Global Village

8

Brain Drain: Why are Cameroonian Medical Doctors Leaving?

April 17, 2006: The news from the Ministry of Health was quite gloomy. In a special report that appeared in the *Cameroon Tribune* last week, it was announced that Cameroon's medical system was in crisis due to a severe shortage of medical doctors resulting from the massive exodus of Cameroonian MDs to countries in the developed world.

According to the report, about 5000 Cameroonian medical doctors are currently plying their trade abroad (with about 500-600 in the US alone, according to the Minister of Health). In an interview with *Cameroon Tribune*, Pr. Tetanye Ekoe, the Vice President of the National Order of Medical Doctors in Cameroon, reveals that some 4200 MDs reside in Cameroon. However, this is only half of the story; of the 4200 listed on the rolls of the Order, only about half are actually practicing MDs. About 1000 are on secondment to the Ministry of Health where they perform a variety of tasks, including purely administrative ones. The rest are either with the Faculty of Medicine and Biomedical Sciences of the University of Yaoundé I, with NGOs, or with the private sector. The nearly 1500 MDs in the private sector handle less that 10-15% of patients.

Pr. Ekoe points out that the limited number of practicing MDs in the country makes the official national doctor-patient ratio of 1 doctor per 10.000 inhabitants largely meaningless. He reveals that the real ratio is closer to 1 doctor per 40,000 inhabitants, and that in remote areas such as the Far North and Eastern Provinces, the ratio closer to 1 doctor per 50,000 inhabitants.

Unfortunately, the country's lone faculty of medicine is unable to meet internal demand because it produces only about 100 MDs annually. To make the already bleak situation worse, the IMF and World Bank have imposed hiring quotas (which do not take retirements and death into account) that limit the number of MDs who can be integrated into the public service each year. The result is that some foreign-trained MDs actually return home to find out to their horror that they cannot be employed... So the internal pool of MDs continues to shrink as more Cameroon-trained MDs move on to greener pastures in the West, while Western-trained MDs don't return home.

The Brain Drain at a Glance

In its *2006 World Health Report*, the World Health Organization (WHO) uses data from the 30-member Organisation for Economic Co-operation and Development (OECD) to shed light on the medical brain drain phenomenon in sub-Saharan Africa:

> It appears that doctors trained in sub-Saharan Africa and working in OECD countries represent close to one quarter (23%) of the current doctor

workforce in those source countries, ranging from as low as 3% in Cameroon to as high as 37% in South Africa. Nurses and midwives trained in sub-Saharan Africa and working in OECD countries represent one twentieth (5%) of the current workforce but with an extremely wide range from as low as 0.1% in Uganda to as high as 34% in Zimbabwe.

According to the report, 109 doctors trained in Cameroon are currently working in OECD countries (p. 100). The effects of this migration are disastrous, according to the WHO report:

> when large numbers of doctors and nurses leave, the countries that financed their education lose a return on their investment and end up unwillingly providing the wealthy countries to which their health personnel have migrated with a kind of "perverse subsidy"...
>
> Financial loss is not the most damaging outcome, however. When a country has a fragile health system, the loss of its workforce can bring the whole system close to collapse and the consequences can be measured in lives lost. In these circumstances, the calculus of international migration shifts from brain drain or gain to "fatal flows".

If the statistics above are to be trusted (and there is no reason not to trust them), then the situation in Cameroon and most of sub-Saharan Africa, has shifted from simple brain drain to that of "fatal flows" with a wide scale system collapse a potential reality.

To begin to adequately address the problem, we must start by clearly understanding the reasons that push MDs to leave and why others are not returning home after their training in foreign countries.

Why They are Leaving

Although the *Cameroon Tribune* special report touches on some of the factors that contribute to the prevailing situation, it tries too hard to sell the patriotism angle, i.e., in spite of the hardship, Cameroonian MDs should be more patriotic and be willing make sacrifices for their country. This, in my opinion, is a rather simplistic analysis of the problem, which can only lead to equally simplistic solutions that will resolve nothing.

In its analysis of the reasons that cause the brain drain, The WHO report states that:

> Classically this is provoked by a (growing) discontent or dissatisfaction with existing working/living conditions – so-called **push factors**, as well as by awareness of the existence of (and desire to find) better jobs elsewhere – so-called **pull factors**. A recent study from sub-Saharan Africa points to both push and pull factors being significant. Workers' concerns about lack of promotion prospects, poor management, heavy workload, lack of

facilities, a declining health service, inadequate living conditions and high levels of violence and crime are among the push factors for migration. Prospects for better remuneration, upgrading qualifications, gaining experience, a safer environment and family-related matters are among the pull factors.

In Zimbabwe, for example, a startling 77% of final university students were being encouraged to migrate by their families (13). Beyond the individual and the family, accelerated globalization of the service sector in the last two decades has helped drive migration in the health field (14–18). In addition, there is a growing unmet demand for health workers in high income countries due in part to rapidly ageing populations. Two important responses in the global market are occurring. First, a growing number of middle income countries are training health workers for international export and second, professional agencies are more actively sourcing workers internationally, raising questions about the ethics of recruitment.

The First Step

Understanding and accepting these reasons – which have little or nothing to do with patriotism or a lack thereof – gives Cameroonian policy makers a better chance of tackling the brain drain issue head-on. In a paper presented at the international seminar on International Dialogue on Migration, Jorge de Regil & Mel Lambert have a word of advice for countries such as Cameroon which are suffering from the migration of indispensable health resources:

> Governments have to be more open and honest about the reality of migration of human resources for health in the country...Given the choice most people would prefer, all things being equal, to remain in their home country. Consequently, in devising policy solutions to migration, making a country a good place to work and to live in must be the starting point: developing a culture where advancement (in education or professional life) depends on quality, not on political affiliation, race, religion, national origin, etc.

Cameroon must therefore go beyond the blame game and look at effective and viable internal solutions to the problem. For example, the Government can seek a moratorium on current Bretton Woods hiring quotas for medical doctors on national security grounds. Or simply go against IMF and World Bank recommendations. There is a precedent here. In 1991, for example, the Government created five new universities in the country, against the specific wishes of the Bretton Woods institutions, which argued that the country could ill afford such an expensive venture. 15 years later, there is hardly anyone in Washington, D.C, who still believes that the creation of these universities was a bad idea.

Without doubt, the medical profession in Cameroon has lost its erstwhile glory and part of the effort to stem the tide of migration must include making it attractive once more in terms of salary, career growth, and social mobility. As long as the situation where a Policeman with a high school diploma earns as much, if not more than an MD persists, the brain drain will continue.

There are a plethora of possible solutions to these problems. According to the *e-Africa* online journal (Sept. 2003), the government of South Africa, for example, set aside R500 million in 2003 and R750 million in 2004 "to adjust the salaries of public-sector doctors and expand the number of rural medical jobs." Regil and Lambert propose a solution along the same lines:

> Developing countries need to try harder to entice their high skilled healthcare professionals back. This could be done, for instance, through schemes where top public officials in countries have their public sector pay 'topped up' through aid assistance schemes so as to encourage them to stay. Schemes could be developed were medical expatriates are brought back for a period of time to impart skills on the home population. However, any such schemes need to be sustainable in their own right and not create artificial situations that could dry up as soon as any funding ends.

In Search of Global Solutions

Beyond what could be termed the "classical solutions" to the brain drain, African governments must craft global, bold, innovate and effective policies that go beyond the case of MDs. Even though theirs is the most visible case, the situation is equally critical across the board. In Cameroon, for example, about 25%-30% of professionals trained in the country are working abroad while 70-80% of Cameroonians trained abroad do not return home after their education.

Creativity is in order. Hence, asking the Diaspora community to visit Cameroonian embassies abroad or the website of the Prime Ministry for possible job opportunities in the country, as Prime Minister Inoni did during his July 2005 visit to the United States, shows a lack of vision and innovation. In the long run, Cameroon may probably have to turn for inspiration to countries such as Nigeria, Ghana, South Africa and the Philippines which are tackling the brain drain crisis in the most innovative manner possible. According to *e-Africa*,

> Nigeria has a special assistant to the president for the Diaspora. Senegal created a ministry of foreign and Diaspora affairs. Ghana changed its laws to allow dual citizenship to make it easier for the Diaspora to return... One lesson from Ghana's effort is that if Africa wants émigrés to return, the process must be easier. In particular, spouses and children born abroad should have the opportunity to claim citizenship easily and be allowed to maintain dual citizenship to make it easier for émigrés to continue to conduct business. The Ghanaian embassy in Washington maintains a computer skills bank on its nationals working in the US.

In 1995, the Filipino government established the Philippine Overseas Employment Administration charged with promoting the return and facilitating the reintegration of migrants. The Employment Administration offers privileges to returning Filipinos such as loans for business capital at preferential rates and eligibility for subsidized scholarships.

There a dozens, if not hundreds of solutions that have been tested around the world. If Cameroon is serious about the brain drain issue, it knows where to start rather than trying to reinvent the wheel…

References

Cameroon Tribune online (December 4, 2006). "Exode des médecins: l'effrayante saignée. » Retrieved on March 15, 2009 from: http://www.cameroon-tribune.net/artrub.php?lang=Fr&oled=j12042006&rub=DOSSIER%20DE%20LA%20REDACTION&olarch=

Herbert, R. (2003). "The African Diaspora – The medicine for what ails Africa." *e-Africa*. Retrieved on March 15, 2009 from: http://saiia.org.za/images/upload/eafricasept03.pdf

Jorge de Regil & Lambert, M. (2006). "Making migration of human resources for health. A win-win situation for all." *International Dialogue on Migration seminar – Migration and Human Resources for Health. From Awareness to Action.* Geneva, 23-24, March 2006

World Health Organization. (2006). *The world health report 2006: Working together for health*. Geneva: World Health Organization.

9

Dual Citizenship (I): Time for a Long Overdue National Debate

May 31, 2006: After Cameroon won the first Afro-Asian football finals against Saudi Arabia in Jeddah in 1985, the Saudis refused to hand over the inter-continental trophy on grounds that Cameroon had fielded an ineligible French player during the first leg encounter in Yaounde. The player in question was none other than the legendary Roger Milla who had showed up for the game with his French passport. The Cameroonian government insisted that even though Roger Milla carried a French passport, he was still a bona fide Cameroonian citizen who had the right, in fact the obligation, to defend the colors of his native land. The issue was resolved months later following high-level diplomatic exchanges and the mediation of the world football governing body, FIFA.

About a decade later, the same Cameroonian Government barred another Cameroonian icon, the irascible novelist and critic Mongo Beti, from running for the 1997 parliamentary elections on grounds that he was not a Cameroonian. The reason? When Mongo Beti returned from exile a few years earlier, he had entered the country using a French passport. Until his death a few years later, the Biya regime continued to describe Mongo Beti as a foreigner who was ceaselessly meddling in the affairs of his host country Cameroon...

These two incidents involving passports from the same foreign country clearly capture the schizophrenic and arbitrary application of Cameroon's outdated and highly restrictive nationality law (*Loi no. 68-LF du Juin 1968 portant code de la nationalité*) which is out of step not only with the reality of Cameroonian society today, but also with current world-wide trends.

According to article 31 of the 1968 nationality code, any Cameroonian who acquires the nationality or citizenship of a foreign country, shall, upon that acquisition, cease to be a citizen of Cameroon. However, as we have seen in the case of Roger Milla and Mongo Beti, the nationality law is generally enforced only when it is in the interest of the regime in power to do so; the only reason Mongo Beti was consistently branded a foreigner and barred from contesting parliamentary elections was because he was a virulent critic of President Biya and his regime. Mongo Beti's treatment was quite different from that of Professor Hogbe Nlend, another prominent Cameroonian who had sought exile in France during the Ahidjo era. Hogbe Nlend, who later became the President of the influential Bordeaux chapter of the ruling CPDM party in the late eighties and early nineties, was eventually appointed a minister in Biya's cabinet in 1999 on the UPC ticket even though he carried a French passport just like Beti...

A Growing Concern...

Until recently, dual citizenship was a marginal issue, which primarily concerned Cameroonian athletes (particularly professional footballers) in Europe. In fact, it is an open secret that practically every European-based player on the Cameroon national team holds a foreign passport. Like other Cameroonian professionals in the Diaspora, footballers take up foreign citizenship for practical reasons (e.g., to avoid UEFA and national league quotas on foreign players that existed before the Bosman ruling of 1996, or current restrictions on non-EU players). In other cases, dual citizenship stems from the fact that some of these athletes were born in countries that grant citizenship by birth, but they later decided to play for Cameroon rather than for their country of birth. This is the case for example, of Joseph Desiré Job and Valerie Mezague both of whom were born in France, and who actually played for the French national team at junior levels before finally opting for Cameroon's Indomitable Lions.

Today, thanks to the establishment of vibrant and ever-growing Cameroonian Diaspora communities around the world (particularly in Europe and America), and the equally growing number of children of Cameroonian parentage born in these foreign countries, the issue of dual citizenship has become a critical one – even though it is yet to become part of the national discourse back in Cameroon. In fact, in the rare occasions when the issue of citizenship has made the headlines in Cameroon, it has been in the context of the fraudulent acquisition of Cameroonian citizenship by foreigners; a situation which according to the Government daily, *Cameroon Tribune* of July 8, 2002, may result in "a person of doubtful nationality could some day become the Prime Minister of Cameroon as was said to be the case elsewhere" (a dubious reference to the case of Alassane Ouattara the former Prime Minister of Cote d'Ivoire)…

Contradictory Signals

During a visit to the United States in 2001, former Prime Minister Peter Mafany Musonge conceded in a press conference in Chicago that the issue of dual citizenship was an important one, and intimated that Cameroon may eventually have to follow the trend towards dual citizenship if it intended to fully exploit the skills and resources of its ever-growing Diaspora community. Dr. Elvis Ngole Ngole, a prominent member of the Musonge delegation, even advised the Cameroon Diaspora in the United States to mobilize its resources and energetically lobby lawmakers back home in view of amending the 1968 Citizenship law. However, when Musonge's successor, Ephraim Inoni, visited the United States four years later, he simply brushed aside the issue of dual citizenship, insisting that Cameroonian law was very clear on the matter, and that change was not in the horizon.

The fact that most Cameroonians in the Diaspora are considered opponents of the Biya regime, and that the dissonant calls for dual citizenship legislation have been coupled with demands for Diaspora voting rights, has not helped matters. It has inadvertently created and emotionally-charged and partisan environment where a reasoned and informed debate on the issue has become virtually impossible since many in the Biya regime consider the granting of dual citizenship rights to the Cameroon Diaspora as an unnecessary and reckless reward for the very people who are trying to bring down the regime in power.

Can Cameroon Afford to Reject Dual Citizenship?

Can Cameroon – a country which proudly celebrates its newfound HIPC (Heavily Indebted Poor Country) status – afford a development policy which shuts out some of its most resourceful and skilled citizens on the spurious claim that their patriotism is questionable because they reside abroad and have taken up foreign citizenship, usually for practical reasons?

Does a country, which is hemorrhaging from the loss of its best brains to other countries not owe it to itself and its unborn progeny to use every strategy and tool at its disposal to turn the brain drain into a brain gain?

Can Cameroon ever attain its development and modernization objectives without a more imaginative, less restrictive and less confrontational relationship with its thriving Diaspora community?

Finally are the reasons that once led to the rejection of dual citizenship still valid in the global village of the 21st century? Isn't it time for a long overdue honest, informed and objective national discussion "over whether dual citizenship is a healthy acknowledgment of a complex cultural identity or a watering-down of patriotic loyalty" (*Chicago Tribune*, July 7, 2002)?

The Case Against Dual Citizenship

The reasons why countries reject dual citizenship are legion (e.g., to avoid complications that may arise from custody disputes or extradition cases involving dual citizens). However, the most common reason advanced is that of "watered down loyalty" which supposedly arises when an individual takes up a second nationality or citizenship.

According to a report by the Australian Parliament on the pros and cons of dual citizenship, opponents of dual citizenship argue that "a person should be totally committed in a legal and emotional sense to one country" because "having more than one citizenship conflicts with notions of national identity and cohesion." The report cites Dr. Katherine Betts of Monash University who insists that "the nation state is still an important political unit. Communities that work have boundaries. Blurred membership leads to blurred loyalty." Other opponents of dual citizenship, cited in the *Chicago Tribune* argue that it commodifies national identity by "treating passports like credit cards to be collected and used interchangeably depending on convenience."

In the specific case of African states, the rejection of dual citizenship is a product of the years immediately following independence when issues of national identity and national belonging were viewed primarily in exclusionary and even confrontational terms. In this context granting citizenship to individuals who still maintained their original nationalities was seen as a weakening the "unifying power" of the nation-state, threatening "National Unity" and slowing down the construction of the "nation."

Current Trends

Close to half a century later, the national and international landscape has changed dramatically as a result of globalization and the dramatic growth of international migration. As the previously-cited Australian report points out:

> There is vastly greater mobility of people and increased incidence of people living and working in foreign countries for extended periods... There is greater acceptance in the modern, internationalised world, that individuals may be citizens of more than one country and satisfactorily meet duties as citizens in relation to each. There is greater acceptance that having dual citizens hasn't done much harm to nations, and that the benefits of dual citizenship extend beyond the individuals concerned.

Today, the issue of dual citizenship in Cameroon is less about excluding foreigners who are reluctant to give up their old nationalities, and more about including bona fide Cameroonians who now live abroad and are part of the highly-skilled, much sough-after and extremely mobile international workforce. Other countries are furiously competing for these skilled workers by offering them attractive incentives ranging from high wages to permanent residence and even citizenship. Cameroon must be willing to offer equally enticing benefits – the most obvious being dual citizenship – if it also intends to compete on an equal footing with these countries and benefit from the skills of these professionals.

To date, there is no evidence to indicate that Cameroonians who have taken up foreign citizenship have become less attached to, or less interested in their homeland, or that they are a threat to national security as a result. On the contrary, the Cameroonian Diaspora is contributing significantly in shoring up the Cameroonian economy. The remittance of Cameroonians abroad amounts to millions of dollars annually; Diaspora-owned business ventures employ thousands of Cameroonians at home; Cameroonian alumni, cultural, professional, and other Diaspora-based organizations carry out thousands of charitable ventures (from scholarships to communal development projects) in Cameroon each year. In the same vein, many prominent Cameroonians in the Diaspora have given the country a visibility on the international scene, which it would otherwise not have had. It is therefore safe to conclude that the contribution of Cameroon's Diaspora to national development has been very significant, and that the color of a dual citizen's passport has little or nothing to do with that citizen's level of commitment and attachment to home and country.

So what are the specific benefits of dual citizenship to individuals concerned and to their countries of origin? Which are some of those countries in Africa and elsewhere that have adopted dual citizenship and what justification was put forth for ultimately embracing dual citizenship legislation?

These questions will be answered in Part II.

References

MacArdle, D. (2000). *From boot money to Bosman: Football, society and the law.* London: Cavendish.

Parliament of Australia & Adrienne Millbank. "Dual Citizenship in Australia." *Current Issues Brief 5 2000-01.* Retrieved March 15, 2009 from: http://www.aph.gov.au/library/pubs/cib/2000-01/01cib05.htm#arguments

10

Dual Citizenship (II): A Win-Win Situation

June 06, 2006: As we saw in the first part of this article, globalization has dramatically altered the dual citizenship debate in many countries. The political reasons that were once used to reject dual citizenship in the 20th century are today steadily giving way to powerful economic and cultural arguments in its favor. As a report by Bella consultants states:

> Dual citizenship is becoming more common in today's increasingly interconnected economy. Countries such as India, the Philippines and Mexico are now seeking the advantages of dual citizenship by liberalizing their citizenship laws. These countries have realized that dual citizenship has the advantages of broadening a country's economic base, fostering trade and investment between the dual citizen's two respective countries.

This view is shared by *Africa's Brain Drain*, an NGO dedicated to turning the brain drain into a brain gain, which argues on its web site that:

> Immigration regulations are cited as one of the barriers to exchange of skills and knowledge across borders. Foreign based professionals need to be assured that they would be able to return to their adopted country once they leave. Immigration laws in some industrialized nations require migrants to remain in the country for a specified period or risk losing their residence status. On the other hand, those who have been naturalized in their new country often have to make a choice between that or their home state, as some African countries do not recognize dual citizenship. Hence the need of more African authorities to allow dual citizenship.

As a leading Ugandan dual citizenship proponent pointed out during Uganda's debate on dual citizenship a couple of years ago: "If dual citizenship is easily available in all of Africa, then it would allow expatriates to return and invest in their birthplace, entice foreign investors and promote cross-border cooperation."

Increasing calls for dual citizenship across the African continent are also driven by a growing recognition that the African Diaspora is making immense contributions to the national economies of African countries, and that this contribution will only increase with the liberalization of citizenship laws. This was the stance taken by Ghana when it finally adopted the *Dual Citizenship Regulation Act* on July 3, 2002. Speaking during the occasion, Dr. Addo-Kufuor, acting Minister of the Interior at the time, stated that:

> The legislation is a tribute to the great support Ghana has received from her citizens who have been living beyond her shores over the years. This

support has been in the areas of economic, technical, social and infrastructural development ... The NRGS contribution of 400 million dollars cannot be treated lightly, and so the importance Ghana attaches to NRGS cannot be overemphasized.

Similarly, when India, a one-time leading opponent of dual citizenship, finally passed a law recognizing dual citizenship in 2003, the motivating factor for this dramatic change of heart was the need to tap into the skills of India's mammoth Diaspora. According to the Government of India:

> Persons of Indian origin settled in economically more advanced countries of the world have skills and expertise in vital sectors. The facility of Dual Citizenship would foster better co-operation in these sectors by way of investments and transfer of skills and resources.
> The need of the PIOs to build emotional and cultural bonds with their will now be strengthened and will facilitate the Diaspora's contribution in India's social Development.
> Dual Citizenship would also help to bring about and establish links of the younger generation of the Diaspora with India as they may be keen to keep in touch with their roots."

Says Bhanoji Rao:

> One can take a sanguine view and extrapolate that India's stand to allow dual citizenship is one more step in its role as an emerging and confident global power which, in the years to come, would help usher in what might eventually lead to the establishment a global citizenry with freedom of movement to pursue opportunities wherever they arise.

A Bridge to the Foreign Born Generation

While the dual citizenship debate has generally focused on first generation immigrants who still have direct ties to their countries of birth, there is increasing interest in the children and grandchildren of these immigrants who are born in these foreign countries, and who have only a tenuous link to their parents' countries of birth. In this case, dual citizenship offers an incentive to reconnect with their roots. Most significantly, it opens up the possibility of them living, working or setting up businesses in their parents' countries of origin. In an article on strategies that African countries can use to tap into the potential of its Diaspora communities ("Good Ideas for Using the Diaspora"), *e-Africa* makes a strong case for extending citizenship to the foreign born children and spouses of Africans in the Diaspora:

> Many countries are examining how to make it easier for those living abroad with foreign-born children or spouses to return home. Dual citizenship would facilitate the freedom of movement of Africans between

developed countries and the continent allowing skills to move as opportunities arise. It will also help prevent well-educated children born abroad from losing touch with Africa.

This is a policy which countries such as Ireland are already benefiting from. Ireland now has one of the fastest growing economies in the world thanks in part to its "citizenship by descent" laws that allow the third and subsequent generation children born abroad to an Irish citizen to become Irish citizens by simply proving that one of their grandparents was Irish, even if none of their parents was born in Ireland.

A Tool for Building Political Clout

One of the rarely-mentioned benefits of dual citizenship, particularly for countries with well-organized Diaspora communities, is the ability of dual citizens to influence economic and political decisions in their host country in favor of their country of descent. For example, the potential influence of Mexican citizens on the American political system was one of the main reasons why Mexico ultimately abandoned its age-old hostility towards dual citizenship in 1998, and started to actively lobby Mexican nationals in the US who were eligible for US citizenship to take up that citizenship. In 2002, the Mexican government even organized a series of "nationality fairs" across the US to educate Mexicans on the benefits of dual nationality, encourage them to organize themselves into a potent political force within the US political system, and to use their political strength to influence key issues of interest to Mexicans such as immigration.

Chicago Tribune was on target when it observed that "Foreign countries are increasingly encouraging expatriates… to claim dual citizenship, hoping to capitalize on the political clout and financial resources of those who have built new lives abroad."

Different Flavors of Dual Citizenship

The list of countries that accept dual citizenship around the world and in Africa keeps on growing by the day. It is worth noting, however, that the form of dual nationality varies from country to country.

Ghana

According to Ghana's *Citizenship Act* of 2000 which went into effect in July 2002, "A citizen of Ghana may hold the citizenship of any other country in addition to his citizenship of Ghana." Citizens who lost their citizenship as a result of the previous law which proscribed dual citizenship can regain their Ghanaian citizenship by apply to the Ministry of Interior for reinstatement. Dual citizens have the same rights as other Ghanaian citizens. However, they cannot occupy certain key positions in the Government, the Army and security apparatus. Some of positions in question include Justices of the Supreme Court, Ambassador, Chief Director of a Ministry, or a Colonel in the Army.

India

In December 2003, the Indian Parliament passed the *Citizenship (amendment) Bill* granting dual citizenship to people of Indian origin around the world. The primary objective of this act is to (a) "simplify the procedure to facilitate the re-acquisition of Indian citizenship by persons of full age who are children of Indian citizens, and former citizens of independent India" and (b) "provide for the grant of overseas citizenship of India to persons of Indian origin belonging to specified countries, and Indian citizens who choose to acquire the citizenship of any of these countries at a later date". Like its Ghanaian counterpart, the Indian citizenship bill lists a number of positions in government that cannot be occupied by overseas citizens of India. For example they cannot become President or Vice President, a Supreme Court or High Court judge, a member of the House of the People or of the Council of States, or a member of the Legislative Assembly or the Legislative Council.

South Africa

The South African *Citizenship Amendment Act of 2004*, which came into effect on 15 September 2004, enshrines the constitutional right to citizenship. Consequently, South Africans can no longer lose their South African citizenship if they become citizens of another country. However, the law requires that South Africans must use their South African passport to enter or leave South Africa, although they can freely use their foreign passports outside South Africa.

A Need for Concerted and Sustained Action

In practically all the cases where national governments eventually adopted dual citizenship legislation, the change of heart was the result of extensive and sustained lobbying by their respective Diaspora communities. Cameroon is no different. For the issue of dual citizenship to register on the national Richter scale, the Cameroonian Diaspora must craft a coherent and organized lobbying strategy, which clearly breaks from the solitary attempts made so far to get the Government interested in the issue.

For starters, the Diaspora community should create a powerful organization whose sole mission and focus will be on changing article 31 of the Nationality code, which prohibits dual citizenship. Such an organization should rally legal experts, historians, economists, political scientists, etc, to produce a series of position papers which make a comprehensive and compelling case for dual nationality. Once completed, these position papers should be given the widest publicity possible in Cameroon and abroad. The campaign should also include taking out full page ads in leading Cameroonian newspapers. Representatives of the organization should be prepared to go to Cameroon to make their case directly to the Cameroonian people, and to Cameroonian politicians, legislators, the Government, civil society activists, the media, and the business and academic communities.

Like every lobbying effort, there is no guarantee that such a campaign will pay off immediately. The case of India, which is now at the forefront of the dual citizenship movement, is instructive in this regard. The Indian Diaspora community began to actively lobby for dual citizenship as far back as the 1970s during the Government of Prime Minister Moraji Desai who was openly hostile to the concept (Desai is famously remembered for his anti dual-citizenship quip that "no man can serve two masters"). It would take close to 30 years of persistent, unflagging and well-funded and very professional lobbying efforts by the Indian Diaspora and its allies in India to convince Indian politicians and legislators that dual citizenship was indeed a win-win situation.

References

Bargblor, E. Z. ((February 28 2006). *Dual Citizenship: Solution to Liberia's Brain Drain?* Retrieved March 15, 2009 from: http://www.liberianforum.com/articles/Bar gblor003.htm

"Dual Citizenship: Who Qualifies?" Retrieved March 15, 2009 from: http://www.info-ghana.com/Dual%20citizenship.htm

"Indian Parliament Approves Dual Citizenship." Retrieved March 15, 2009 from: http://www.immigration.com/newsletter1/dualpio.html

Rao, B. (January 18, 2005). "Dual citizenship — Driven by pride and pragmatism." *Business Line Internet edition.* Retrieved March 15, 2009 from: http://www.blonnet.com/2005/01/18/stories/2005011800060800.htm

11

Citizenship in the Age of Globalization

May 14, 2008: During the African Athletics Championship, which took place earlier this month in Addis Abeba, Ethiopia, one of the star attractions was Cameroon's hammer throw representative, Georgina Toth. Georgina attracted lots of media attention because she is white. A 26-year old native of Hungary, Georgina moved to the United States in 2006 after she obtained a scholarship for the Northern Arizona University where she is a Business major. Georgina's story an intriguing one because she does not have any tangible connection to Cameroon; she is not married to a Cameroonian, does not have children of Cameroonian ancestry and has never lived in Cameroon.

A fortuitous meeting in 2006 with Ange Sama, President of the Cameroon Athletics Federation resulted in a suggestion that she compete under the Cameroonian flag. She was granted Cameroonian citizen one week prior to the African Athletics Championship after Hungarian Athletics Federation (She was a member of the Hungary U23 National Team from 2003 to 2005) authorized her to compete for Cameroon. This allowed her to bypass the two-year wait imposed by the International Athletics Federation on athletes who switch national federations.

Georgina did not win a medal in Addis Abeba. She came in fourth with a hammer throw of 55.71 meters not enough to qualify for the Beijing Olympics (She has until July 23rd to obtain the required minimum). Heavy rains were blamed for her performance which fell short of her personal best of 62.78m which she set on March 28, 2008 in Tempe, Arizona, and far short of the world record of 78.61m set in 2007 by Russia's Tatyana Lysenko. Nonetheless, she broke Jeanne Ngo Minyemeck's national record of 51.78m set in 1988.

Stormy Nationality Debates

Since Georgina competed for Cameroon, there have been stormy debates on many Cameroonian internet forums over her Cameroonian citizenship. Some have argued that granting talented foreigners "fast track" citizenship is a major step forward, and is part of the process of the reversing of the "brain and muscle drain." As Ange Sama declared: "We always complain about the departure of our athletes to more prestigious federations. Therefore, I didn't hesitate at the opportunity of bringing a European athlete to Cameroon. Thankfully, my country backed me." Others, however, argue that by granting Cameroonian citizenship to an individual with absolutely no connection to Cameroon, the government is cheapening and auctioning that citizenship – particularly when that individual is not the top athlete in her field.

The Georgina Toth citizenship has also revived the never-ending debate over Cameroon's nationality law, which does not recognize dual citizenship. Says one Cameroonian,

> It is one thing for the government to turn a blind eye on the fact that

practically every player on the Cameroonian football national team has dual citizenship, while at the same time making life difficult for less prominent Cameroonians in the same situation. It is however a different ball game when that same government grants Cameroonian citizenship to someone who has not given up her Hungarian citizenship and doesn't intend to do so, while demanding that native born Cameroonians give up their Cameroonian passports when they become citizens of other countries.

Proponents of this school of thought argue that the case of Georgina Toth is another clear indication that Cameroon's continuous repudiation of dual citizenship is outdated and anachronistic, even within the Cameroonian context, and should therefore be modified.

So where do you stand in this debate? Is Georgina Toth's newly minted Cameroonian citizenship the way to go? Or did authorities cheapen Cameroonian citizenship by making her a Cameroonian citizen? Also, it is time for Cameroon to finally recognize dual citizenship?

Part Three

Collective Memory

12

Individual Memory and Collective Amnesia: Where are the Political Memoirs?

April 15, 2007: Andze Tsoungui, the one time Vice Prime Minister and one of the longest serving cabinet Ministers in both the Ahidjo and Biya governments died early last week in Brussels, Belgium. Andze's career spanned close to half a century, beginning in 1958 when he was appointed assistant to the sub-divisional officer of Nanga Eboko. That same year, he was transferred to Douala as assistant to the head of the Wouri region. This was at the height of the UPC insurgency of which Wouri, along with the Sanaga maritime was a hotbed. After a brief stint in the East, he was appointed the Divisional officer for Mungo in 1961. By this time, the UPC insurgency had ended in the Sanaga Maritime, and the area of operations moved further west to the Mungo and Bamileke regions.

Andze Tsoungui's primary mission was to crush the UPC rebellion by any means necessary. He carried out his mission "without concession" until 1963 when he was promoted to the position of Federal Inspector for the entire Littoral region (which included Mungo and Wouri). In 1965 he was transferred to the Western region still as the Federal Inspector (During the days of the federal republic, Cameroon was divided into six regions, each headed by a Federal Inspector whose job was similar to that of today's provincial Governor). It was under his watch that Ernest Ouandié, the last historic leader of the UPC was arrested in 1970 alongside Bishop Ndogmo, and executed in January 1971 thus ending the decade-long UPC rebellion.

With the dissolution of the federation in 1972, Tsoungui became a Minister in Ahidjo's first cabinet under the new "United Republic". He subsequently held a series of key cabinet positions in both the Ahidjo and Biya region, including the position of Vice Prime Minister under Biya – a position he held until 1997 when he left Government for good...

As Paul Biya's Minister of Territorial Administration (interior) in the early 1991 and 1992, he played a central role in crushing the nationwide opposition insurrection and the Ghost-town. Even more critical, he was the brain behind infamous the October 1992 presidential elections, which President Paul Biya won thanks to what observers unanimously agree was a massive and well-oiled rigging machinery controlled by officials of MINAT. As the National Democratic Institute (NDI) stated in its 1992 interim report:

> The election system provided civil administration officials responsible to President Biya — including the Minister of Territorial Administration, divisional officers and sub-divisional officers — with excessive discretion in matters of voter registration and ballot tabulation, which many officials abused to further the political interests of the incumbent president.

Without doubt, *Père Andze*, as the French-language media dubbed him back then, was one of the last survivors from that generation with an intimate knowledge of the unknown details of pre and post colonial history, from the bloody decolonization, the crushing of the UPC rebellion, the reign of terror under Ahidjo, to the emasculation of the Cameroon opposition in the 1990s.

Alas! The world will never get to know Andze Tsoungui's version of these landmark events. Like the majority of key players in Cameroon's pre- and post-independence history, he died without writing his memoirs or an autobiography. He therefore joins a long list of prominent Cameroonians on both sides of the Mungo who never bothered to write their memoirs thereby depriving future generations of Cameroonians of the right to know and understand their past. It was Francis Wache who once wrote in *Cameroon Tribune* (February 16, 1990) that "our historical heritage would be compromised if not jeopardized if those who are participating in the hurly-burly of our national life were to leave the stage without a written legacy." Time is proving him right.

Beginning with the former British Southern Cameroons, neither EML Endeley nor John Ngu Foncha who served as Prime Ministers of the territory wrote their memoirs before their death. Similarly, neither Augustine Ngom Jua nor S.T. Muna who all later served as Prime Ministers when the territory became known as the federated State of West Cameroon wrote their memoirs.

Similarly, of the original 13 Southern Cameroons representatives who sat in Nigeria's Eastern House of Assembly in Enugu in 1952 (the *Cameroon bloc*), only one, Nerius Namaso Mbile, wrote his memoirs which were published in 1999. In this regard, Bate Besong was on target when he lamented some two decades ago (*Cameroon Post*, July 29, 1988) about the "paucity of Anglophone Cameroon autobiography, i.e., for its first generation politicians". [As a side note, of the original 13, only Pa Lainjo is still alive today.] As Dr. Julius Ngoh pointed out in the case of Dr. EML Endeley (*Cameroon Tribune*, August 5, 1988), "There is no perfect human being – and this failure to leave behind an autobiography or memoirs may likely play into the hands of his detractors."

It was the same song heard 17 years later when George Ngwane lamented in his eulogy to former OAU Secretary-General, Nzo Ekhah-Ngaky, that in the three decades after his resignation from the OUA and until his death in 2005, Nzo "became as politically silent as [his] Nguti grave... chose the path of retreat and reticence." As Ngwane rightly points out, the absence of a memoir from Eka-Ngaky has been a great disservice to Cameroon and Africa as a whole. This lament was also echoed by Xavier Luc Deutchoua (*Quotidien Mutations*, June 18, 2005) who regretted that:

> Nzo Ekangaki died in Yaounde without talking or writing, just like Charles Assale, Théodore Mayi Matip, Samuel Kame, Dooh Kinguè, Paul Soppo Priso, John Ngu Foncha and other personalities who guided the newly independent Cameroon. He has gone to the afterworld without writing his memoirs. (My translation)

Today, it is most likely that second and third generation political personalities from the former trust territory of British Southern Cameroons – former Prime Ministers Achidi Achu and Mafany Musonge immediately come to mind – will keep up this disheartening tradition as there is no indication that they are working on their memoirs or have commissioned anyone to write their biographies.

Praise must therefore be given to rare gems like Albert Mukong who published two tomes of his memoirs (*Prisoner Without a Crime* and *My Stewardship in the Cameroon Struggle*) both of which shed light on some of the dark practices of the Ahidjo regimes and Biya regimes and covered a 30-year period.

Although the situation is only slightly better in the French Cameroons, especially in recent years, it is still the same sad story. The territory's first Prime Minister Andre Marie Mbida died without writing his memoirs; the same with former president Ahmadou Ahidjo. Others who played critical roles in Cameroon's post independence history such as the notorious Jean Fochive who was the head of the secret police from 1960 until his dismissal in 1996 (save for a few years) also died without memoirs.

To date, none of the prominent actors of the new multiparty era have written a personal account of their roles in the major events of this period – the Ghost town campaign, the controversial elections of 1992, 1997, 2002, etc, numerous attempts at establishing viable opposition coalitions, student activism in the multiparty era, rebirth of Anglophone nationalism, etc. To their credit, some players such as journalists Boh Herbert and Ntemfac Ofege (*Prison Graduate*) and Rtd. Justice Nyo Wakai (*Behind the Fence*) wrote about their experiences behind bars in 1990 and 1992 respectively. Cho Ayaba, a student leader in the mid-1990s and a founder of the Southern Cameroons Youth League (SCYL) has also published an account of his clandestine departure from Cameroon to Germany (*Not Guilty: We Versus Them, the Experience of an African Refugee*). Similarly, Ebale Angounou, the president's "Young Friend" who was the brains behind the 1991 arrest of University of Yaounde student leader, Senfo Tonkam, also published his memoirs regarding his alleged ties to the Biya regime (*Paul Biya, the nightmare of my life, or, The other side of my destiny*).

The Broader Problem

The absence of memoirs, autobiographies and biographies in Cameroon is merely one facet of a much broader problem, i.e., the collective inability (or unwillingness) of Cameroonians to keep historical records for posterity or to even consider these records as important contributions to the national collective memory. For example, there are very few publications containing key political speeches, landmark declarations and documents of our times (save those of Presidents, Ahidjo and Biya).

How many of us can still remember the content of the document that sent Yondo Black, Albert Mukong and others to jail, and opened the political floodgates in 1990? Who still remembers Jean Jacques Ekindi's famous "the single party is dead" speech that silenced the multiparty holdouts within the then single party the CPDM in 1990 or Celestin Monga's open letter to Paul Biya in 1991?

How many Cameroonian scholars ever mention the speech made by Ben Muna, then President of the Cameroon Bar Association on March 27, 1990 at the Meridien Hotel in Douala which brought the Yondo affair to the public attention, transformed the bar association into a pro-democracy organization and served as a catalyst for the public rejection of one-party rule in the country?

> I am convinced that the time has come for lawyers to take a stance... We are not behind bars but we are prisoners of our fear... Barrister Yondo might be behind bars, but here we are, the real prisoners, tiptoeing in order not to awaken our conscience... I call on the Cameroonian Bar to express in one clear voice, the problems of human rights in our country. I hope they will have the courage to do it.

How many people are even aware that John Fru Ndi made a speech at the launching of the SDF on May 26, 1990? And what about all those historic speeches made at the All Anglophone Conference (AAC) in Buea in 1993, including the *mea culpa* from Muna and Foncha? Did the AAC ever bother to publish a compilation for posterity?

The result has been a collective memory that borders on collective amnesia. To borrow from Peyi Soyinka-Airewele, our collective memory is like "a chessboard of colored and blank patches" – blank patches that will never be filled up.

It should be pointed out, however, that the responsibility for this state of affairs is not solely that of politicians. The fact that someone is a leading public or political personality does not automatically make him or her a writer. Hence, historians, writers, journalists and other scholars also have a responsibility to assist key political figures in documenting their individual memories – memories which in their aggregate help build our collective memory. Did anyone, for example, ever approach Nzoh Ekangaki to co-author a memoir about the Lonrho scandal that led to his resignation as OAU Secretary-General, or about his prominent role in the pre-plebiscite unification debates as President of NUKS? Or has anyone bothered in these last few years to get 96 year-old Pa Lainjo to finally tell his Cameroon story? I doubt it.

For decades Cameroonians could end up in Tchollire, Mantoum or other political prisons if they dared – even in private – to articulate ideas that were contrary to the official discourse. This partially explains why entire generations of Cameroonians died without putting anything on paper, especially when their narratives of key events conflicted with the official narrative. People rarely kept incriminating documents that the Secret Police could stumble upon. Today, however, that excuse is no longer tenable. Even people still in active service such as General Pierre Semengue have written memoirs that not only talk about their role in key national events, but also give their personal take on the ongoing political process (*Le Geìneìral Pierre Semengue: toute une vie dans les armeìes*).

It is our hope therefore that the current crop of Cameroonian politicians and other public figures will break from the past and start writing for posterity. Wishful thinking?

13

The Cultural Alienation and Historical Amnesia of Public Spaces in Cameroon

March 07, 2006: On November 5, 1891, a German expeditionary force, led by *Karl Freiher Gravenreuth* and *Lieutenant Von Stetten*, was dispatched to Buea to crush the Bakweri resistance to the German colonial machine. In the epic battle that ensued, the Bakweri, led by Chief *Kuv'a Likenye*, killed Gravenreuth, repulsed the German attack, and chased the German-led forces across the Fako Mountain as they fled back to Victoria. It would take another four years for the German war machine to defeat the Bakweri..

In his analysis of the impact of Kuv'a Likenye's victory over the Germans, Edwin Ardener writes in *Kingdom on Mount Cameroon* that:

> Kuva's case is of more than local interest. This remote and ideologically merely intuitive tribesman held up the march of events, by an unexpected veto on the foreign economic exploitation of the mountain. The veto only ended with his death. During its existence, it revealed serious weaknesses in German Colonial administrative and military practice... the resistance of the mountain people provided one of the important shocks of the early colonial system in Kamerun. As a resistance movement, it was before its time...Kuva must receive credit for diverting the curse of Gravenreuth and his slave-troops upon the colonial masters themselves.

Kuv'a Likenye died shortly after the Bakweri defeat of 1895, and was buried in an unmarked grave somewhere in Buea. On the other hand, Karl Freiher Gravenreuth, whose forces had been humiliated during the 1891 battle, was buried with honors and a monument built in his honor in Douala. That monument still stands to this day... But no one can pinpoint exactly where Kuva Likenye is buried...

Defacing General Leclerc

Kuva's story is being retold today because it goes to the heart of a "nationalist" trial currently taking place in Douala. It is the trial of Mboua Massok ma Batalong, the "Father of the Ghost Town". His crime? On January 29, 2006, Massok, the self-styled leader of the "moral rebellion" against the Biya regime, was arrested in Douala for defacing the monument of General Leclerc located at Douala's Independence Square. Massok wrote the words, "to be destroyed, our martyrs first, 180 days" on the commemorative wall behind Leclerc's statue. Mboua Massok proudly accepted his crime in open court.

Massok's defense, as reported by the French language daily, *Quotidien Mutations*, is simple: The trial is not about his person but about "colonization, acculturation, and alienation." According to Massok, the real issue here is not about defaced public property, but about Cameroonian national identity, and the imperative to

Camerooniz̧e public spaces such as streets, public, buildings and monuments: "Does General Leclerc, a French soldier, deserve to be honored at the Bonanjo [Douala] independence square of all places, at the expense of Cameroonian martyrs such as Douala Manga Bell and Ngosso Din?" Billion dollar question...

And, going back to our original story, does Gravenreuth, a German who not only fought the Bakweri but also brutally crushed a revolt of the Abo people of present-day Mungo division in February 1891, deserve a monument in Douala, when there is not a single street in Buea honoring Kuv'a Likenye, or even a plaque commemorating the German-Bakweri wars?

In an article on how national identity is invented, Anne-Marie Thiesse lists a number of "symbolic and material items" that "any real nation needs to possess." These include,

> a history establishing its continuity through the ages, a set of heroes embodying its national values, a language, cultural monuments, folklore, historic sites, distinctive geographical features, a specific mentality and a number of picturesque labels such as costume, national dishes or an animal emblem.

It is easy to see why Cameroon has been confronted with the problem of nationhood (be it linguistic or ethnic) since independence. For decades, successive Cameroonian regimes imposed a watered-down version of the country's history on citizens, and virtually banned any public reference to Cameroonian nationalist figures; there are virtually no public spaces in their honor, and to this day, they are barely a footnote in Cameroonian history books. Instead, the most important public spaces in Cameroon are a tribute to colonial and neo-colonial actors; the Leclerc monument, Avenue Charles de Gaulle, Avenue Giscard d'Estaing, Avenue Kennedy, Rue du Maréchal Foch, Rue de Nachtigal, Avenue Winston Churchill, etc., etc. The result? A people with no roots who have little or no pride in their heroes and martyrs, or in their indigenous cultures which have instead become sources of discord and division. The colonialism of the mind continues...

> Emancipate yourself from mental slavery,
> None but ourselves can free our minds...
> How long shall they kill our prophets,
> While we stand aside and look? Ooh!
> Bob Marley (Redemption Song)

Mboua Massok's moral rebellion is therefore a timely one aimed at stemming the tide of cultural alienation and historical ignorance. As African nationalist, Marcus Garvey wrote in "African Fundamentalism":

> The time has come for the Blackman to forget and cast behind him his hero worship and adoration of other races, and to start out immediately to create and emulate heroes of his own. We must canonize our own martyrs

and elevate to positions of fame and honor Black men and women who have made their distinct contributions to our racial history.....

Africa has produced countless numbers of men and women, in war and in peace, whose lustre and bravery outshines that of any other people. Then why not see good and perfection in ourselves? We must inspire a literature and promulgate a doctrine of our own without any apologies to the powers that be. The right is the Blackman's and Africa's. Let contrary sentiments and cross opinions go to the winds. Oppositions to Race Independence is the weapon of the enemy to defeat the hopes of an unfortunate people.

From this perspective, the Mboua Massok trial (actually, it should be the *General Leclerc trial*) is arguably the most important trial of the year. Too bad that the Cameroonian press and the public are too distracted by stories of sex and financial impropriety in high places to pay any attention ...

References

Ardener, E., & Ardener, S. (1996). *Kingdom on Mount Cameroon: Studies in the history of the Cameroon Coast, 1500-1970*. Cameroon studies, v. 1. Providence: Berghahn Books.

Thiesse, A. (1999). Democracy softens forces of change: Inventing national identity. *Le Monde Diplomatic* (English Edition online). Retrieved March 15, 2009 from: http://mondediplo.com/1999/06/05thiesse

14

France's Dirty War in Cameroon: The Assassination of Félix-Roland Moumié

> The use of political assassinations against key leaders of liberation movements has had a major impact on the course of history in Africa and the Middle East. Not only have some of the greatest of Third World leaders been killed but so, too, has the hope for political change they embodied – *Victoria Brittain*

October 15, 2006: Early in October 1960, Dr. Félix-Roland Moumié, the exiled leader of the Camerounian nationalist movement, the Union *des Populations du Cameroun* (UPC), traveled to Geneva, Switzerland, on a mission. On the eve of his return to Conakry (Guinea) where the UPC had set up its headquarters in exile, he was invited to dinner by an individual whom he had met earlier in July in Accra, Ghana. The individual, 66-year old William Bechtel, claimed to be a journalist interested in the UPC's armed struggle against the French-backed regime of Ahmadou Ahidjo. But William Bechtel was no ordinary journalist. A former member of the French Foreign Legion and one of the first soldiers to rally De Gaulle's Free France Forces in London in 1940, he was also a reserve officer in the French secret service, the *Service de Documentation Extérieure et de Contre-Espionage* (SDECE). Most importantly, he was a member of the "Main Rouge" (Red Hand), a covet unit within the SDECE charged with assassinating anti-French and pro-independent African nationalists and their supporters in Europe.

According to Richard Belfield in *The Assassination Business: A History of State-Sponsored Murder*,

> Moumié knew he was at risk as the French were running a major assassination programme at the time, targeting and murdering African Nationalists, as well as journalists and academics who supported them (or even wrote about them from anything other than the French government point of view). Moumié believed that while he was in Geneva he would be safe, a big mistake as Swiss neutrality meant nothing to the French.

In their award-winning investigative book on the French secret service titled *La Piscine*, Roger Faligot and Pascal Krop give a detailed account of the Moumié assassination as narrated to them by General Paul Grossin, the head of the SDECE from 1957 to 1962. According to Grossin, Moumié showed up for the dinner at the *Plat d'argent* restaurant on Saturday October 15, 1960 with Jean Martin Tchaptchet, the President of the French section of the UPC. Upon their arrival, Moumié was informed that he had a phone call. Surprised that anyone knew of his whereabouts at that moment, Moumié left the table to answer the phone. Bechtel distracted Tchaptchet with some documents on Cameroon and then poured a lethal dose of

Thallium into Moumié's aperitif. Moumié returned shortly, complaining that no one had answered the phone. He did not touch his aperitif. When it became obvious that Moumié did not intend to drink his aperitif, Bechtel seized on a moment of distraction during diner to pour another dose of Thallium into Moumié's wine.

This time Moumié literally swallowed the bait.

Bechtel was ecstatic: The poison would take effect only after Moumié arrived in Conakry where the doctors would be unable to figure out what was wrong with him. And, in a classic case of killing two birds with one stone the French expected that Guinea's rabidly anti-French President, Sekou Toure, would be blamed for Moumié's death. But things would not go as planned. According to Belfield,

> It was the first time this particular poison had been used and the French doctors who had made it were incompetent. The poison was poorly refined and did not work in the way it was supposed to. This was just the beginning of the ineptitude of the French: their assassin then administered the wrong dose."

Krop and Faligot however quote General Grossin as saying that the plan went awry when, just before the end of the dinner, Moumié suddenly picked up his untouched aperitif and drank thereby taking a double dose of the Thallium poison! The poison, which had been carefully prepared at the "carsene Mortier" was now too strong, and took effect before Moumié could catch his flight for Conakry. The next day, a very ill Moumié was admitted into the *Hôpital Cantonal de Genève* where he lived in great pain and agony for two weeks before dying on November 3, 1960 at the age of 34. News of his death was received with dismay and outrage within anti-colonial and African nationalist circles. As Franz Fanon recalls,

> We hardly felt his death. A murder, but a bloodless one. There was neither volleys nor machine guns nor bombs. Thallium poisoning. It made no sense. Thallium! How was one to grasp such a cause? An abstract death striking the most concrete, the most alive, the most impetuous man. Felix's tone was constantly high. Aggressive, violent, full of anger, in love with his country, hating cowards and manoeuvres. Austere, hard, incorruptible. The essence of revolutionary spirit packed into 60 kilos of muscle and bone.
>
> In the evening we went to comfort the Cameroon comrades. The father, his face seamed, impassive, inexpressive, listened to me speak of his son. And progressively the father yielded place to the militant. Yes, he said, the program is clear. We must stick to the program. Moumie's father, at that moment, reminded me of those parents in Algeria who listen in a kind of stupor to the story of the death of their children. Who from time to time, ask a question, require a detail, then relapse into that inertia of communion that seems to draw them toward where they think their sons have gone.

On the Trail of an Assassin

As a result of the botched operation, the Swiss police quickly realized that Moumié was the victim of foul play. They initially suspected 25-year old Liliane Friedli, described either as Moumié's secretary or as a "woman of the night" with whom he spent his time in Geneva. Their suspicion even extended to Jean Martin Tchaptchet who had accompanied Moumié to the *plat d'argent*. Eventually their attention turned to Bechtel. The Swiss police found traces of Thallium in Bechtel's apartment and on his clothes. In spite of this, no arrest was made as the investigation painfully dragged on, ostensibly because of immense political pressure from the French. The French ultimately whisked Bechtel out of Geneva while the Swiss turned a blind eye, and was resettled in Southern France. Switzerland eventually issued an international warrant of arrest for Bechtel. However, no real efforts were made to arrest and bring him to justice. It was some 30 years later that he was "accidentally" arrested in Belgium in 1979 and extradited to France. In 1980 he was set free without a trial after a French judge inexplicably rendered a judgement of nonsuit.

According to Frank Garbely, producer of the 2005 documentary on the assassination of Moumié (*L'assassinat de Félix Moumié – L'Afrique sous contrôle*), the Moumié case was a political hot potato that both France and Switzerland badly wanted to go away. On the Swiss side, there were fears that the Moumié case would reveal how the allegedly neutral Swiss collaborated with, and covered the tracks of the French secret service as it persecuted and eliminated African nationalists. For France the stakes were even higher; an in-depth investigation of the Moumié case would have revealed that the SDECE had carried out an « Operation Homicide » on the nationalist leader, and would have invariably exposed France's brutal "pacification campaign" in Cameroon, which was being carried out far from the scrutiny of the international community, distracted at the time by the ongoing Algerian war of Independence.

William Bechtel died in a French military hospital shortly after he was set free without paying for his crime.

So who exactly ordered the hit on Moumié and how high up in the French government did the crime and cover-up go?

For years, French authorities strongly refuted any French government involvement in the Moumié assassination. Initially they even denied that Bechtel was a member of the French intelligence service, even though all the evidence pointed to the contrary. It wasn't until after Bechtel's death that tongues began to loosen. And it became apparent that the plot against Moumié directly involved the Matignon and even the Palais de l'Élysée.

True Confessions

As we saw earlier, General Grossin made one of the first public admissions of French government involvement in the assassination of Moumié to Roger Faligot and Pascal Krop in July 1984. In a forthcoming book by Faligot and Guisnel titled "*Histoire secrète de la Ve République*" (November 2006) which deals with the state secrets of the French Fifth Republic, General Grossin sheds more light on the Moumié assassination. In an excerpt published in *La Lettre du Continent*, the authors write:

> Questioned 20 years after the Moumié affair, General Grossin crudely shed light on the manner in which the SDECE set up the Moumié assassination, at a time when Prime Minister Michel Debré, just like Foccart, was troubled by the situation in Africa.
> One day, Debré says to me: There is a rebellion in the South of Cameroon, we have to do something. Do you have any information [on the rebellion]? I reply: Because of their tribal system, if you kill the leader, it is over. Moumié is the leader and he is in Switzerland. We can get rid of him... We decide to poison him but the dose is too strong, or he drank some coffee. In short, he was supposed to die upon his arrival in Conakry the next day.
> But he died in Geneva, hence the scandal... [My translation]

Recently in 2005, Pierre Mesmer, the former French High Commissioner to Cameroon from 1956 to 1958, and former French Prime Minister from 1972-1974, confirmed French responsibility for Moumié's death in Garbely's documentary. He justifies the assassination by arguing that the UPC was a communist party led by ruthless communists who deserved absolutely no mercy from the French...

Most significantly, two years before his death, Jacques Forccart, De Gaulle's Chief of Staff for African Affairs and the "father" of the *Francafrique* network finally conceded in an interview with *Jeune Afrique* (16 février 1995) that the Moumié assassination was the handiwork of the French. As he coyly stated in the interview: « *Je ne crois pas que cela ait été une erreur* » / "I don't think that it was an error." Foccart was even more forthcoming in *Foccart Parle: Entretiens avec Phillip Gaillard 1* which was published in 1995. According to Kaye Whiteman in his 1997 Foccart obituary,

> One revealing moment comes when Foccart admits that the French secret services eliminated the Cameroonian Marxist leader Felix-Roland Moumié in 1960. First, he volunteers the information that there had been an "execution." Asked who decided it, he responds evasively that "the archives will one day answer your question", a fall-back position he often adopts. Gaillard then quotes a book by Pascal Krop in which it is written, "Debré, advised by Foccart, decided to eliminate the irritant", which produces the cool response, "To tell the truth, not particularly Foccart." However one reads this, Foccart is conceding that he was among those who took the decision to murder someone who was inconvenient to French interests.

Moumié's Second Death

After his death in Geneva, Moumié's body was embalmed and taken to the Republic Guinea where he was buried in a sarcophagus in Conakry. This was supposed to be a temporary resting place for Moumié until a time when it would be possible to repatriate his body to Cameroon. The Cameroon government has always opposed the repatriation of Moumié's corpse to Cameroon.

On October 3, 2004, Felix Moumié's widow, Marthe Moumié, traveled to Guinea Conakry in the company of Frank Garbely to visit Moumié's grave. When they arrived at the cemetery, they were in for a nasty shock: the sarcophagus was empty! Moumié's grave had been vandalized and his embalmed body stolen. We will probably never know if this was a simple act of vandalism or yet another chapter in the decades-long attempt to erase the memory of Felix Moumié and other historic leaders of the UPC. One thing is certain, however: Moumié's remains have disappeared forever, and he will never be buried in his native Cameroon as he wished, neither will Cameroonians ever have the opportunity to pay their last respects to a man who, in spite of his shortcomings, had a nationalist vision for his country that was totally at odds (and rightly so) with what the French and their surrogates had in store for the French Cameroons, and ultimately the bilingual Cameroon Republic.

In this fairy tale the heroes do not live happily ever after…

Postscript: In a most tragic conclusion to the Moumié story, Marthe Moumié was brutally murdered in Ebolowa in the South province of Cameroon in January 2009 during what was officially described as a robbery. She was 78 years old.

References

"Appointment in Geneva. Monday." (November 14, 1960). *Time Magazine*. Retrieved March 15, 2009 from: http://205.188.238.109/time/magazine/article/0,9171,711950-1,00.html

Belfield, R. (2005). *The assassination business: A history of state-sponsored murder*. New York: Carroll & Graf.

Brittain, V. (2006). They had to die: assassination against liberation. *Race & Class*. 48 (1), 60-74.

Faligot, R., Guisnel, J., & Kauffer, R. (2006). *Histoire secrète de la Ve République*. Cahiers libres. Paris: La Découverte.

Faligot, R., & Krop, P. (1989). *La piscine: The French secret service since 1944*. Oxford, UK: B. Blackwell.

Fanon, F. (1988). *Toward the African revolution: Political essays*. New York: Grove.

Foccart, J. (1995). *Foccart parle 1995. 1*. Paris: Fayard.

« L'aveu de l'assassinat de Moumié. » (12 decembre 2006). *La Lettre du Continent* N°503.

Whiteman, K. (1997). The Man Who Ran Francafrique. *National Interest*. (49), 92-100.

15

Once Upon a Time... Osende Afana

March 26, 2007: On March 15, 1966 Osende Afana, one of the last of the "intellectual revolutionaries" died in Ndélélé subdivision deep in the dreaded Djoum forest in what is today Kadey division in the East Province of Cameroon. The circumstances of his death are still unclear to this day but what is known is that he was tracked down by Ahmadou Ahidjo's security forces, ambushed, killed and then beheaded. While his headless body was buried in an unmarked grave, legend has it that his head was taken to Yaounde and put on display for some members of the Ahidjo regime as a "war trophy."

The death of Osende Afana, one of the most influential but least known historic leaders of the Cameroun nationalist resistance, was another watershed in the nationalist struggle against the French-backed Ahidjo regime. It also closed the chapter on the brief and improbable life of one of the continent's leading intellectuals who could have become a professor in any top ranking French university if only he had been willing to make compromises and become a systems man like many of his contemporaries, but who abandoned academic robes for military fatigues in a revolutionary war in the jungles of Eastern Cameroon.

So how did the 36-year old Osende Afana, Cameroun's first PhD in Economics and one of the precursors of African economic nationalism, along side Amilcar Cabral, Antar Diop, etc, end up being hunted down and slaughtered like a wild animal deep in the forests of Djoum? This is his story.

Early Interest in the Politics of Liberation

Born in 1930, the young Osende became interested in politics at a very tender age. In 1947, for example, when he was barely 17 years old, he made the case for independence before visiting United Nations Visiting Mission to the French Cameroons as a representative of the *Association des etudiants camerounais* (see the 1947 edition of the *Yearbook of the United Nations*). After he was dismissed from the Major Seminary for insubordination, Osende Afana moved to lycée général Leclerc in Yaoundé where he was actively involved in student politics. Upon graduation, he left for the *Université de Toulouse* in France where he ultimately obtained a doctorate in economics. It was at Toulouse that he went into full bloom politically; he formally joined the *Union des Populations du Cameroun* (UPC) and helped found the Toulouse branch of the nationalist movement, along with a local chapter of the *Association des etudiants camerounais* (AEC).

Student Activist Extraordinaire

In 1954, Osende Afana represented the AEC in the radical Federation of Students from Black Africa in France - *Fédération des étudiants d'Afrique noire en France* (FEANF). Created in December 1950 during the Bordeaux congress of the African student associations of Bordeaux, Montpellier, Paris and Toulouse, FEANF quickly became

65

a thorn in the flesh of the French government. The association was at the forefront of the clarion call for immediate and unconditional independence for African countries still under the yoke of colonial rule. Even after the independence, FEANF continued its fight and was, according to Gonidec, "accused of systematically disparaging African governments and propagating the 'inoperative concepts' of neo-colonialism and imperialism." During its 8th Congress in 1957, FEANF formally adopted a series of resolutions that called for the total independence of Africa. This historic congress was chaired by none other than Osende Afana, then Vice-President in charge of communications.

By 1958, France began to openly discuss the possibility of granting independence to its African colonies. At the same time the French began a frenzied search for the "right people" to groom for an eventual take-over of positions of power in various African states upon their departure. Members of FEANF and other student associations who formed the elite of the soon-to-be-independent African states were suddenly confronted with a dilemma – either submit to the call of pseudo-independence being offered by France or keep fighting for real and unconditional independence – a dilemma that would continue long after the flurry of independence in the early 1960s. As Gonidec points out in *African Politics*:

> During struggles for national liberation, it is easier for intellectuals to lean on the side of (political) revolution, because the aim is to destroy a system which blocks their chances of acceding to jobs at higher levels...
>
> After independence, the situation becomes more complex. It is no longer merely a matter of replacing European rulers by African rulers, but of radically transforming society. Faced with this problem, intellectuals do not show evidence of the same cohesion, and finally split into three groups, adopting different class positions.
>
> Some of them rally to the cause of the minority dominant classes who wield the power of the State and who are the allies of imperialism...
>
> The Second group of intellectuals is constituted by those who are apparently revolutionaries because they believe that progress can result from the partial substitution of private (especially foreign) capitalism with state capitalism...
>
> Lastly, there are the truly revolutionary intellectuals. They are those who having realized that they cannot constitute an independent political force, have decided, as Franz Fanon puts it, to plunge into the mass of the people, to listen to the voice of the exploited people and to awake their political awareness. (p. 73 - 74)

The Revolutionary Option

For Osende Afana, there was no dilemma; he would continue the revolution. So in 1958 he left France clandestinely and headed for Cario, Egypt, where the UPC had set up its headquarters in exile. Osende Afana later explained that the choice to leave France and abandon his dreams of a teaching job in a French university was an easy one:

> I would not have had the courage to look at myself in the mirror every morning. I love Cameroon and I my heart bleeds when I see her being exploited in the worst possible manner. Even the most prestigious economic professorship in the world cannot stop that bleeding. The land of our ancestors deserves better than the scallywags at its head.

Osende Afana soon became one of the closest collaborators and advisers to the historic leaders of the UPC in exile – Félix-Roland Moumié, Ernest Ouandié and Abel Kingué – and was a member of the UPC delegation that went to the United Nations to defend the case for immediate independence for Cameroon. He was also the UPC representative at the Permanent Secretariat of the *Afro-Asian Peoples' Solidarity Organization* (AAPSO), which was headquartered in Cairo.

An unapologetic panafricanist who strongly believed in the resolutions of the Bandung non-aligned conference particularly its endorsement of South-South cooperation, Osende Afana worked hard at the AAPSO to establish a credible and mutually beneficial framework for Afro-Asian relations (See for example, Osende Afana, "Consolidating Afro-Asian Solidarity," 1960).

By the time UPC leadership moved the party's headquarters to Conakry in Guinea, he had become an indispensable piece in the UPC edifice.

Pan-Africanism and Economic Nationalism

Osende Afana was among the select group of African intellectuals who realized early on that political independence was meaningless if it was not accompanied by economic independence. Hence, he advocated for new economic models that were not subject to foreign control. It was in this context that he warned against the dangers of foreign aid. (see for example, Osende Afana, "Les dangers de l'aide exterieure", *Revolution Africaine*, No. 12, Alger, 1963). This was a view shared by Mamadou Dia who argued that:

> African Intellectuals would be wrong to think that they can discard or toy with Economic Sciences in order to achieve their cultural objectives. That would be tantamount to ignoring one of the fundamental tenets of Negro-African culture and resigning oneself to half-culture which will not stand the test of time or the assimilationist tendencies of other cultures because it has no root. The African man of culture cannot, under pain of serious mutilation, ignore the relationship that exists between the evolution of economic structures and that of the various phases of civilization (...). He cannot but realize that the genius of each people marks with an indelible seal not only his works of art, his philosophy but also his economy, i.e. his grip on the reality. (quoted by Elikia Mbokolo)

Alongside other African revolutionary intellectuals such as Majhemout Diop of Senegal, Amilcar Cabral of Guinea-Bissau or Issa Shivji of Tanzania, Osende Afana sought to establish the "reality of social classes and the class struggle in Africa." It was in this context that he developed his "theory of accelerated growth of the African economies," which he expounded in his publication, *l'économie de l'ouest africain, perspectives de développement* (1966), which Gonidec summarizes thus:

> On a purely theoretical level, some Africans have tried to gain acceptance of a conception of transition to socialism close to either the new democracy or national (or revolutionary) democracy. The former trend may be illustrated by the work of Osende Afana, Osende Afana, former leader of the FEANF and a UPC militant, killed in the Cameroon resistance. Here we find a Marxist analysis of African societies: the existence of social classes and the reality of the class struggle, and the setting of imperialism against the African people as the main contradiction. The remedies draw their inspiration from Chinese methods; compulsory planning, nationalization of all key sectors of the national economy, self-reliance, the necessity of a proletarian party, and the creation of a united front - a 'dictatorship of all revolutionary classes combined, led by the proletariat'. (p. 137)

While many might be baffled today at the Marxist-Leninist and socialist tendencies of the first generation of African revolutionaries (Neto, Cabral, Toure, and even Kenyatta and Nyerere, etc.), Ali Mazrui explains that:

> After the war, European communist parties continued to play a relatively important role in French-speaking Africa, but less so in English-speaking Africa where the British communist party, unlike its French counterpart, had not established strong roots... Marxism gained a stronger and more lasting foothold in other parts of Africa. The ....(FEANF) included in its rank, and especially among its cadres, a majority of Marxists, like Osende Afana of Cameroon, author of an important work on the economy of West Africa. Through communist study groups founded during the Second World War or soon after, and the General Confederation of Labour, many trade-union cadres became receptive to Marxism and to techniques for organizing the masses. (p.801).

But *l'économie de l'ouest africain* was not just another publication regurgitating sterile Marxist-Leninist dogma that would be discredited some three decades later with the fall of the iron curtain. As Nga Ndongo has pointed out, Osende Afana's work was part of a nationalist economic 'school' which offered an uncompromising – and accurate – critique of imperialism and neocolonialism, sought to demystification of monetary integration and cooperation, and unmasked the nefarious and debilitating effects of foreign debt and investment, among other things.

Most important to some, *l'économie de l'ouest africain* was also a blueprint for true Pan-Africanism. Afana believed that the creation of a multiplicity of regional organizations in Africa – Maghreb Union, Casablanca group, Monrovia group, etc. – was a threat to African unity, and that Pan-africanism had become a distant and even unattainable dream because of the inward-looking nature of these organizations:

> These regional groups could have set the basis for true African unity. Unfortunately, imperialists... deploy every effort to foil the realisation of the revolutionary unity of our continent. Thus even after the pan African Conference of Independent African Heads of State and Government that held in Addis Ababa in 1963, they continue the work of division under the guise of regional decentralization...
>
> At [the continental] level just as at the national level, the fight for unity and the fight against neocolonialism are one and the same fight. Only the liquidation of neocolonialism will make it possible to unite the entire continent under one government at the service of African people. The road to this ultimate goal passes through different phases made up of unity of action, strengthening of cooperation in the areas of politics and organization, and even through progressive regional organizations. (p. 197)

Some 40 years later, true African Unity is still a distant dream even after the creation of the African Union (AU), which has so far promised more than it has delivered. As the Elikia Mbokolo points out:

> The misfortune of Pan-Africanism lay in the new balance of power between the political leaders and the intellectuals after independence. Until then, there was more than collaboration between the two groups, a veritable osmosis in the sense that the political and intellectual functions were performed by the same movements and, often, by the same people.
>
> Afterwards, in an Africa dominated by "parties-states-nations", the political leaders appropriated all the powers to themselves and sidelined, sometimes with brutality and violence, the intellectuals from the political scene and from government. Economic thinking, though relevant, novel, bold and brilliant, was thus confined within university walls and nuclei of dissidence, while in the circles of princes there were all kinds of busy and shrewd "advisors" bent on keeping African States in the neo-colonialist structures.
>
> This produced disastrous consequences. Whilst on the political scene the Pan-African ideal was sluggishly moving toward the full emancipation of the continent, the latter was indeed paralysed (S. Amin) from the economic standpoint, incapable or unwilling to map out a development strategy for the entire continent, leaving it to each State to define its short term interests. By hanging onto the European Economic Community, particularly through the Lome Accord, African States found themselves bound hand and foot in traps against which they were warned by the first generations of Pan-African activists like Kwame Nkrumah (*Africa must unite*, 1963; *Neo-Colonialism*, 1965).

The Death of Moumié and the UPC Split

Following the assassination of UPC President Felix Moumié in Geneva, Switzerland in November 1960, cracks began to appear in the hitherto solid edifice of the UPC in exile. This ultimately led to a split within the party. It is generally accepted that the split was simply an offshoot of that between the Soviet Union and China. Donald Buskey writes, for example, that:

> The pro-Soviet group formed in 1961 was called Commité revolutionaire de l'UPC, or Revolutionary Committee of the UPC, led by Ernest Ouandie, second Vice President of the UPC. It also had close ties with the French communist party. The pro-Chinese faction called the Comité directeur de l'UPC, or Directing Committee of the UPC, led by Osende Afana, and headquartered in Brazzaville. (Page 114)

The UPC split was, however, only indirectly linked to differences between the Chinese and Soviet factions. It was triggered by the power struggle, which erupted after the sudden death of Felix Moumié in 1960. With the return of second Vice President Ernest Ouandie to Cameroon to lead the UPC rebellion, the leader of the UPC in exile was its first Vice President Abel Kingue. Kingue's authority was contested by "young Turks" such as Woungly Massaga who had abandoned his doctorate in Mathematics in France a few years earlier to join the UPC.

That power struggle reached its peak following the assassination attempt on Nkwame Nkrumah in the town of Kulungugu in August 1962. A few weeks after the assassination plot, a bomb exploded at the residence of Ndeh Ntumazah (President of the One Kamerun (OK) party, the Southern Cameroons offshoot of the UPC) shortly after a UPC meeting. In the confusion that ensued, scores of UPC exiles in Ghana were rounded up and jailed. It was while most of the UPC leadership was locked up in jail that the Revolutionary Committee was created.

Ntumazah and Abel Kingue later insisted that the mass arrest was the handiwork of the dissidents of the revolutionary committee led by Massaga. [See 1963 document written by Kingue and Ndeh Ntumazah titled *La vérité sur le comité révolutionnaire*, and Mongo Beti's 1981 clarification interview with Ntumazah published in *Peuples Noirs Peuples Africains* no. 25 (1982), pp. 48-66.] However, in his famous memoirs *Prisoner Without a Crime*, Albert Mukong, who spent 14 months in jail following these incidents, claims that Ghanaian security forces that were unhappy with Nkrumah's continued support of African Liberation Movements were behind the massive arrest of Cameroonian exiles.

When members of the UPC Steering Committee eventually left Ghana, they set up shop in Congo-Brazzaville, which shares a border with Cameroun. While in the Congo, this UPC faction collaborated militarily and politically with groups such as the *Popular Movement for the Liberation of Angola* (MPLA) and Pierre Mulele's Maoist *Parti Solidaire Africain*. The goal of exiled groups in Brazzaville was to create a revolutionary framework for politicizing and organizing the masses in view of waging a people's war. As Ludens has pointed out with regards to Pierre Mulele, he believed that it was

> ...necessary to politicize the masses, according to a scientific, anti-

imperialist, and socialist ideology. It is the only way to liberate a country from imperialism. The masses have to know who is their enemy, what is imperialism, and who are the agents of imperialism. Otherwise, national and social liberation is impossible.

It was on this basis that Mulele, who studied guerrilla warfare in China, launched a peasant uprising in Eastern Congo – the first ever in Africa - which lasted from 1963 to 1968 (the Kabila movement that ultimately ousted the Mobutu regime in Zaire in 1997 – and in which famed Marxist Che Guevara briefly participated in 1965 - was a remnant of the Mulele insurrection). In 1968, Mobutu lured Mulele back to Kinshasa with promise of Amnesty and then brutally murdered him... Mulele's insurgency was the blueprint for many revolutionary groups, including Osende's faction of the UPC. According to the *Yearbook on International Communist Affairs*:

> A new phase in the history of the UPC began in 1964 under the leadership of Osende Afana, who was elected Secretary-General of the "Provisional Committee of the UPC." The first plenary session of the Provisional Committee, in May 1965, adopted a 10-point program based on Marxism-Leninism and on the thoughts of Mao Tse-tung...

By the following year, the UPC was ready to begin its armed insurrection in Southeastern Cameroon, which it was hoped, would serve as a catalyst for a popular uprising against the Ahidjo regime.

The Eastern Front Opens

On September 1, 1965 UPC guerrillas "personally led by Afana" as Buskey points out (p. 114) attacked Southeast Cameroon from the Congo; Osende Afana's cherished dream of taking his nemesis Ahmadou Ahidjo head-on had become a reality...

> but the child returned
> with his luggage and dreams intact
> broad dreams
> but with hard words
> ...
> the child returned
> to the forest that he had chosen
> beforehand in the construction
> of the monument to his belief
> in the honor of his people
> (Patrice Nganang, *Elobi*)

Unlike the UPC insurgency in the Bamileke region, the rebellion in southeastern Cameroon promised more than it could deliver and the popular uprising never materialized. It was an insurgency carried out in a hostile natural environment and a relatively indifferent population – a recipe for failure, if not disaster. Major General Pierre Semengue, the head of Cameroonian armed forces, writes in his memoirs that:

> The rebellion of the peasants [i.e., in the Bamileke region] was rustic and pragmatic. That of the intellectuals (Ossendé Afana, Woungly Massaga, Samson Mondjengué) was a pitiful failure, even though they had better weapons than the national army; it did not last up to a month.

Woungly Massaga who is very much alive today insist that the General's statement is mere hyperbole, and points to the fact that as late as 1969 he was still personally carrying out insurgent attacks against government installations in Southeastern Cameroon.

Whatever the case, there is a general agreement that the insurgency ultimately failed. And there is a widespread view, even within UPC circles, that the insurgency was precipitated. This is the view shared by Ndeh Ntumazah who insisted in the 1981 interview with Mongo Beti that it was ill-conceived to start the insurgency without prior mobilization and organization of the masses, and without solidly implanting the UPC in the region. Ntumazah laments that as a result of this oversight, scores of brilliant and highly-educated UPC officials, many of them PhD holders, lost their lives in the forests of Southeastern Cameroon.

Evidently, by launching the guerrilla war when it did, the UPC deviated from the successful the Mulele blueprint whereby,

> In every village Mulele formed a group of young partisans in order to wage guerrilla warfare. Out of a population of 500,000 in the liberated zone of Kwilu, Mulele enrolled 100,000 young people in the guerrilla army! Moreover, in every village there was a revolutionary committee that directed community life. He started the formation of cadres to lead the revolutionary organization.

The End

On March 15, 1966, some six months after the beginning of the guerrilla campaign, Osende Afana became a casualty of war. There are conflicting versions about events leading up his death, but there seems to be a consensus that he was betrayed, ambushed by Ahidjo's security forces deep in the equatorial forest, then killed and beheaded:

> but the paths refused him their
> shade
> but the paths refused him
> refuge
> but the animals turned away
> from him

but the swamps refused him the
refuge of their reeds
and the jungle was closed to him
(Patrice Nganang – *Elobi*)

Dr. Castor Osende Afana was 36 years old when he died. It is alleged that no one was allowed to publicly mourn his death and that even his own mother had to go deep into the equatorial forest to cry for he lost son. The outpouring of emotion and anger after Osende Afana's death was best captured in a virulent editorial of the Paris-based *l'Etudiant d'Afrique noire* (no. 46), the radical student journal which he once headed in the 1950s – not only had the UPC lost one of its top officials, Africa had lost one of its most brilliant minds: Here is a an excerpt of that editorial which appears in Jacques Lantier's *l'Afrique déchirée (1967)*:

An Example of Self-Sacrifice: Osende Afana Falls at the Service of Africa

On March 15, 1966 at 10:30 am, comrade Osende Afana, Secretary General of the bureau of the Steering Committee of the UPC gloriously fell at the battlefront, his heart cowardly pierced by bullets of the imperial armed forces and their Kamerunian lackeys (UPC communiqué)...

Osende Afana, our comrade, our friend, our brother was thus cowardly assassinated by French mercenaries.

Osende Afana, our comrade, a longtime official of our journal l'Etudiant d'Afrique noire, dynamic militant, courageous, and an unapologetic and logical patriot.

Osende, our friend, who, after serving the Kamerunian revolution as a student, continued to serve as an official of the UPC; the representative of the UPC to the Afro-Asian group in Cairo for a number of years, he quit this position and became the Secretary General of the bureau of the Steering Committee (P) of the UPC.

French imperialism, along with its sinister manservant Ahidjo, has perpetrated a horrible crime against the Kamerunian people.

1958: Um Nyobe, the great leader of Kamerunian nationalism falls under a hail of bullets by French mercenaries.

1960: Felix Moumié, the Secretary General of the UPC dies in Geneva after being poisoned by the "Red Hand".

March 1966: Osende Afana.

As a result of this heinous act perpetrated against Africa, French imperialism has shown its true face; that of a relentless enemy of our people. It is not the balderdash about France's alleged favorable attitude towards the Third World which can mask this glaring fact. Ahidjo, the manservant of French imperialism, hangman of the Kamerunian people, continues in his crimes because he knows he is finished; finished because condemned by the valiant Kamerunian people: Ahidjo is a finished man. Given the level of popular discontent, no sorcerer can save this most reprehensible character that bears prime responsibility for the tragedy that has befallen our country (UPC press release 012-DE-CR-CP-66 of the UPC revolutionary committee) ... [My translation]

Conclusion

Osende Afana was a product of a time when African nationalism, anti-imperialism and socialism were natural bedfellows. And his actions and ideology must be understood in that context. With hindsight, he was overly optimistic about the ability of Marxism to resolve Africa's socio-political and economic problems. But he was not alone in that regard. However, in spite of his romanticization of Marxism, he was a visionary who understood that the battle for Africa's soul would ultimately be won – or lost – on the continent itself and nowhere else; not in Paris, London, Moscow or Peking. He also clearly understood that for Africa to be able to hold its own against the West both politically and economically, she had to imperatively resolve what historian Elikia M'bokolo refers to as the "quagmire of underdevelopment." Which is why he spent his last years not only planning for his revolution but also mulling and devising viable operational frameworks for resolving this quagmire.

> the majority of them... when they returned to Africa shamefully betrayed the noble ideals which they defended... in Paris. They joined the ranks of the bourgeoisie and adopted the motto FVVA (*Femmes, Villas, Voitures, Argent*). Only a few militants like Osende Afana practised what they had preached and died for the causes in which they believed: that of revolution.

Sadly for Africa, they don't come like that anymore ...

References

Busky, D. F. (2002). *Communism in history and theory: Asia, Africa, and the Americas*. Westport, Conn. ;London: Praeger.

Eyene, C. A. (2002). *Le Général Pierre Semengue - Toute une vie dans les Armées*. Yaounde, Editions Clé.

Gonidec, P. (1981). African politics. *African politics*. The Hague: M. Nijhoff.

Lantier, J. (1967). *L'Afrique déchirée, de l'anarchie à la dictature, de la magie à la technologie*. Paris: Planète.

M'bokolo, E. (2004). *Pan-Africanism in the 21st Century. First Conference of Intellectuals from Africa and the Diaspora*. Dakar, 6 - 9 October 2004. African Union. Retrieved March 15, 2009 from http://africa-union.org/CIAD_NEW/Documents/Elikia%20M'Bokolo%20En.pdf

Mazrui, A. a. A., & Wondji, C. (1999). *General history of Africa*. Unesco general history of Africa, V.8. Oxford: J. Currey ; Paris : UNESCO.

Mukong, A. W. (1989). *Prisoner without a crime* (Second Edition). Paris: Editions Nubia.

Kingue, A. & Ntumazah, N. (1963). *La vérité sur le comité révolutionnaire. Union Des Populations du Cameroun*. Retrieved March 15, 2009 from http://etoilerouge.chez-alice.fr/docrevinter2/cameroun1.pdf

Martens, L. (1997). "A New Development in the Congolese Revolution (interview)." *Solidarité Internationale*, April 1, 1997.

____. 1990. *Pierre Mulele and the Kwilu peasant uprising in Zaire*. London: Zed Books.

Nga Ndongo, V. (Janvier-Juin 2002) « De Castor Osende Afana à Georges Ngango : continuité et puissance d'une pensée économique nationaliste au Cameroun.» *Revue Africaine des Sciences Economiques et de Gestion*, Vol. IV, N° 1, pp. 43-74.

Nganang, A. P., & Goldblatt, C. (2006). *Elobi: Poems*. Trenton NJ: Africa World Press.

Traore, S. (1973). *Responsabiliteìs historiques des eìtudiants africains*. Paris: Eìditions Anthropos.

16

Repaid in his Own Coins: Ahmadou Ahidjo and the Politics of Ostracism

November 30, 2006: On November 30, 1989, Ahmadou Ahidjo, Cameroon's first President, died in exile in Dakar, Senegal, far away from the country that he had ruled with an iron and bloody fist for over two decades. Ostracized by the Biya regime which considered him public enemy number one, scorned by Cameroonians for his alleged role in the bloody 1984 coup attempt against his successor; and banished from official Cameroonian discourse and memory (bank notes with his image were withdrawn from circulation, public spaces that bore his name – such as the Ahmadou Ahidjo stadium – were renamed, his name a taboo in the official media, etc.), Ahidjo like the UPC exiles of the 50s and 60s, became, in his final years, a sad and lonely figure in exile, moving from Morocco, to France, and then finally to Senegal. According to a report in *Jeune Afrique* cited in *Cameroon Life Magazine* (1991), "[Ahidjo] was bitter. And sad. He felt profound grief at the way things had turned out between him and his successor. Saddening news about the daily worsening economic situation in Cameroon exacerbated his illness."

As soon as Ahidjo's death was announced, messages of condolence poured in from all over the world, except from Cameroon whose government was visibly irritated by the interest generated by his passing. His death was merely a footnote in the national news. Barely a month earlier, on October 31, 1989, the Government of Cameroon had reacted angrily to rumors that secret negotiations were underway between Biya and Ahidjo. In a statement in the national daily *Cameroon Tribune* (no. 4506, 31 octobre 1989, p. 1), Simon Nko'o Etoungou, Cameroon's ambassador to Paris and former Minister of Foreign Affairs under Ahidjo in the 1960s, lashed out against the rumor in very acerbic terms reminiscent of Ahidjo's own declaration at the UN some 30 years earlier:

> *Le gouvernement camerounais, sous la houlette de son chef, le président Paul Biya, a mieux à faire... que de ressusciter les morts* / The Cameroonian Government under the leadership of President Paul Biya has better things to do than to resuscitate the dead.

Ahidjo was buried at the Muslim Cemetery in Yoff, Dakar, where he still lies today, his grave tended by his wife, Germaine Ahidjo – a sad end for the "Father of the Cameroonian nation" whose regime left a trail of blood and tears...

Since his death, there have been regular calls for his full rehabilitation and the repatriation of his corpse to his native Garoua for a burial befitting of his status and stature in Cameroonian history. These attempts have been met with indifference and even hostility from Cameroonian authorities although a 1991 amnesty law (no. 91/022 of December 16, 1991) rehabilitated Ahidjo, along with Um Nyobe, Felix Moumié, and Ernest Ouandie (the rehabilitation of the hunter and the hunted...)

What is Good for the Goose…

There are many who are however not shedding a tear for Mr. Ahidjo, and who believe that his ignominious end is merely retributive justice for the leader who perfected the art of ostracizing and inflicting violence upon the dead. As Ahidjo himself vehemently argued at the UN in 1959, rehabilitating the UPC and its leaders would also "rehabilitate violence and crime, resuscitate the memory of mourning and tears, provoke individual score-settling and private vengeance, and insult the victims."

"We have forgotten. Why do they want us to remember again?" he asked.

The list of those whom Ahidjo "forgot," whom he refused to "remember," and whom the entire nation was ordered not to remember, is a very long one. That list begins with the historic leaders of the UPC.

The Roll Call of Infamy

The most famous among those whom Cameroonians were asked to forget was Ruben Um Nyobè, the leader of the *Union des Populations du Cameroun* (UPC) who was ambushed and executed on September 13 1958 (when Ahidjo was already Prime Minister of the French Cameroons). That he was dead was not enough for the regime. His body was dragged for miles to his village, completely disfiguring and dehumanizing him in the process. His mutilated body was then put on display – a shocking warning to all those who dared oppose Ahidjo and his French masters.

But that was not enough.

Before being buried at the Presbyterian mission cemetery in Eseka, Um Nyobe's body was entombed in cement to prevent anyone from having access to his body. Today the burial site of Cameroun's foremost nationalist is a nondescript one. Attempts by his family to bury him in a more befitting location in his village have been resisted by authorities.

Even that too was still not enough. As one historian put it, "even his ghost was hunted down." During Ahidjo's entire reign, and until recently, every effort was made to erase every trace of Um Nyobe's existence. His pictures and his writings were systematically destroyed, his family, friends, and sympathizers were persecuted. Anyone who mentioned his name, even in private, could be arrested and jailed for subversion.

Next on the list of infamy is Félix-Roland Moumié who succeeded Um Nyobe as the leader of the UPC. After his assassination in Geneva in 1960, Moumié was buried Conakry in the Republic of Guinea. Unlike Ahidjo, there is not even the slightest hope that his body will ever be repatriated to Cameroon - His grave was vandalized and his body stolen.

Abel Kingue, the UPC's first Vice President, also died in exile. He is buried in an unknown grave in Egypt.

Also on the list is Osende Afana, Cameroun's first PhD in economics and leader of the UPC's "eastern front" who was decapitated in 1966 in the South Province. His headless body lies in an unmarked grave somewhere in the forests of Djoum. Another national hero without even a street named in his honor…

The same is the case of Ernest Ouandie, the last historic UPC leader executed in Bafoussam in 1971. Like Um Nyobe, his grave is known but it is largely nondescript. In 1990, some members of the Cameroon opposition decided to lay a wreath at the spot where Ouandie was executed. A narrative of what happened next is found in Achille Mbembe's *On the Postcolony* (p.119):

> On Friday 18 January [1991], a communiqué issued by the Governor of Western Province invited the population to stay at home and to refrain from going into the streets for any reason whatsoever. Troops had been placed on alert since dawn on January 19. The municipal airport was closely guarded. Surveillance at all strategic points in the city had been increased, and extra vigilance ordered. Anyone remotely suspicious had to be identified and questioned as necessary.
>
> The spot where Ernest Ouandie was executed on the 15th January 1971 was taken over by men in uniform. The place is just behind the BICIC [bank] at Bafoussam and is [today] covered with grass.
>
> ...The forces of law and order, alerted by the gathering crowds, descended on the site, dispersing the crowd and seizing the bouquet of flowers. [Some people] were arrested by soldiers and taken to the office of the provincial Governor; there they were interrogated.

Without doubt, it is one of the cruelest ironies of modern Cameroonian history that Ahmadou Ahidjo, the man who made it his mission to erase all traces of the UPC historic leadership from Cameroonian history, is today suffering the same fate – buried in anonymity in a foreign land, and virtually forgotten in his native Cameroon.

Which Way Paul Biya?

Some have argued that by making Ahidjo's corpse *persona non grata* in Cameroon, Paul Biya may be inadvertently setting himself up for the same fate that befell his one-time "illustrious predecessor" turned mortal enemy. To Biya's credit though, the amnesty law of 1991 allowed the return of many Cameroonians who had gone on exile in the 1950s and 1960s, among them, Ndeh Ntumazah, founder of the One Kamerun party; Woungly Massaga, who with Osende Afana opened the UPC's "eastern front"; Mongo Beti, renowned for his virulent criticism of Ahidjo and who until his death in 2001 was a veritable thorn in Biya's flesh; and even Bishop Ndogmo who had the opportunity to visit Cameroon before his death.

In Need of National Healing

Ahmadou Ahidjo is just one piece of the puzzle in Cameroon's dire need to come to terms with its history and collective memory. What the country desperately needs is a recognition of all its heroes - from early nationalists such as Kuv'a Likenye who defeated the Germans in 1891 but lies in an unmarked grave in Buea while his German adversaries are immortalized in grandiose monuments across

Cameroon; to Duala Manga Bell, Martin Paul Samba, the historic leaders of the UPC, and even Ahidjo himself. As Francis Wache rightly pointed out in 1991, "Let us make no mistake; until we exorcise the ghost of our political forefathers – Ahmadou Ahidjo, Um Nyobe, Felix Moumié, Ernest Ouandie, Osende Afana… the center of this triangle called Cameroon can never hold."

Part Four

The University in Crisis

17

When History Repeats Itself: The Government Spin Machine and the UB Crisis

December 18, 2006: As I watched the tragic events at the University of Buea unfold in the past couple of weeks, and listened to the official narrative of events regarding the shooting of two students by the Cameroonian security forces, it all sounded so eerily familiar. And with good reason; we had been down this path before. The Government's reaction to the death of the students reminded me of its reaction to another student demonstration some 16 years earlier at the University of Yaounde.

Just as in Buea this year, the government narrative of what actually occurred at the university of Yaounde campus in Ngoa-Ekele on May 26, 1990 did not square in with the facts. And in a bizarre twist of fate, one of the central figures in the events of May 26, 1990 also happens to be at the center of the UB maelstrom of November 2006...

May 26, 1990. Cameroonians apprehensively await the outcome of the inevitable confrontation between the Social Democratic Front (SDF) and the Biya regime in the town of Bamenda. Officials of the SDF, a political party created a couple of months earlier, have chosen this day to officially launch the party in Bamenda, in spite of a government order formally banning the event on grounds that the SDF is illegal – a view not shared by SDF members and sympathizers who are determined to go ahead with the launching come what may. Bamenda is flooded with troops sent in to crackdown on any SDF-led public manifestation while thousands of SDF sympathizers from all over the Northwest province and beyond converge on the city under siege. Against all odds, the party is successfully launched at the Ntarikon motor park where John Fru Ndi, the party's Chairman, reads the inaugural speech. By the end of the day, however, six teenagers lose their lives, "trampled to death" at the rally, according to an official communiqué from the Government.

On the same day students at the University of Yaounde organize a pro-democracy rally on campus in support of multiparty politics which is disrupted by security forces. What follows is a six-hour orgy of violence and destruction as troops spread their dragnet across campus and into the nearby student *quartiers* where, with the assistance of university-appointed "student delegates," they zoom in on residential areas with a high concentration of English-speaking students. Hundreds of rooms are broken into, their occupants severely beaten and then carted away to detention centers around town. About 400 students are arrested by the end of the day.

Even before the arrested students settle down in their respective detention centers later that evening for their first dose of "coffee", the official spin machine is already working in overdrive. According to a communiqué repeatedly broadcast on radio and TV, the University of Yaounde demonstration was not a "national affair", contrary to the claims of the international media, but an ethno-regional venture spearheaded by a "handful of misguided students" of from the Northwest province who had gone on rampage after being confronted by a larger group of patriots made up of students from "all ten provinces of Cameroon."

Worse, continued the communiqué, these "vandals" had committed a most treasonous act by singing the national anthem of "*un pays voisin*" (a neighboring country). Anyone remotely familiar with Cameroonian politics knows that when a "pays voisin" is mentioned with regards to Cameroon's English-speaking minority, the country in question is none other than Nigeria. The communiqué also stated that the crowd at the rally in Bamenda was made up primarily of thousands of Nigerians imported from across the border for the occasion by the SDF, and that SDF leader, John Fru Ndi, had fled to where else? Nigeria!

In Cameroonian politics, linking "les anglophones" with "le Nigeria" or "un pays voisin" in times of crisis is not an innocent act; it is a powerful tool for demonization and exclusion which is meant to conjure images of the *Biafrazation* of the country; of a fifth column serving the interests of Nigeria rather than Cameroon's; and of a powerful neighbor busy manipulating the "Anglophone Trojan horse" to its advantage. Expectedly, the communiqué resonated quite well with large segments of the Francophone majority which generally believes in the inherent (pre)disposition of English-speaking Cameroonians to betray *la patrie*.

"Enemies in the House"

Within hours of the communiqué being broadcast, pseudo-patriots of all stripes rose up in unison to condemn those "Biafrans" in Yaounde and Bamenda who had finally showed their true colors. The opening shots were fired on May 28 by the Mfoundi section of the ruling CPDM party whose President, Emah Basile (also Mayor of Yaounde at the time), declared on national radio that Anglophones were "*Enemis dans la maison*"(enemies in the house). In an interview published in the Government-owned *Cameroon Tribune* the next day, Ibrahim Mbombo Njoya, the Minister of Territorial Administration lashed out at the alleged traitors: "Those who do not feel Cameroonian should go elsewhere" (*Ceux qui ne se sentent pas camerounais peuvent aller ailleurs*).

The patriotic fervor that gripped the French News desk of CRTV reached fanatical proportions as otherwise level-headed journalists did their best to outdo each other in spewing out the most virulent anti-Anglophone vitriol which had nothing to envy from the kind of material that would be heard a few years later on Rwanda's *Radio Milles Colines*. One of these notorious commentaries titled "*La cinquième colonne*" (The Fifth Column) was read by Zacharie Ngniman (later CPDM Member of Parliament from Mayo Banyo) on the French Newscast of Monday May 28, 1990. The opening lines went straight for the jugular:

> When an individual claims to be a patriot, and believes that it is his right to demonstrate on the [university] campus and in the streets, this presupposes that the said individual has nothing but respect love and fidelity towards his nation.

What should we therefore make of the individual who, claiming to express this right, sings the national anthem of another country?

Isn't that the manifestation of an inherent disposition to betray one's own nation and compatriots?

This blasphemous and divisive act, which is an insult to the nation, was indeed committed on May 26 by a handful of activists at the University of Yaounde and in the streets of Bamenda. Individuals who were victims of intoxication and manipulation sang the national anthem of a neighboring country". [My translation]

Even the usually critical French language private press swallowed this tale, hook, line and sinker. The Douala-based *La Détente* best captured the general mood East of the Mungo River with a three-word headline: *"Ils ont osé!"* (They had the guts!).

The Spin Machine Unravels

As with most lies, it was not long before cracks started appearing in the Government's story. First, pictures and leaked autopsy reports from Bamenda confirmed that the six youngsters had died of bullet wounds – "trampled by bullets" as the French language private press would later put it, once it regained its senses. Also, a painstaking effort to reconstitute the events at the University of Yaounde eventually proved that university students never sang anything close to the Nigerian national anthem.

Zacharie Ngniman and Antoine-Marie Ngono, respectively Editor-in-Chief and Chief of Service for Political Affairs on CRTV Radio, the two Francophone journalists who had led the vicious attack against the Anglophone community, would later write a pathetic open letter to the Minister of Information, complaining that Government officials had deliberately misled them.

> By making us say things like 'the dead in Bamenda were trampled upon' did we lie or were we misled? By making us announce that Mr. John Fru Ndi had escaped to Nigeria when he was relaxing in his bookshop in Bamenda... we were sacrificed to public vilification.

In his 1993 book, *Cameroun: la démocratie emballée* (Yaoundé, 1993) Ngniman tries explain how he unwittingly became part of one of the most shameful episodes in recent Cameroonian history.

The *coup de grace* was given by Cardinal Tumi during a Press conference on June 11, 1990 when he berated the journalists of the official media and lashed out: "You have lost all credibility in the eyes of the public you are merely 'your master's voice.'"

The Puppet Masters

While the French language official media was roundly condemned – and rightly so, for their overzealous pursuit of the "treacherous Anglophones," they were nonetheless mere pawns in a macabre puppet show put up by puppet masters pulling the strings in the shadows. It would be eventually revealed that the tale of "Anglophone treason" had been concocted at the highest levels of Government, precisely by the infamous "cellule de communication" at the Presidency. This communications cell, whose notoriety would increase during the "smoldering years" of 1991-1992, was headed by none other than ... Jacques Fame Ndongo .

Neither Fame Ndongo nor anyone else was ever sanctioned for their role in the "Nigerian treason" scandal. Instead, Fame Ndongo continued his meteoric rise within the Biya regime, which began in the early 1980s with the publication of his overly effusive treatise titled *Paul Biya ou l'incarnation de la rigueur* (Paul Biya or the incarnation of rigor). After the events of May 1990, he would subsequently be rewarded with the position of Chancellor of the University of Yaounde I, then Minister of Communication, and Minister of Higher Education (while still maintaining his position as a *Chargé de mission* at the Presidency – a position he has held since 1984...).

Today, Fame Ndongo is the central player in the University of Buea crisis, which culminated in the death of two youngsters. And like 16 years earlier, he is one of the brains behind the "police self defense" narrative, which has been used to justify the killing of unarmed students in Buea.

Self Defense of Excessive Force?

According to a communiqué that the Minister published in *Cameroon Tribune* on November 29, 2006, a violent mob armed with machetes, stones and locally-made hunting guns, invaded the university campus with the "strong determination" to ransack the university computer center. After being pushed back by forces of law and order, the communiqué goes on, the assailants turned their attention to the Molyko police station and began firing at the police. Two of the assailants were killed when the Police returned fire in self-defense, the communiqué claims. During a stormy question-and-answer session at the National Assembly a few days later, the Vice Prime Minister of the Republic, who also serves as Minister of Justice, added insult to injury by declaring that the "student vandals" had it coming: "Ils se sont livrés à des actes de violence et de vandalisme, et mal leur en a pris."

However, eyewitness reports tell a completely different story. For example, according to an article in *The Post* newspaper in its online edition of November 30, 2006 (a version confirmed by a variety of sources including some UB officials):

> Earlier at 7.00 pm, that same day, heavily armed anti-riot police had entered the University campus and began beating students indiscriminately. They also fired tear gas at them. Some of the students who were reportedly beaten had been hospitalised by press time.
>
> As the anti-riot police descended on the campus, the students dispersed

and filled the main road. They pulled down kiosks, billboards and other structures, setting them on fire. The police followed them and a running battle ensued.

More tear gas was fired and the students replied with a volley of stones. That is when gunshots rang out felling two students. By press time, it was alleged that more deaths had occurred in the Molyko neighbourhood.

The indiscriminate nature of the violence unleashed by the security forces was seen in the case of Laura Ambang, a hairdresser who was shot in the neck as she tried to close her saloon in the vicinity of the University. This particular case was confirmed by the Mayor of Buea, Mbella Moki, who in an interview to *The Post* (online edition of 06 December 2006) described how he "braved all the teargas and bullets to come to the succour of the lady" as she lay dying in a local clinic that lacked the facilities to save her life – a snapshot of the havoc that security forces wrought during the "peacekeeping" mission.

A Culture of Impunity

The UB crisis has once again demonstrated in the most macabre way, the culture of impunity and arrogance which reigns in Cameroon – a country where the Government never accepts responsibility (even if only moral responsibility) for acts committed in its name; where government officials are never punished for crossing the line as long as they are "toeing the line" of the regime in power; and where dissenting voices that deviate from the official discourse are considered criminal and treated as such. As a foreign observer of the UB crisis rightly put it:

> While the violence has ended and students have resigned themselves to the government's initial position, the government has only succeeded in proving to Anglophones (and many Francophones) once again … that they are welcome to participate in the political process as long as they support the "correct" positions.

18

Deconstructing Regional Balance and Higher Education in Cameroon

Should admissions into state-owned universities be based solely on merit or should "sociological balance" be taken into account?

January 14, 2007: At the root of the deadly crisis that engulfed the University of Buea in November / December 2006 were deep-seated disagreements over the application of the principle of "regional balance," Cameroon's attempt at affirmative action. The crisis began when Prof. Fame Ndongo, the Minister of Higher Education invalidated the list of successful candidates eligible to participate in the oral part of the entrance examination into the Faculty of Medicine which had been published by that university's Vice Chancellor.

According to the Minister, the Vice Chancellor's list was null and void because it was based solely on merit (it consisted of the best 127 candidates who sat for the written part of the exam) and failed to "respect of the sociological balance [of Cameroon], the guarantor of national integration and stability". As the Minister pointed out in a press release carried by the national media:

> the list of eligible candidates to sit the oral part of the examination [was] composed of 127 Anglophone candidates and no francophone candidate, whereas out of the 870 candidates who sat for the written part of this examination, there were 292 francophone candidates, that is 33.56% of the total... As a result... 26 best francophone candidates were added by the Jury to the list of eligible candidates to sit for the oral part of the examination, without suppressing a single name of successful Anglophone candidates, thereby bringing the total number of candidates eligible to sit for the oral part of the examination to 153.

And when the final list of the 85 successful candidates was made public, an accompanying press release stressed that the list was driven by "regional balance" considerations. For the first time in the history of public examinations in Cameroon, official results included a detailed breakdown of the linguistic and provincial origins of the successful candidates: - 25 Francophones were admitted against 60 Anglophones with the following provincial breakdown: 39 students from the Northwest province; 21 from the Southwest; 6 for the Western province; 4 from Adamawa; 4 from the South; 4 from the Center, 3 for the North; 2 from the Littoral; 2 from the Far North, and 3 from the East.

Although the Minister insisted that this balance was in conformity with texts governing Higher Education in Cameroon, it was definitely not in conformity with the ministerial decision signed by the same Minister in August 2006 organizing the examination into the UB medical school. According to Article 10 of the decision:

"A l'issue de l'étude du dossier et des épreuves écrites, le jury dresse et publie par ordre alphabétique la liste des <u>72 meilleurs candidats admissibles</u> à l'épreuve orale." (i.e., after the review of student files and the written examination, the jury shall publish, in alphabetic order, the list of the **best 72 candidates** eligible to take part in the oral exams).

According to article 12 (1) of the same decision, *"à l'issue de l'entretien, le jury établit une liste des candidats proposés à l'admission au concours <u>par ordre de mérite</u> en tenant compte des notes obtenues aux trois épreuves"* (i.e., after) the orals, the jury shall establish a list of candidates proposed for admission **by order of merit.**

Lambi Erred

As an aside, it is noteworthy that article 12(2) of the ministerial order clearly states that *"les résultats définitifs sont publiés par Communiqué du Ministre de l'Enseignement Supérieur"* (i.e., the final results are published through a communiqué issued by the Minister of Higher Education). On this point at least, Fame Ndongo was right to insist that dismissed Vice Chancellor Cornelius Lambi overstepped his authority when he unilaterally published a list of successful candidates without consulting the Minister of Higher Education – but that is another story for another time which goes to the failings of Cameroon's over-centralized system which one foreign observer argues, "will either drown itself, or kill any hope of innovation and advancement."

Outrage across the land

Predictably, the entire UB saga sparked outrage across the country, particularly among English speaking Cameroonians. As *The Post* newspaper stated in a commentary,

> The lessons from the recent University of Buea saga are numerous. When it comes to Anglophone institutions, the government voraciously announces 'regional balance'. Where, one may ask Prof. Fame Ndongo, is regional balance in CUSS, Polytechnic, School of Public Works, Police College(s), CEFAM, P&T School, ENAP, ESSTIC, ENAM etc, etc.?

The reaction was largely the same among Francophone Cameroonians as evidenced by a stinging commentary by *Le Messager* columnist, Shanda Tonme:

> The Minister published the results, indicating the percentage of successful candidates by ethnicity, in effect by Bantustan, like in the worst days of the Apartheid regime in South, all in the name of regional balance. Why is there no balance in the number of Vice Chancellors [in state-owned universities]? Why are two out of six Vice Chancellors from the same ethno-tribal group as the Minister? ...
> Why is regional balance not applied everywhere? Does the Minister know

that his native province has one Member of Parliament for every 24,000 inhabitants against one Member of Parliament for more than 350,000 inhabitants in the Littoral, West and North-West provinces? Does the Minister know that one out of five Police Commissioners, one out of three Police Officers, one out of four Army officers, one out of three cabinet ministers, are natives of the Centre-South? Where then is the (regional) balance that the Minister talks about, if not in the voracious determination to control and grab everything by practicing exclusion and marginalization, and by encouraging the spread of sentiments of hate and revenge, to the greatest misfortune of the country?

During his ten-year reign as the head of Cameroon's lone state-owned school of journalism... one out of three student journalists trained in that institution were from the Centre-South

So, where is the balance?

Topsy-turvy Regional Balance?

Was *The Post* right in claiming that UB had been singled out as a testing ground for this nebulous concept called regional balance? Was the whole "regional balance" talk simply a means to hide the fact that the ruling elite tried to force their "dull kids" on UB at the expense of meritocracy and competence as Tomne argued? In short, was the application of "regional balance" at UB really an anomaly within Cameroon's higher education system?

It is not possible to answer this question conclusively without a detailed study of the ethno-regional breakdown of the origins of students admitted into the different institutions of higher learning across the country. However, anecdotal evidence clearly indicates that ethno-political favoritism rather than regional balance has governed the admission process into the *Grandes Ecoles* in the last couples of decades – just as the Biya regime tried unsuccessfully to artificially create a Beti business class in the mid 1980s to rival the Bamileke, so too did it try (this time with great success) to create a new Beti elite within the higher echelons of the public service, the police and the army by manipulating the admissions process into professional schools...)

Until November last year, the website of the Ministry of Higher Education carried detailed admission results for the country's professional schools. However, the website went offline during the UB crisis. It was brought back online only last week, but stripped of all the professional school results for the 2006-2007 academic year (was this a technical problem or a political decision???) Fortunately, due to an obvious oversight, the site still has the admissions results for the *École Polytechnique* (School of Engineering), which is Cameroon's most prestigious scientific and technical institution of higher learning (modeled after the French Polytechnique and not to be confused with the far less prestigious polytechnic in the Anglo-Saxon system).

Communiqué N° 06/0182/MINESUP/DDES/PEEX of 11 August 2006 signed by Fame Ndongo "To admit candidates into the first year of the School of

Engineering (ENSP) of the University of Yaoundé I, for the 2006/2007 academic year" states that:

> The following candidates **ranked in order of merit** are definitively admitted into the first year of the School of Engineering of the University of Yaoundé I for the 2006/2007academic year, subject to the presentation of the originals of the required certificates.

Note that admission into this institution is by "order of merit" with no reference to "sociological balance" as was the case with admission into the UB medical school. Also, a cursory glance at the list of 100 admitted students shows that the regional balance so stridently demanded in Buea has been largely ignored. While some might be argue that the *Polytech* case alone does not prove a pattern, it nonetheless confirms that the "regional balance" demands that were at the center of the discord in Buea are not universally applied across the board.

It is said in some quarters that the ruling elite is not interested in institutions such a *Polytech* where you cannot survive "without brains" and whose graduates generally end up in unglamorous – technical/scientific jobs that offer little or no access to state rents and prebends [use of public office for private enrichment]. The political elite are more interested in sending their progeny to "lucrative" schools such as the Police Academy or the School of Administration and Magistracy (CENAM) which trains high-ranking administrators, treasury inspectors, etc., who have direct access to budgets and quickly become key players in the prebendal system.

A Legitimate Debate

Without doubt, the regional balance debate is a legitimate one in a multi-ethnic and bilingual country such as Cameroon. In principle, regional balance, like affirmative action in the United States, is one which makes lots of sense in a country where history and geography have created regions that are lagging behind others, and where colonialism and post-colonial politics also created favored and disfavored ethnic groups. However, if regional balance is to truly become the cornerstone of Government policy (be it in admissions into state-owned institutions of learning, in appointments to high-level positions in government, or in the creation of road infrastructure and social amenities), then is should operate within a framework which is transparent, objective, accountable and public. And to avoid situations such as that which happened in the University of Buea, "regional balance", if it must be applied in higher education, MUST operate under guidelines that are publicized before competitive exams and not during or after.

Regional balance is too emotional, too divisive and too explosive an issue to be left to the whims and caprices of politicians and bureaucrats with hidden agendas who discard the policy when it suits them. For regional balance to succeed, clear laws must be adopted to govern its implementation. Until that happens (please don't hold your breath...) regional balance will continue to be seen (and rightly so) as a tool to promote mediocrity and ethnic dominance at the expense of excellence and the masses.

19

University of Buea: What is the Cost of Quality Education?

March 05, 2007: Students attending state-owned universities in Cameroon do not pay tuition. Instead they pay an annual registration fee of 50,000 FCFA [98 US Dollars]. This fee was instituted in the wake of the 1993 university reforms, which decentralized the University of Yaounde (then the country's lone university) and created five new universities across the country.

According to a report on these reforms published by the University of Buea,

> This fee was irrespective of degree programme or kind of degree pursued. Although the fee amount is a substantial increase from the 3,500 CFA francs (about $6) charged to students previously, it remains far below the fees paid by students in the country's private primary and secondary schools. Registration fees paid by students have quickly become one of the universities' principal sources of income, contributing about 30% of their recurrent budgets. The rest of the funds (over 70%) are provided by government.

In the past decade, attempts by state universities to increase this fee through a variety of mandatory fees has generally been met with stiff resistance by students and even higher education authorities (e.g. the University of Buea's discontinued annual development fund). In fact, some have even advocated the cancellation, pure and simple, of the registration fee on grounds that it is still too expensive for the average Cameroonian family – this in spite of the fact that, as another article by Ngwana has stressed, "parents and students were still able to respond to the calls of private universities paying tuition fees, which were three to eight times the registration fees in state universities (at least $250)."

In May-June 2005 for example, the University of Buea (UB) was crippled by a strike initiated in part because additional fees were tagged to the 50,000 FCFA registration fee. The strike action ended only after the Minister of Higher education signed an agreement with the student union stating that:

> the school fees of the University of Buea has been reduced to FCFA 50.000 flat, with all other additional payments like medical fees, Departmental & Faculty fees scraped; with the assurance that the students' caution fees should be refunded to them at the end of their programmes.

The same scenario repeated itself during the November/December 2006 strike at the same university. Earlier that year, the University Senate instituted a series of professional-oriented graduate programs (such as the much sought-after MBA) for the 2006/2007 academic year. A number of distance-learning programs were also planned for the same academic year. However, the university did not have the financial resources to get these programs off the ground and the State was not ready to dish out the necessary funds. Consequently, university authorities sought to make the new programs self-sustaining by instituting tuition. Students, however, insisted that the proposed tuition be scrapped and the cost of all graduate programs maintained at the 50,000 FCFA.

In an interview with *The Post*, former Vice Chancellor, Prof. Lambi – under whose reign the new graduate programs had been instituted – explained the rationale behind the increases:

> It should be noted that the state had fixed the amount for university registration at FCFA 50,000 and up to this moment, we have been paying that even for postgraduate programmes. Since many students request for programmes which we do not offer at the postgraduate level; considering that it entails bringing experts from out of the country and other costs, I had suggested to the Minister that they pay something extra. Since we made the proposal, the Minister is yet to reply and that is why we have not given out admission letters to anybody. But if they take postgraduate programmes that we already run, there is no problem; they will pay the FCFA 50,000. For specialised programmes like Masters in Business Administration, MBA, which has been demanded by many, we are proposing that they pay FCFA 750,000, but the Minister has not given his accord, so we are yet to give admission to anybody. You would want to know that mostly those in industries and big business enterprises have demanded the MBA programme.

This explanation literarily fell on deaf ears and in the end, the students prevailed. In another agreement, this time between the Student Union and the new university administration, university authorities agreed, according to an article in The *Post* titled *UB Strike Pays Off*, "to step down fees at all levels of degree programmes in the university to FCFA 50,000, while those who had paid more than the amount for postgraduate programmes would be refunded the balance."

Pyrrhic Victory?

The students had won yet another battle against the university administration but was this victory really to their advantage? One of the primary goals of the 1993 reforms was to "make [university] programmes more varied, professional, adapted and responsive to the needs of the job market, by providing more programmes that would enable graduates find employment in the private sector as well as create self employment." However, as a result of the students' victory, most of the new graduate programs were put on the back burner due to a lack of funding. Distance-learning programs, which were to be based on partnerships with top foreign universities and academics, are yet to see the light of day due to prohibitive costs. The result is that UB will continue the old-age tradition of producing thousands of unemployable "generalists" with no specific marketable skills. From the university's perspective, the result has been the loss of revenue streams particularly from companies that were willing to pay the "big bucks" to (re)train their staff.

Whatever one's stance on the issue of tuition at state-owned universities, it is obvious that UB and UB students are the ultimate losers here... And the irony is that other state universities – even those like the university of Yaounde whose students always lead the call for the abolition of registration fees – are making major strides in setting up professional degree programs.

The Example from other State Universities

It will come as a surprise to many that other Cameroon state universities have degree programs where students pay tuition which, in some cases, is more than 10 times the official registration fee. One of the flagship programs of the Fotso Victor Institute of Technology in Bandjoun (which is part of the University of Dschang) is the undergraduate program in Information Technology created under the auspices of the *Projet Comètes*. This program has become so popular that it is being offered as an e-learning degree to students in Central and West Africa (The « licence *de Technologie Informatique, option Informatique et Réseau, spécialité Concepteur-Développeur Réseaux-Internet (LTCDRI3)*. The annual tuition of this program is 400,000FCFA [784 US Dollars] for Cameroonian students and 600,000FCFA [1176 US Dollars] for foreign students. [As an aside, Monday's issue of *The Post* carries an interview with the French ambassador to Cameroon who reveals that plans are underway to extend the *Projet Comètes* to the University of Buea. Will UB students allow this program to take root?]

A similar program is offered by the Computer Science department of the University of Douala, in collaboration with the University of Laval in Canada and the African Virtual University. Courses are beamed in real time from the University of Laval with students in both universities following the same lectures. Tutoring is however done by local faculty in Douala. The tuition for the joint program is 630,000 FCFA [1235 US Dollars] per year (as opposed to about 10.000 US Dollars for students at the Laval campus).

The newly inaugurated Digital Law Center at the University of Yaounde II in Soa will begin offering graduate and doctoral degrees in Fundamental Law, Ethics and Human Rights during the 2007/2008 academic year. The degree programs are offered in collaboration with the University of Nantes in France. The courses were already being offered to students through the Yaounde Digital Campus of the *Agence Universitaire Francais* (AUF). According to the University's Vice Rector, tuition is expected to be "FCFA 650,000 and above."

This is just a small sample of the plethora of tuition-based degree programs currently being offered by state-universities in Francophone Cameroon. It is estimated that about 90% of students who graduate from programs such as the one offered by IUT Bandjoun are employed within six months. Students in these programs have understood that quality education does not come cheap, and that in this age of globalization and knowledge economy, marketable skills are what matter most.

Getting Student Buy-in

Without doubt, UB students are short-changing themselves by consistently rejecting all degree programs that cost more than the official registration fee, irrespective of the cost and infrastructure needed to launch and sustain the programs. That said, high tuition fees do not automatically translate into good quality programs; university authorities should be able to demonstrate that these new courses are actually worth their weight in gold.

Also, if these programs stand a chance of ever getting off the ground, then UB authorities must device new strategies for involving students (through the student union for example) when these programs are still in the design or conceptual stages. This might be the only way of getting the indispensable student buy-in –a tough call in a system where dialogue and conciliation are generally seen as a sign of weakness.

As long as students believe that proposed fee hikes are merely get-rich-quick schemes by university authorities, then it is unlikely that they will ever agree to any fee hike. And in the end, it will be the University of Buea, that famous "place to be," that will ultimately lose its luster and become the lame duck of Cameroon's university system.

References

Njeuma, D., Endeley, H. et al. (1999) *Reforming a National System of Higher Education: The Case of Cameroon*. A Washington DC, Report of the ADEA Working Group On Higher Education, World Bank.

Ngwana, T. A. (2003, December 12). "University strategic planning in Cameroon: What lessons for Sub-Saharan Africa?" *Education Policy Analysis Archives*, 11(47). Retrieved March 15, 2009 from http://epaa.asu.edu/epaa/v11n47/.

20

Regional Balance, Educational Quotas and (Under)development in Northern Cameroon

January 11, 2009: The year 2008 ended in Cameroon with a major controversy over competitive examinations into the Teachers' Training College (ENS) of the newly-created University of Maroua in the Far North Province. It is alleged that prior to the launching of the competitive exams, the Head of State personally guaranteed the elite of the *Grand Nord* (i.e., Adamoua, North and Far North provinces) that 60% of registered candidates from the three northern provinces would be admitted into ENS Maroua.

When the results were released, 760 candidates from the *Grand Nord* were among the 2253 admitted into the first and second cycles of the School. These results incensed the northern elite who pointed out that only 14% of registered candidates from the northern provinces had been admitted, far short of the 60% promised. The Minister of Higher Education presented his own figures, which showed that 36% of candidates from the Grand Nord had been admitted. In any case, Members of Parliament from the *Grand Nord* demanded an additional 500 places, failing which they would organize sit-ins and protest rallies, and also disrupt the seventh edition of the National Arts and Culture Festival (FENAC), which was scheduled to begin in Maroua on December 19, 2008.

The MPs were roundly condemned in the media and elsewhere for trying to sacrifice "meritocracy" on the altar of "ethnic politics." Northerners retorted by pointing out that the entire *Grand Nord* was an "educationally backward region," and that this backwardness was largely due to the fact that teachers from the Southern parts of the country (who form the bulk of the country's teaching corps at all levels) generally refuse to take up teaching positions in the northern provinces which are considered too remote. There is even a running joke that only Peace Corps Volunteers who don't know any better are excited about living in the *Grand Nord*. In fact, the government itself routinely sends civil servants who have fallen out of grace to the northern provinces as a punitive measure. They also pointed out that less than three per cent of students in existing Teachers' Training Colleges, all of which are in the Southern regions of the country are from the *Grand Nord*. The MPs therefore argued that it was imperative that the University of Maroua and the ENS in particular be used to resolve the "Educational imbalance" between the North and South. In other words, the University of Maroua and its institutions should be the preserve of Northerners.

On December 18, one day before the FENAC began, the government caved in to the Northern demands. However, instead of simply granting the region the additional 500 places demanded by the MPs, it added a mind-boggling 4899 candidates to the original list of successful candidates (including every northerner who registered for the exams), thereby increasing the total number of students to 7152 – this for a new university with no infrastructure of its own and which was supposed to kick off with 1,500 to 2,000 students. So after spending 100 million Francs CFA to organize the *concours* into ENS, the government threw a wrench into the entire process in order to satisfy the northern elite.

The Issues

The ENS Maroua controversy and its controversial *denouement* raises a plethora of issues, primary among them, the government's continued use of an undefined "regional balance" policy and a hazy quota system driven primarily by political expediency; the inability of successive "affirmative action" policies to pull the three northern provinces out of the bottom rungs of educational achievement in Cameroon; ongoing doubts about the quality of teachers who will eventually graduate from ENS Maroua, and their potential impact on the quality of education not only in the north but in the entire country; why the Biya regime, which is usually intransigent towards "sectarian" demands (remember the bloody crackdown on protests over admissions into the UB Medical school in 2006) gave in without a fight to the demands of the northern elite; how northern MPs successfully created a "Northern Bloc" in Cameroon's national assembly at a time when Anglophone MPs in the same assembly were refusing to take a common stance on development issues concerning their region on the spurious claim that a Member of Parliament represents "the entire country and not a specific locality", etc., etc.

Regional Balance and the Ethnic Weighting of Examination Results

The use of quotas and the ethnic weighting of examination results is not a new phenomenon in Cameroon. In fact, these were the cornerstone of Ahidjo's "balanced development" policy, which was officially supposed to "redress regional inequalities by providing education, infrastructures and the public amenities necessary for bridging the country and the town." Defending this policy, Ahidjo argued that,

> As the regulator of the nation's economic and social activities, the state must encourage, through appropriate incentives, those regions which for historical and sociological reasons, are lagging behind... our policy of balanced development must be applied not only in the distribution of infrastructure and public amenities, but also in the training of individuals.

In examinations for recruitment into categories B, C, and D of the civil service, two lists were established; an "A" list for natives from "educationally backward regions" and a "B" list for the rest of the country. Those on the "A" list were admitted following less rigorous criteria than those on the "B" list. This ethnic weighting of results was also applied in the admission into top professional schools such as the Joint Forces Military Academy (EMIAC), which trains the country's military brass, and the National Center of Administration and Magistracy (CENAM) which trains leading administrators and judicial officials. Also, at the University of Yaounde, students from these educationally backward areas were eligible for scholarships at age 25, while those from regions considered to be educationally advanced were eligible if only they were not above 18 years of age.

Like all other elements of the balanced development policy, the reason behind the use of ethno-regional considerations in recruitment and admission was a laudable one; that of bridging the gap between disfavored regions and those regions favored by history. But here again the result was the exacerbation of ethnic frustration and antagonism because the beneficiaries of the system were almost exclusively from one region – the Muslim North. Individuals from other educationally backward groups such as the Toupouri, Moundang and other non-Muslim and non-Fulani tribes of the *Grand Nord*, or the pygmies of the Eastern province, rarely benefited, if at all, from this policy. The hegemonic ambition of the Fulbe/Fulani ruling class and not social justice was the determining factor in a policy that became a tool for the establishment of a Fulani civil and military elite that dominated the higher echelons of the state bureaucracy and the army.

Under the Biya regime, the balance of power swung to the South, and members of Biya's Beti ethnic group replaced the Muslim North as the primary beneficiaries of admission policies into the *Grandes écoles*, even though the Beti were among the most educationally advanced groups in the country. In fact, it is safe to say that under Biya, regional balance was mentioned and implemented in a haphazard manner only when it served a specific purpose that benefited the regime, e.g., admitting unqualified Francophones into the UB medical school, or admitting every candidate from the Grand Nord who applied for a place in ENS Maroua, irrespective of their qualification, in a blatant attempt to garner political support of the *Grand Nord*.

A Tool for Political Control

Although the *ethnic arithmetic* formula has been hailed as an astute means of ethnic management in multiethnic African states, Kofele-Kale and Banock convincingly show that in Cameroon the formula has rarely served as a tool for ethnic accommodation and harmony. It has been more of a "device for ethnic fragmentation and mass control." By astutely pitting ethnic groups against each other in the struggle to control or protect principal sources of state rents (such as strategic ministries, lucrative public corporations, and coveted seats in the *Grandes écoles* whose graduates are automatically admitted into the civil service which is the main avenue for social mobility in Cameroon), the Biya regime (like the Ahidjo regime before it) has successfully tightened its grip on power as competing ethnic brokers are increasingly placed in a situation of dependence vis-à-vis the state which is the only institution capable of mediating in their favor.

From this perspective, Biya's "goodwill gesture" to the *Grand Nord*, particularly the Far North Province, is not an altruistic act, but a calculated political move to put the region and its elite in his corner at a time when he needs the broadest support possible to stay in power beyond 2011 – or negotiate a dignified and safe exit. This is however a shortsighted policy because while it satisfies the *Grand Nord* and makes it indebted to the regime, it creates a heightened feeling of marginalization in the other provinces who have been sidelined by the policy.

Still an Educationally Backward Region...

To Ahidjo, regional balance might have been a success because by the time he left power in 1982, northerners controlled all the levers of power in Cameroon, from the civil service, to the military, the gendarmerie, public corporations, etc. However, the North province (which Biya broke up into three separate provinces in 1983) remained an educationally backward region, unable to compete with the rest of the country – even as the northern elite occupied key positions in all strata of national life. In short, the preferential treatment extended to the region failed to fundamentally change the educational landscape of the region. In fact, many have argued that these preferential policies ironically held back northerners and contributed to the underdevelopment of the Grand Nord.

References

Banock, M. (1992). *Proceìssus de democratisation en Afrique: Le cas camerounais*. Paris: Harmattan.

Kofele-Kale, N. (1980). *An African experiment in nation building: The bilingual Cameroon Republic since reunification*. Westview special studies on Africa. Boulder, Colo: Westview Press.

21

Stuck on the Fringes of the Knowledge Economy

May 08, 2006: The email from the IT department of a US-based company was a simple one:

> Due to civil disturbances in Bangalore, India, there is limited IT Services staff available in our Bangalore help desk location to provide telephone support. Our help desk locations in Ottawa and Dublin are providing extended services to alleviate this situation, but you may experience extended delays when contacting IT Services via phone.

This brief email, which would have raised eyebrows two decades ago, is now just another mundane piece of workplace communications in the United States. And, it succinctly sums up Thomas Friedman's now famous assertion that the world is "flat" – i.e., that national boundaries are no longer relevant in today's global economy, and that people and companies can now compete for jobs and market share on an equal footing, from anywhere in the world. According to Friedman, the dramatic developments in Information and Communications Technologies (ICTs) in the past decade, particularly the Internet and computer technologies, have created a new global economy where

> intellectual work, intellectual capital, [can] be delivered from anywhere. It [can] be disaggregated, delivered, distributed, produced and put back together again — and this [gives] a whole new degree of freedom to the way we do work, especially work of an intellectual nature.

The result, says a recent World Bank report, is a new economic reality where

> comparative advantages among nations come less and less from abundant natural resources or cheap labor and increasingly from technical innovations and the competitive use of knowledge – or from a combination of the two, as is illustrated by the success story of Bangalore, the capital of the Indian software industry.

As I read the email on disturbances in Bangalore, I could not help but marvel at how India, a country which for all intents and purposes is still a "third world country" quickly understood the opportunity – and vacuum – created by the digital revolution of the 1990s, and how it quickly adapted to the exigencies of new economy that ensued.

A decade ago, India was no different from most developing countries in Asia or even Africa. As an Indian financial expert quoted in Friedman's book points out, "India had no resources and no infrastructure. It produced people with quality and by quantity. But many of them rotted on the docks of India like vegetables. Only a relative few could get on ships and get out." However, India was able to capitalize on the Internet boom of the late nineties and place itself at the frontline of the 21st century "knowledge economy." It did this by creating an enabling environment characterized by a renewed emphasis on science education, particularly in engineering and computer sciences at the tertiary level; huge investments in ICTs, particularly in a robust and reliable Internet system, and a world class software industry; the establishment of business-friendly laws aimed at attracting foreign investment and multinationals; the adoption of less restrictive citizenship laws to harness the potential of India's mammoth Diaspora community, etc.

The results are there for all to see. Today, India's graduates are no longer rotting "on the docks of India like vegetables" but have become frontline soldiers in a global digital economy. As the Indian financial expert puts it, "…we built this ocean crosser, called fiber-optic cable. For decades you had to leave India to be a professional. Now you can plug into the world from India. You don't have to go to Yale and go to work for Goldman Sachs."

Cameroon's Unfulfilled Potential

Inevitably my thoughts turned to Cameroon, that country so strategically situated in the "armpit" of Africa, with the additional advantage of having one of the highest literacy rates in sub-Saharan Africa and being officially bilingual in French and English. This is also a country with a huge unexploited ICT potential, particularly the high-performance fiber optic *SAT3/WASC* Submarine cable which has a terminal in Douala, and the COTCO fiber-optic link which runs across the entire length of the country along the Cameroon-Chad oil pipeline. No serious effort has been made to build the infrastructure within the country necessary to take advantage of these fiber optic links. So a country that has the potential to be at the forefront of the ICT revolution not only in the central African region but also in the rest of Africa is trailing the pack.

Today Cameroon is where India was some two decades ago — and it has the potential to become what India (or even Mauritius) is today. However, unlike India, Cameroon is crippled by the "civil service mentality," and it lacks a crop of creative economic and political visionaries similar to those who transformed Bangalore from a sleepy backwater Indian town into an IT outsourcing and software Mecca.

Nowhere has that absence of vision been most manifested than in the country's higher education system, which was established primarily to train administrators for the post-colonial government. Time has not changed the focus of Cameroon's higher education system even as the world has moved on. Apart from a few exceptions such as the Yaounde Polytechnic or the three Institutes of Technology in Bandjoun, Douala and Ngaoundere which graduate a meager 100 or so students annually, Cameroon's university system still churns out thousands of "pen pushers" each year rather than technology-savvy and innovative graduates with higher-order skills who are able to tackle the challenges globalization and knowledge societies. In

Cameroon's universities, there is no particular emphasis on science and technology in general, or on research and development in particular, which are the cornerstone of the new economy.

An editorial in the economic monthly, *The Entrepreneur* (Vol. 1 No. 3 Jan. 2006 p. 2) brilliantly sums up the consequence of this misaligned educational system:

> The deficit of knowledge and learning is killing Cameroon and Africa softly. Despite a proliferation of schools and colleges, the lack of true learning and creativity has held the African captive to underdevelopment. In Cameroon we have graduates who are just producing what they were taught in school, instead of producing new things...This has left Cameroon with millions of qualified illiterates and graduates who are failures as far as life and service is concerned. A Master's degree holder moves with little or no creativity. Thousands of poorly educated Cameroonians only wait for opportunities to work where others have worked. Few are involved in the creation of new things. The outdated education they received then gives birth to confusion.

Some might consider this analysis a little too bleak and apocalyptic. But the truth remains that Cameroon's educational system is a relic of colonization, which creates a dependent consumer society with little or no capacity for creativity, innovation and productivity. In this regard, Jeremy Weate's observation about Nigeria (http://naijablog.blogspot.com/) is truer for Cameroon:

> The longer I live here, the more I realise that technological interventions or money pumped in by donors will do little to transform, unless there is a primary focus on business processes (whether in the commercial or the public sector)... Nigerians enjoy the benefits of cars, laptops, mobile phones and other modern technology, but live in a society which does not understand the discipline and rigour it takes to produce such technology. This creates an alienated culture where technology and modern industrial processes are seen as a mystery. No one seems to be able to solve the aviation crisis. No one seems to be able to create value-added manufacturing processes; no one seems to stem the tide of an import-economy, turning into an export-economy. So few technological interventions (in any sector) meet with any kind of success.

Being part of the knowledge economy is not just about benefiting from IT outsourcing opportunities. For developing countries, it is the most effective way of competing in the global economy, increasing economic productivity and improving general living standards. Countries that fail to become part of the knowledge society will therefore be stuck in a vicious cycle of poverty, dependency and underdevelopment. As the World Bank report stresses,

> Lagging countries will miss out on opportunities to improve their economies through, for example, more efficient agricultural production and

distribution systems— which would increase yields and lower the proportion of food wasted due to poor distribution—or by making exports more competitive through better metrology, standards, and quality testing.

References

Friedman, T. L. (2005). *The world is flat: A brief history of the twenty-first century.* New York: Farrar, Straus and Giroux.

World Bank. (2002). *Constructing knowledge societies: New challenges for tertiary education.* Washington, DC: World Bank.

Part Five

Presidential Politics

22

President Paul Biya: 25 Years and Counting

November 06, 2007: When Paul Biya became president on November 6, 1982, he seemed determined to break away from, and put an end to the clientelist policies of the Ahidjo era; to establish a more humane nationalist agenda that respected ethnic and linguistic diversity but frowned on tribalism; encourage state decentralization; and introduce grassroots democracy within the single party. These ideas formed the bedrock of Paul Biya's "New Deal" philosophy, which he articulated during the first five years of his rule, and whose core principles were later published in a 1987 political manifesto titled *Communal Liberalism*.

Unlike Ahidjo who insisted that national unity could be possible if and only if "particularist loyalties (identifications) are systematically suppressed in the interest of national consciousness," Paul Biya argued that a Cameroonian Fatherland would become a reality not by obliterating ethno-regional frames of reference, but by using them as stepping-stones to nationhood. Therefore, creating a single nation out of Cameroon's numerous fatherlands was,

> ...certainly not going to be a question of embarking on a forceful and arbitrary elimination of the present ethnic and regional peculiarities. These, in some respects, are national socio-cultural resources, given their unquestionable contribution to the dynamism and co-operation for which our country is well known. Not only is it difficult to find the magic wand for this purpose, it is also evident that any such attempt could generate more social frustration.

However, like Ahidjo, Biya believed that the state remained "the best politically organized human grouping and the most complete from the standpoint of its authority," but felt that the state should derive its strength from popular legitimacy and not "solely from the concentration of legal prerogatives even if they are accompanied by an enormously strong force for law and order." The best means of obtaining this legitimacy, he asserted, would be – again unlike Ahidjo's philosophy – through the devolution of powers to local administrative communities (such as rural and urban Councils, *Départements* or administrative divisions, and provinces) which were to be "transformed into real decentralized territorial communities with extensive prerogatives to chose their leaders democratically and manage their own affairs."

With regards to the single party, Paul Biya, like Ahidjo before him, insisted that it remained "the only suitable institutional framework for bringing together Cameroonians of all origins," but saw its existence as temporary:

> After moulding the unitary spirit of the Cameroonian people, and making real its triumphant march towards democracy, the single party will, when

the time comes, appear as having been the best laboratory for a truly pluralistic democracy in Cameroon, the necessary prelude to multipartism, the measured, methodic and responsible birth of which will constitute a very important phase in the accomplishment of our democratization project which should immediately take shape within the state machinery.

Abandoned Vision

In practice, however, Paul Biya failed to transform his nationalistic and progressive political vision into reality. By the end of the 1980s he had jettisoned all the key principles of his "New Deal" doctrine that had won him widespread national support and international acclaim early in his presidency. Many reasons have been advanced to explain Biya's inability to carry out the agenda that he set for himself, the most common being that the 1983-84 succession crisis – that pitted him against his former mentor Ahmadou Ahidjo – and the April 1984 Muslim-backed coup forced him to abandon his nationalist agenda and cave in to the hegemonic ambitions of the various Beti factions that sprung up during this period, and on whom he increasingly came to rely for survival.

Whatever the reasons, the result was a gross disparity between the president's political discourse and his actions. Increasingly, his regime became exclusionist in nature, deriving its support from and controlled principally by what became known as the "Beti Lobby." Rather than modifying the principles and mechanisms underlying the prebendal system inherited from Ahidjo, the Biya regime sought to ease out previous beneficiaries, particularly the Bamileke (who dominated the commercial sector) and Fulani (who controlled the political establishment and had a firm grasp of the public corporations), in favor of this budding Beti lobby.

The northern-backed coup attempt of 1984 was thus a golden opportunity to settle old scores with the northern elites, and replace northern political domination with Beti hegemony. The failed coup attempt was followed by a nation-wide purge of Cameroonian institutions of northern influence, and the stripping of the hitherto powerful Fulani elite of privileges acquired through three decades of Ahidjo patronage. The majority of northerners occupying key positions in the army, the Gendarmerie, the police force, public corporations and the civil service, were stripped of their positions. Those rightly or wrongly suspected of having participated in the failed coup (and this group included practically the entire political, military and economic elite of Northern Cameroon), were arrested, jailed and/or summarily executed and their property seized, including that of former president Ahidjo. Thereafter, the Beti lobby took control of virtually all strategic positions in the army, national security apparatus, the public corporations and the civil service.

Just as the coup attempt had served as a pretext to destroy the Fulani political network, the so-called policy of "rigour and moralisation" which was the key component of Biya's New Deal policy, was used essentially to deprive Bamileke networks of their share of rents, which they controlled under the previous regime, in favor of the Beti lobby. Mbembe argues that the deliberate opening of Cameroonian markets to Indo-Pakistani businessmen with the help of the infamous

Bank of Credit and Commerce International (BCCI), was also part of a strategy to deprive the Bamileke of lucrative business networks which they had seized from the Greeks and Lebanese in the 1950s particularly in the wholesale and export trade.

Still as part of its strategy of dominance, the Biya regime made a determined effort to promote entrepreneurship among the Beti elite, and to create a Beti economic class that would rival the Bamileke and serve as the financial backbone of the regime.

The "Beti Lobby"

In a country where, as Michael Rowlands has pointed out, there is a "natural affinity between the stream of power and the stream of money or credit," it is no surprise that the Biya regime used its political influence to obtain bank credits for its clansmen on very liberal bases, especially between 1983 and 1987. By the mid-1980s, a quarter of the total portfolio of the state-controlled banking sector – amounting to 120 billion FCFA francs (roughly $240 million US at the time) – consisted of unrecoverable loans, most of them being politically mediated loans to elites. The Biya regime also dug deep into the coffers of public institutions created to supply credit and guidance to local entrepreneurs such as the BCD, FONADER, CAPME and FOGAPE in its bid to create a Beti economic class.

According to Van de Walle, the Beti elite – whom he calls the Beti Barons – particularly benefited from a more than liberal access to sources of state rents such as public contracts, export-import licenses, scholarships, loans, employment, public contracts, equipment, and customs fraud, which all aid in setting up patronage networks.

Along with the attempt to take over the private sector, the Beti lobby tightened its stranglehold on the public sector, particularly the public corporations, which became the target of extreme neopatrimonial practices tolerated and even encouraged by the government. In spite of glaring evidence of widespread corruption and the embezzlement of funds, the managers of these public corporations went unpunished. Instead, they continued to be recipients of huge government subventions even when their corporations were being consistently indicted for mismanagement by the Financial Commission. Jua argues that bad management was deliberately tolerated and financed by the regime as part of its neopatrimonial control system;

> By enabling members of the development coalition to appropriate funds with impunity, the state staved off even the threat of any momentary political deficiency a la Gramsci, which could unleash a struggle among members or factions of the development coalition for political office and control of the patronage system. In the face of this Cameroonians now claim that managers of parastatals have "titres fonciers" (in this case a free hand) over their concerns.

However, the powerful Beti bourgeoisie that the state had attempted to create by manipulating economic conditions to its advantage never became a reality. Plagued by what Rowlands describes as "an ethos of ostentatious consumption" and "unproductive patterns of investment and reliance on the state patronage for accumulation," they failed to offer competition, let alone overtake Bamileke entrepreneurs who continued to dominate their traditional areas, albeit with more difficulty. In the process, however, the national banking sector, the principal public corporations and state-owned financial institutions all went under, the victims of the extreme prebendalism of the first five years of the Biya reign. Historian Achille Mbembe best sums up public sentiment in Cameroon in the early 1990s when he describes the venal proclivity of the Beti lobby as,

> the rampant [and] ostentatious colonization of the state, the central administration, the banks, the public media, the diplomatic corps and the army by an arrogant regional elite with little mastery of monetary issues and more inclined towards the ethos of lavishness than production. In addition to the ensuing waste is the [general] feeling that the redistributive Party-state of the Ahidjo era has been replaced by a crude and sectarian state.

Although available evidence suggests that Cameroon's economy was already on its knees by the end of the 1970s, and that the collapse had simply been postponed thanks to the oil boom of the early 1980s; and although there is evidence that the plundering of public corporations and banks by regional elites began under Ahidjo, the fact is that when "the state's offices and treasury ceased to provide orderly profitable circuits for well connected, opportunistic patrons and clients" in the mid-1980s, there was a frenzied "inter-elite competition for shrinking resources" and in this competition, the Beti elites "were identified as the ever more exclusive beneficiaries of the state's remaining largesse."

Unlike Ahidjo who was able "to frustrate somewhat the appetite of Northerners in order to stabilize his personal power" by carefully "cultivat[ing] ties with every ethnic group and [by] placat[ing] all the provincial elites with access to state resources," Biya "demonstrated less ability to control corruption and rent-seeking than Ahidjo had." He therefore allowed the "Beti barons" to increase "rent-seeking, corruption, and patronage beyond what Ahidjo ever allowed," and in the process, established a political system based on "ethnoclientelism".

Thus, rather than enlarging his public support, Biya narrowed it by his politics of exclusion. The result was an exacerbation of ethnic consciousness in the country, and systematic attacks against the political system by ethno-linguistic and regional forces which became commonplace during the multiparty years.

References

Biya, P. (1987). *Communal liberalism*. London: Macmillan.

Rowlands, M. (1993). "Accumulation and the Cultural Politics of Identity in the Grassfields." In Geschiere, P., & Konings, P. *Itineìraires d'accumulation au Cameroun = Pathways to accumulation in Cameroon*. Paris, France: Karthala.

Jua, N. (1993). "State, Oil and Accumulation." In Geschiere, P., & Konings, P. *Itineìraires d'accumulation au Cameroun = Pathways to accumulation in Cameroon*.

Krieger, M. (1994). "Cameroon's Democratic Crossroads, 1990-4." *Journal of Modern African Studies*. 32 (4).

Mbembe, A. (December 22, 1992) "Perspectives Politique: Comment le Cameroun est Parvenu a Offrir l'Image Desormais Largement Repandue d'une Caricature de la Démocratie." *La Messagère*, 22 Décembre

_____ (1991) "Dix Notes en Vue de la Conférence Nationale," *Challenge Hebdo*, 10-17 Juillet.

Van De Walle, N. (1994). "Neopatrimonialism and democracy in Africa, with an illustration from Cameroon." In Widner, J. A. (ed). *Economic change and political liberalization in Sub-Saharan Africa*. Baltimore: Johns Hopkins University Press.

23

How to Eliminate Presidential Term Limits (Notes from the Biya Playbook)

> Term limits are an important instrument of democratization in electoral-authoritarian countries: this is not just because they constrain the power of individual leaders, but also because they tend to promote political party alternation, as in Croatia in 2000 and Kenya in 2002, which in turn fosters democratization – *Gideon Maltz*

January 03, 2008: Following the arrest of Yondo Black and nine others in February 1990, the Biya regime insisted that contrary to popular belief, the "Douala 10," as they came to be known, had been arrested not because they called for the reinstitution of multipartyism, which regime officials pointed out was enshrined in the constitution, but because they had insulted the Head of State. Realizing however, that this statement could open the floodgates of pro-multiparty advocacy in the country, the regime immediately initiated stage-managed a nationwide campaign against "precipitated multipartyism." At the end of the campaign, President Biya declared in a nationwide address that "the people" – and not the regime! – had "unequivocally rejected political models and formulas imported from abroad." In other words, even though the constitution allowed for multiparty politics, the Cameroonian people had rejected it as being unsuitable to Cameroonian realities.

Two years later, when the regime decided to outmaneuver the weakened and divided opposition by calling for early Presidential elections, the Biya playbook was once again put to good use. On June 27, 1992, a delegation of 15 prominent Cameroonian business magnates – practically all of whom had been financially compromised by the ghost town campaign of 1991and the violent and merciless tax recovery drive of 1992 – were dragged to Unity Palace where they "appealed" to the President to call for early presidential elections. The very next day, the Secretary General of the CPDM Central Committee sent a confidential telex to all provincial governors asking them to work with CPDM sections to organize meeting and rallies in favor of early presidential elections and a Biya candidacy. The telex also included the draft of a "spontaneous motion of support" to be issued at the end of these rallies. On August 25, 1992, President Biya announced that as a result of demands by "the people" early elections would take place on October 11, 1992 and that he would also seek reelection.

Over the years, President Paul Biya has elevated feigned disinterest into an art form in order to create the illusion that his actions are dictated by and even imposed upon him by "the will of the people." Thus, when he was asked during his September 2007 interview on France 24 about calls by some members of his party to eliminate presidential term limits, it was an apparently disinterested Paul Biya who declared that "I think that these questions about the 2001 elections are premature." He nonetheless added that "I'll allow the debate take place, but for now the constitution does not allow me to run for a third term.... The people will decide what is good for them... we are listening..." That, of course, was part of a well-orchestrated plan to set the constitutional amendment plan in motion. What followed was a flurry of motions of support, rallies and meetings by CPDM stalwarts across the country, all calling for a constitutional amendment scrapping term limits. And at the end of the process, President Biya once again "caved in" to the demands of "the people."

The President who argued only a couple of months ago that discussions on presidential term limits were "premature" now states that these discussions are "normal and even encouraging." The President even goes farther to argue that the current constitution is undemocratic because it limits the presidential mandate to two terms:

> In fact, there are arguments for a revision, particularly of Article 6 which indeed imposes a limitation of the people's will, a limitation which is out of tune with the very idea of democratic choice.

No longer is Paul Biya a disinterested and passive spectator in a "premature" debate over term limits. He is now the principal actor in a "normal" process which will, without doubt, culminate in a constitutional revision that will virtually make him President for life. And at the end of that stage-managed process, the President will claim that he didn't stay on because he wanted to, but because he was virtually forced into that course of action by "the people" who begged for "continuity." That then is Cameroonian "democracy" at its finest. And as usual, the President will most definitely get away with it mainly because Cameroonians actually tolerate and even actively participate in this politics of make-believe...

The Dance of the Absurd: President Paul Biya in His Own Words
Paul Biya - Paris, September 2007

> The 2011 elections will definitely take place but I consider them distant. I have a seven-year mandate, half of which I have already completed. Presently, we have other priorities and the constitution does not permit me to run for a 3rd term... I think that these questions about the 2001 elections are premature... but I leave it up to those who want to launch this debate. There are some people who say that the president should take part in the [2011] elections for continuity. I'll allow the debate take place, but for now the constitution does not allow me to run for a third term. I also know that the constitution is not etched in stone. The people will decide what is good for them. So we are listening, however, I urge my compatriots to focus on more urgent tasks.

End of Year Message, December 31, 2007

> ... I cannot fail to mention a problem that was raised by journalists during my recent stay in Paris and which, I am aware, has been the subject of much speculation in Cameroon for several months now. I am referring to the possible revision of our Constitution and particularly Article 6, Paragraph 2, which provides that "the President of the Republic shall be elected for a term of office of seven years renewable once".
>
> Even though the next presidential election is only due in 2011, it is normal and even encouraging that Cameroonians take an interest in this issue since it concerns the future of their institutions. Many calls in favor of a revision are reaching me from all our provinces. I am obviously not indifferent to them.
>
> In fact, there are arguments for a revision, particularly of Article 6 which indeed imposes a limitation of the people's will, a limitation which is out of tune with the very idea of democratic choice.
>
> I want to add that in itself a constitutional revision is nothing unusual. Our present Constitution (which is itself the outcome of a revision of our Constitution of 1972) contains revision procedures which enable, if necessary, an adjustment of the text to changes in our political society. Moreover, the procedures are of a general nature and do not concern anybody in particular.
>
> We are therefore going to reconsider, in this spirit, those provisions of our Constitution which would need to be harmonized with recent developments in our democratic system so as to meet the expectations of the vast majority of our population.

Reference

Maltz, G. (2007). The Case for Presidential Term Limits. *Journal of Democracy*. 18 (1), 128-142.

24

Biyaism Without Biya? The Battle for Regime Change in Cameroon

<u>January 20, 2008:</u> After close to a year of subtle and not-so-subtle calls by members of the ruling CPDM for an amendment of Article 6(2) of the constitution of Cameroon, which imposes presidential term limits, President Paul Biya finally took a stance on the debate last December 31. During his nationwide end-of-year address, Paul Biya backed the opponents of term limits by arguing that: "In fact, there are arguments for a revision, particularly of Article 6 which indeed imposes a limitation of the people's will, a limitation which is out of tune with the very idea of democratic choice."

Expectedly, the President's declaration, which will most definitely put the amendment process in motion, has generated a firestorm of protest among Cameroonians, even within his own CPDM. Understandably, most Cameroonians are fed up with the Biya presidency, which has lasted for a quarter of a century, and desperately want someone else to step in and, hopefully, put the country back on track, politically and economically.

Implicit in the arguments against the amendment of Article 6(2) is the belief that it is actually possible for regime change to occur in Cameroon in 2011 within the framework of the current constitution and current political system. I believe that this faith is largely misplaced. Today, Paul Biya does not simply represent an individual – himself – whose disappearance from the political scene will automatically lead to the kind of change that Cameroonians dream about. He also represents a deeply entrenched political system, which has the potential to survive his departure, that is, if no major systemic change takes place before then.

This political system is what some have referred to as "Biyaism" – a prebendal and predatory system where rules and institutions governing the polity are heavily skewed in favor of the incumbent; a pseudo-democratic political system characterized by political pluralism and authoritarian continuity where (rigged) elections are organized not to inject new blood into the political class, but to give the President and his regime a veneer of legitimacy. It is a system, which actually thrives on institutional corruption and the ethnitization of political life, and maintains a firm grip on the country by relying heavily on the repressive structures inherited from the one-party era.

Thus, while it is understandable that the majority of Cameroonians want to see the last of Paul Biya, he is, nonetheless, just part of a much larger puzzle. "Biyaism" is, in my opinion, the greatest obstacle to the democratization and the establishment of the rule of law in Cameroon.

Proponents of maintaining the constitutional status quo argue, however, that Biya is the main obstacle to regime change, and that with him out of the way in 2011, the playing field will be leveled, making it possible for a new leader to emerge, most probably from the ranks of the opposition. This, I believe, is based on yet another misreading of Biyaism, which has elevated electoral manipulation into a science, and controls the entire electoral process from beginning to end – including picking out the winner. As the NDI report on the 1992 presidential elections clearly stated:

> ...President Biya and his government retained control over the appointment of every election official, issued every electoral decree... established all vote counting procedures, staffed every electoral bureaucracy and strictly controlled governmental release of partial results - for which no provision existed in the electoral code. The result was a flawed and heavily rigged electoral process.
>
> The manipulated electoral process has failed the people of Cameroon. A democratic political system requires political leaders to contest elections fairly and to work within the political system whether they win or lose. Absence of such a system, Cameroon is likely to regress into authoritarian rule.

12 years later in 2004, it was the turn of the Commonwealth to call for:

> an electoral process which is truly independent of all contesting political parties and not subject to direction or abuse by the government of the day" but "At present the whole electoral process is run by, and the key decisions are taken by, the Ministry of Territorial Administration and Decentralisation and its agents in the local Administration. This is the principal obstacle to the holding of credible elections.

It is obvious therefore that if left unchanged, the existing system, which has ensured that Biya and the CPDM win every single election organized since the reinstitution of multipartyism – with ever increasing margins of victory – will, in the unlikely event that Biya steps down, also ensure that Biya's hand-picked candidate wins in 2011. If that scenario comes to pass, then Biyaism will still be very much around, albeit with a new face.

So how do Cameroonians make sure that a new political system is in place by 2011, which will establish true political pluralism, viable democratic institutions, the separation of powers and the rule of law, and a transparent and fair electoral process? This, in my opinion, is one of the greatest, if not the greatest challenge facing the forces of change in Cameroon today.

I therefore agree with those who have argue that a constitutional revision may not be such a bad thing after all, that is, a complete overhaul of the 1996 constitution and not just cosmetic changes meant for King Biya alone. Not only is the 1996 constitution a poorly written and short sighted document, it is so cut off from Cameroonian realities that some of its clauses will never see the light of day.

To conclude, making sure that the Biya regime does not scrap constitutional term limits is a legitimate fight. But it is just one battle. The war will be won only when the political system is completely overhauled to give birth to a truly democratic polity. Once such a system is in place, then the issue of regime change will become largely insignificant – with or without Biya...

25

«La Politique de Pourrissement»: Why Biya Remains Defiant

February 28, 2008: Some 72 hours after riots broke out in Douala before spreading to most major towns of the country including Yaounde, the capital city, President Biya officially responded to the ongoing crisis in a nationwide televised address. Prior to that speech, there was hope, and even an expectation, in many quarters that the president would be conciliatory in his remarks, and probably make some concessions to the rioters whose demands ranged from the respect of presidential term limits to the scrapping of recent hikes in the price of fuel. Instead, President Biya refused to budge an inch and delivered a speech that was defiant:

> Our country is witnessing a situation which brings back unpleasant memories of a period we thought was long gone... For some people, who by the way, did not hide their intentions, the objective is to obtain through violence what they were unable to obtain through the ballot box... The apprentice sorcerers who manipulated these youths behind the scenes, were not bothered about the risk that they made them to run by exposing them to confrontations with the forces of law and order...
>
> Those behind these manipulations definitely did not have the good of our people in their mind. A country cannot be built through destruction... Cameroonians know that disorder can only bring about calamity and misery. We cannot allow that to happen. To those who are responsible for manipulating the youth to achieve their aims, I want to tell them that their attempts are doomed to failure. All legal means available to Government will be brought into play to ensure the rule of law.

The speech was reminiscent of Biya's (in)famous June 27, 1991 speech made at the height of the "Ghost Town" civil disobedience campaign in which he lashed out at opposition parties for promoting violence and described the national conference as "sans objet":

> Violence, vendetta, vandalism, terrorism risk becoming the order of the day. Intimidation, threats, illegal strikes are all used to destabilize our country. Is this what Cameroonians expect of democracy? – Cars, houses, schools have been burnt down, shops and factories looted and plundered, citizens molested. Is this what Cameroonians expect of democracy? – Institutions are called into question. Leaders as well. Intolerance, sectarianism and tribalism have become the order of the day. Is this what Cameroonians expect of democracy? – To humiliate the people, to want to bring the government to its knees, to paralyze the country and its institutions... Is this what Cameroonians expect of democracy?... Order shall reign...

These are the "unpleasant memories of a period we thought was long gone" that the President referred to in yesterday's speech... Since that televised address, Cameroonians have been asking themselves why the President chose to stoke the flames rather than outline a strategy for easing the tension and addressing the root causes of the riots. Some have even argued that Biya's reaction can only come from someone is completely cut off from the reality of what is going on in the country. But Biya is neither senile nor ignorant of the Cameroonian realities; there is a method to his madness. His strategy of defiance is rooted in a careful analysis of the forces at play and their (in)ability to maintain a sustained uprising against the regime.

An Explosion of Pent Up Anger, not an Organized Uprising

The Biya regime is banking on the fact that the same reasons that ultimately led to the collapse of the six-month civil disobedience campaign of 1991 are still very present today; an emasculated civil service which cannot join any anti-regime movement for fear of losing its privileges; an embryonic civil society which is in no position to take control of, and organize the protest movement; a security and military apparatus so steeped in corruption and repression that it has little option but to support Biya, in spite of occasional rumblings of discontent within the ranks, etc. In addition, the ongoing rioting is not part of an organized popular uprising with effective control structures, but a spontaneous explosion of pent-up anger. History has shown that such explosions usually peter out if no organized force steps in to channel all that energy and anger towards clearly defined objectives.

So the situation today is unlike that of 1991 when close to 30 political parties and associations, working under the banner of the *National Coordination of Opposition Parties and Associations* (NCOPA), were able to take complete control of the streets in seven of the country's 10 provinces. To make matters worse, the political parties which dominated the political terrain in the early 1990s such as the SDF, UNDP and UPC have been severely weakened by internal wrangling and regime maneuvers, and are in no position to step in and fill the void at a national level.

La politique de Pourrissement

Based on this assessment of the political terrain, the Biya regime has decided to wait it out in the hopes that the protesters will eventually tire out and simply walk off the streets. This is the famous *politique de pourrissement* (loosely translated as the "policy of decay") whereby the regime allows the political situation to rot, with the expectation that those who have taken to the streets will ultimately be worn down or beaten into submission by the repression and the government's intransigence. This strategy worked in 1991 and regime hardliners believe that it will work again this time around. Thus, in spite of concerns within the Biya regime that the situation might degenerate into a nationwide revolt or even a coup, the regime is nonetheless confident that it will eventually weather the storm thanks to the largely uncoordinated nature of the riots and the repressive machinery of the state.

So is the Biya regime correct that a sit-tight policy will eventually defeat the hydra-headed monster that has taken over the streets? Or, will it ultimately pay the price for misreading the situation and for its arrogance?

Whatever the outcome, this week's events have peeled back that illusion of "stability" that Cameroon has cloaked itself in for close to two decades, and has exposed the level of deep-seated discontent with and contempt for the Biya regime. The regime will probably survive this time around, but it might not be so lucky down the road...

Part Six

Political Pluralism

26

Indigenous Minorities and Political Pluralism in Cameroon

January 30, 2006: The concept of "Indigenous Minorities" as used in Cameroon refers to ethnic groups located primarily in the coastal and urban areas of the South-West, Littoral and Center provinces. The common denominator among these ethnic groups is that they are numerically outnumbered in their native lands by non-natives who have emigrated from other parts of the country. The numerical superiority of these non-native communities (whose members are commonly referred to as "strangers") is usually accompanied by their domination of the political, economic and social life in these areas.

Indigenous Minorities have been wary of political pluralism because of fears that majority rule will institutionalize their minority (and hence marginal) status within their respective communities, and exclude them from the decision-making centers within these communities in favor of the demographically superior and more influential "stranger" community.

The fear of non-native majorities in certain regions of Cameroon has given birth to some very controversial theories on political participation and representation, the most notable being the *Automatic Majority* theory and the *Electoral Village* theory, both of which will be discussed later. These minorities therefore insist that any new political system must include clear constitutional provisions that give them a representative, if not predominant, political voice within their local communities.

Ascriptive Majority Rule

The case of the indigenous minorities is a regional variation of what Donald Horowitz has described at national level as "ascriptive majority rule." This is the situation where the nature of a country's political landscape in general, and the outcome of its elections in particular, are predetermined by demography. In such a system, elections are "tantamount to a census, and.. lock[s] out the minority from any significant political power save when it can pry loose by violence or disruption" (97-98). Horowitz argues that democracy is

> a 'system of processing and terminating intergroup conflicts' without foreordained outcomes, a way of institutionalizing uncertainty... The indeterminacy of these conceptions of democracy implies that no group should indefinitely be denied the opportunity to participate in government. (244)

In this regard, therefore, he concludes that "rigidly ascriptive majorities and minorities can hardly be said to be conducive to democratic rule," because their existence makes a mockery of the concept of democratic uncertainty. This is the same argument being put forward by Cameroon's indigenous minorities.

Indigenous Minority Representation: The Quandry

Is Horowitz's theory applicable in Cameroon? Are Cameroonian indigenous minorities victims of "Ascriptive majority rule"? Whatever the case, the underlying issue is essentially one of political representation in a democratic system. Put differently, it is about the respect of majority rule and the protection of minority rights.

Many have argued that the one-man-one-vote rule is the only real gauge of democracy, and that any tinkering of this core democratic principle in Cameroon or elsewhere in Africa will lead to disaster. However, as Francis Nyamnjoh has argued in *Africa's Media: Democracy and the politics of belonging*,

> The African experience in liberal democracy where ethnicity and belonging have continued to play a major role and voluntary associations have failed to take root, reveals the need for a fresh theoretical space, addressing not only individual rights and freedoms, but also the interests of communal and cultural solidarities. (37)

It is in this context that indigenous minorities in Cameroon insist that the one-man-one-vote theory would be valid in Cameroon only if voters generally made political choices on the basis of ideology, which is not the case.

The late Francois Sengat Kuo, a former political strategist and speech writer for both Presidents Ahidjo and Biya, best captured this argument in his famous "Automatic Majority" concept. A native of the minority Duala ethnic group, Sengat Kuo argued back in 1985 that Indigenous Minorities needed special political protection and privileges, particularly in the selection and election of candidates running for multi-candidate positions within the ruling single party, the CPDM. He argued that the electoral choices of individuals from the Cameroonian western grasslands such as the Bamileke (who constitute the single largest ethnic group resident in Douala) were determined solely by ethnic solidarity rather than by ideology or competence. This, he argued, meant that in practice, grasslanders running for elective office in areas such as Douala would always have an "automatic majority" on their side because of the ethnic factor.

He, therefore, insisted that the only way to protect the rights of the Indigenous Minorities against the "automatic majority", and thus give them a participatory voice within their own local communities, was by selecting indigenous candidates over non-indigenous ones by "consensus" rather than through majority vote. This principle was effectively applied during the 1985 multi-candidate elections within the then single CPDM party. As a result of "consensus" a candidate of Bamileke origin was forced to abandon the race for the top party position in the Douala region in favor of a "son of the soil" candidate who eventually won.

In 1991, it was the turn of Yaounde University law professor, Gabriel Nlep, who argued that the best way to solve the problem of under-representation of Indigenous Minorities in their indigenous regions was to constitutionally oblige all Cameroonians to vote and run for office only in their respective regions of origin, which he referred to as their "Electoral Village." This, he emphasized, would eliminate the potentially explosive grievances stemming from predominant political role that "stranger" elites generally play in their non-indigenous areas of residence, at the expense of the native elites who rarely have any control over the majority and politically decisive "stranger" votes.

In Search of a Workable Formula

The main question, therefore, is whether Cameroonians can successfully come up with an acceptable/workable formula for political coexistence that takes into account the clamor for minority rights protection by the coastal and urban indigenous minorities, along with the equally valid calls for the respect of majority rule by the dominant "stranger" population. In other words, can Cameroonians craft an inclusive democratic political system that will address what Nyamnjoh describes as the failure of liberal democracy "to provide for an ethnic cultural citizenship that blends well with African notions of civic citizenship..."?

References

Collectif C3. (1992). *Le Cameroun éclaté: Une anthologie commentée des revendications ethniques*. Yaoundé, Cameroun: Editions C3.

Horowitz, D. (1991). *A Democratic South Africa? Constitutional Engineering in a Divided Society*. Berkeley: University of California Press.

Nyamnjoh, F. (2005). *Africa's Media: Democracy & the Politics of Belonging*. London: Zed Books.

27

Cameroon: Why So Many Political Parties?

June 17, 2007: According to the website of Cameroon's Ministry of Territorial Administration and Decentralization (MINATD), 45 political parties will take part in the July 22, 2007 legislative elections, while 33 will take part in municipal elections also scheduled for the same day. To the casual observer, this would seem like a lot of political parties for a country with the size and population of Cameroon. However, these figures pale in comparison to the actual number of registered political parties in the country – a whopping **207** as of June 1, 2007! (See official list of registered political parties at http://www.minatd.net/). Even though these political parties exist on paper, most of them are completely absent from the national and local political scene. In fact, since the reinstitution of political pluralism in Cameroon in 1990, there has never been an election in which all registered parties participated:

- In 1992, 32 of the 69 registered political parties in the country took part in the legislative elections, while five political parties took part in the presidential election;
- In 1996, 36 of the 123 political parties took part in municipal elections. Councilors from 15 parties were elected into local councils;
- In 1997, 9 of the 152 political parties each fielded a candidate in the presidential election while 72 political parties registered to take part in legislative elections (only 44 eventually participated). The National Assembly which came out of the elections consisted of MPs from seven political parties;
- In the 2002 legislative elections, only 48 of the 178 political parties in existence participated, with five ending up in parliament;
- In the 2004 presidential elections, candidates representing 16 of the 188 political parties participated;
- And now in the 2007, a miserly 45 political parties, out of 207 will take part in both legislative and municipal elections.

It should be noted that in all the above mentioned elections, many of the participating parties could only compete in just one constituency. For example in 1996, 13 of the 36 parties that took part in municipal elections competed only in a single constituency. Evidently, quantity is not a problem when it comes to the number of political parties in Cameroon. However, quality is a very scarce commodity with very few viable parties that can effectively compete and win elections at the national and local levels.

So what explains the very high number of political parties in Cameroon, and their evident inability to take part in the political process and compete in elections, which is the essence of political parties?

Integral Multipartyism

The law governing political parties in Cameroon (Law no. 90/56 of 19 December 1990) allows for an unlimited number of political parties – what has been described as *"Le multipartisme integral."* Creating a political party is a fairly easy and inexpensive administrative process in Cameroon. It is even less cumbersome than creating a Not-for-Profit organization. Officially, this is to give every Cameroonian the chance to have a voice in the country's political process if he or she so desires. Conventional wisdom, however, holds that the Biya regime crafted Cameroon's multiparty law in 1990 with an eye on (opposition) party multiplication and fragmentation as a means to perpetuate the CPDM's grip on the political process and system. As Nyamnjoh has argued (in *Africa's Media: Democracy And The Politics Of Belonging*), "The Multiplicity of parties, most of which had no existence outside the personality of their founders, can be explained partly by the government's interest in dissipating real democratic opposition..."

The CPDM is routinely accused of sponsoring the creation of dummy parties whose role is to muddy the political waters, serve as relay points for the government's unpopular positions issues of the day, and dilute the strength and votes of the opposition. In fact, many of the political parties created during the early years of Cameroon's multiparty experience (1991-1992) were suspected of being CPDM moles charged with either infiltrating opposition groupings such as the *National Coordination of Opposition Parties* (NCOPA), or passing off as the "responsible opposition" constantly challenging the "radical and irrational" policies of the "hard-line opposition." Virtually all of these parties eventually joined what became known as the *Majorité présidentielle*. To this day, many political analysts still insist that Dakole Daisalla's *Movement for the Defense of the Republic* (MDR), which teamed up with Biya in 1992 to give the latter a parliamentary majority in 1992, was in fact created by the regime.

Nyamnjoh adds an ethnic explanation to the debate by pointing out that "in a plural society like Cameroon, it was difficult for any one political party, founded on ethnic, linguistic or religious lines, to cater for every group's interest" (113). Hence every ethnic group or region sought to have its own political party which increased its chance of getting a share of the national pie.

No Independent Candidates

Other seasoned observers of the Cameroon political scene such as Churchill Ewumbue-Monono have attributed the plethora of political parties to (a) the "extreme partitisation" of Cameroonian politics symbolized by the rejection of independent candidates in municipal and legislative elections on the one hand, and the largely unfulfillable conditions for running as an independent in presidential elections on the other, and (2) the administrative and political harassment of civil society organizations that are interested in politics.

According the laws governing elections in Cameroon, independent candidates are barely tolerated (presidential elections) or simply outlawed (legislative and municipal elections). In fact, the conditions for running as an independent in presidential elections are so stringent that no candidate has ever been able to fulfill them since the reinstitution of multiparty elections. Candidates are required to furnish signatures from 300 "grand electors" (i.e., Members of Parliament, Councilors, First Class Chiefs, etc.,), 30 from each of the 10 provinces.

Political parties are therefore the only form of legitimate political expression in Cameroon. And, individuals who would normally participate in the political process or contest elections as independents are forced to create political parties. Ewumbue-Monono highlights the fact that "the electoral behavior and capacity pf most of the political parties in Cameroon have been similar to those of independent candidates who could present lists or candidates in only one constituency" (p. 180). In short, the majority of political parties in Cameroon are "independents in party garments, and which cannot present candidates or lists in more than one constituency."

Little Tolerance for Civil Society Participation in the Political Process

Ewumbue-Monono also points out that "In Cameroon, when a political party is criticizing the Government, it is seen as constructive, but when such criticism comes from the civil society it is seen as subversive." A good example was the July 1991 banning of six civil society organizations for allying with the NCOPA to promote the *Villes Mortes* and support calls for a Sovereign National Conference. No political party suffered a similar fate for the same crimes. Ewumbue-Monono therefore argues that,

> To avoid harassment, therefore, most civil society organizations have merely registered as political parties. In effect, over 70% of the registered political parties in Cameroon as of 2004 are nothing short of civil society organizations in scope of activities and objectives dressed in party uniforms. Many civil society organizations aimed at empowering vulnerable groups like the youth, women, children and the handicapped, the elderly, and workers have been registered pure and simple as political parties, which explain the high number of parties in the country.

The result has been the "partitisation" of the civil society as civil society organizations simply morph into political parties in order to survive. This is the case, for example, of Fritz Pierre Ngo's *Cameroon Ecological Movement* (environment), Tchoungui Francois-Xavier's, *Movement for Justice and Freedom* (human rights), and Boniface Fobin's *Justice and Development Party* (Anglophone minority rights).

Conclusion

Whatever the original intentions of the various laws that govern political parties and elections in Cameroon, the outcome has been a political landscape that promotes the mushrooming of non-viable political parties, many of whose entire membership can fit in a phone booth, as they say in Cameroon. Worse, these laws exclude huge segments of Cameroonian society from the political process. As the head of the OAU election monitoring team for the 2002 municipal and legislative elections stated, "The texts of the law which do not permit independent candidatures have prevented many competent citizens of the civil and society from participating in the management of municipal and parliamentary affairs."

References

Ewumbue-Monono, C. (2006). *Men of Courage: The Participation of Independent and Civil Society Candidates in the Electoral Process in Cameroon. A Historical Perspective, 1945-2004*. Limbe: Design House.

Nyamnjoh, F. (2005). *Africa's Media: Democracy And The Politics Of Belonging*. London, ZED Books; Pretoria, UNISA Press.

MINATD. (2007). *Liste des partis politiques legalisés*. Retrieved March 15, 2009 from http://www.minatd.net/fr/cadrejuridique/partis.xls

28

State Funding of Political Parties: A Democratic Imperative or Hush Money for the Opposition?

July 18, 2007: On July 1, 2007, the Government of Cameroon announced that it had earmarked 1.5 billion CFA francs to fund political parties taking part in the July 22 parliamentary and municipal elections, although it did not shed light on how that money was to be distributed among the 44 parties participating in the election. However, a few days later, the Secretary General of the opposition SDF revealed that her party had been promised 217 million FCFA. She added that 108 million FCFA would be used for the council elections and 109 million CFA for Legislative elections. Given the very tense, acrimonious and sometimes violent relationship between the government and the opposition, particularly the SDF, many Cameroonians still have serious reservations about public or state funding of opposition parties. They believe that public funding of the opposition cannot occur without some sort of *qui quo pro*; that the subsidy to political parties is simply a slush fund used to bribe the opposition from protesting too loudly about pre and post electoral irregularities. At a minimum, opponents of public funding argue that by taking money from the State, the Cameroonian opposition legitimizes both the Biya regime and a largely unfair electoral process skewed in favor of the CPDM. It also prevents them from actively building grassroots support and seeking private sources of funding.

The Case for Public Funding

Proponents of public funding however point out that the Cameroonian situation is not unique, and that even in Western democracies where political parties have the ability to raise lots of money through private sources, they are still eligible for public funding. This is the case, for example, of the Presidential Campaign Fund in the United States which offers matching funds to presidential candidates. As Samuel Fambom has pointed out:

> The issue of public funding of political parties has been debated for a long time in old democracies. Three main arguments militate in favour of political parties. The first is that political parties must be treated as public services for the same reason as other services whose products are ideas, political socialisation and the renewal of the political class... The second argument is that the public funding of political parties provides a living space to the opposition, which of a nature to encourage the spread and diversification of ideas, the opening up of debates and political alternation. According to the third argument, the public funding of political parties enable to respect a basic democratic principle, that of equality, by evening up the chance of the participants in the electoral game.

In the specific case of Africa, Fambom argues that:

> ... the consolidation of democracy requires as a precondition the enhancement of the capacities of the political actors for action which, in the African case, can only be achieved by an equitable allocation of public resources among the actors... In the new African democracies, where the majority of the citizens are poor, it is difficult for political parties to gather significant amounts of funds from contributions of their members. Under these conditions, the only sources of finance available are assistance from foreign donor and the subsidies of public moneys.

(It is worth noting that law no. 90-56 of 19 December 1990 instituting multipartyism in Cameroon stipulates in Section 9 that "No party shall be authorized to exist if it receives subsides from abroad...")

So where exactly does the money used to fund political parties in Cameroon come from? How come parties are simply "promised" state funds as if it is a favor from the State and not a specific budgetary allocation? And, are there any checks and balances to ensure that the money given to political parties (including the ruling CPDM) is solely used for its intended purpose? Or does the government simply turn a blind eye thereby effectively making it the hush money that critics insist it is?

Public Funding of Political Parties in Cameroon
The Theory

In Cameroon the funding of political parties is governed by:
1. Law No. 2000/015 of 19 December 2000 relating to the public funding of political parties and election campaigns and Financing political parties, and
2. Decree No. 2001/305 of 8 October 2001 to define the organization, composition, duties and conditions of functioning of the Committee on the control of the use of public funds earmarked for political parties and election campaigns.

According to the law on the public funding of political parties;

- Public funding shall serve to cover regular political party activities as well as for the organization of election campaigns;
- Each year, the finance law shall include a subsidy to cover certain operating costs of legally recognised political parties;
- The subsidy shall be an allocation of public funds by the State to a political party to cover inter alia :

- √ recurrent administrative expenses;
- √ the dissemination of its political programme;
- √ the co-ordination of the political activities of its members;
- √ preparation for elections.

Apart from the funds that political parties receive annually for running expenses, they also get additional funds during the campaign period. Section 9 states that:

> The State shall contribute to the funding of election campaigns by defraying some of the expenses of political parties during elections; that the funding shall concern expenses relating in particular to the preparation, publishing and printing of circulars, manifestos and posters.

These election campaign expenses include expenses resulting from the organisation of election meetings and logistics. These funds, according to Section 11,

> shall be shared in two equal parts among the political parties taking part in the elections as follows:

- √ a first part shall be allotted to the political parties which took part in the last legislative election, proportionately in the number of seats ;
- √ A second part shall be served to all political parties proportionately to the lists submitted and endorsed in the various constituencies.

To ensure that the funds are used for their designated purpose, the law stipulates that:

> Any person who, acting on behalf of a political party, uses the funds provided for within the framework of public funding, for purposes other than those specified in the law shall be punished as provided for in Section 184 of Penal Code.

To this end, Decree No. 2001/305 of 8 October 2001 institutes a Control Committee with the task of auditing political parties that receive state funds, and establishing "cases of embezzlement of public funds allocated to political parties in accordance with the laws in force." The Committee produces an annual report, which is forwarded to the President of the Republic.

The Reality of State Funding in Cameroon

Although the laws governing the public funding political parties are fairly straightforward, their implementation is fuzzy at best and characterized by a lack of transparency. For example, instead of a specific parliamentary allocation based on an objective assessment of the political landscape, it appears that the global sum allocated for elections is arbitrarily decided upon by the regime in power. Which explains why the amount earmarked for elections changes from one election to the next without any clear pattern. For example, for the 2004 presidential elections, the SDF was promised 400 million FCFA (of which it allegedly received only 46 million FCFA). Yet for the twin legislative and municipal elections of 2006 which require much more resources, the SDF will receive 217 million FCFA , that is, about half of what it was supposed to get in 2004.

Also there are no effective checks and balances to ensure that the taxpayers' money is used for its intended purposes. First, the control committee lacks the human and financial resources, and even the expertise, to effectively monitor the activities of the recipients or to audit their financial records. In fact, the committee is yet to carry out an exhaustive audit of political parties who have so far received state funds, in spite of widespread allegations of misuse and outright embezzlement of these subsidies by party stalwarts.

Finally, even in the hypothetical case where it functions as planned, the committee is unlikely to serve as a deterrent for embezzlement because its activities are shrouded in secrecy. It cannot make its findings or its annual reports public. Instead, it sends them directly to the President who decides what to do with them. Even in cases of obvious mismanagement, the President is likely to turn a blind eye because the existence of political parties that can effectively participate in local and national elections creates the much needed illusion of a free, vibrant, and plural political landscape...

As a result of these shortcomings, political parties who receive state funds virtually have a free hand to use these funds as they see fit – either for their intended purposes or for personal enrichment. We can safely conclude that although the principle of public funding is a great one in theory (creating an active and egalitarian democratic system), its main role in Cameroonian politics seems to be to "soften" and domesticate the opposition.

Reference

Fambom, S. (2003). *Public Funding Of Political Parties In Africa*. Paper submitted at the Africa Conference on Election, Democracy and Governance 7-10 April 2003, Pretoria, South Africa. Retrieved March 15, 2009 from: http://www.whofundswho.org.za/pubs/conf/fambom.pdf

29

Social Democratic Front (SDF): A Dream Derailed?

May 26, 2006: On May 26, 1990, thousands of SDF militants and sympathizers gathered at Bamenda's Ntarikon Park to take part in the launching of the Social Democratic Front (SDF) in defiance of a Government ban. In his speech, the SDF Chairman, Ni John Fru Ndi, fearlessly lashed out at Cameroon's monolithic and oppressive political system, amidst heavy military presence. Speaking directly to the militants who had braved the threat of repression to be at the party's launching Fru Ndi declared:

> Thank you for your faith and determination. Make no mistake, and don't allow yourself to be misled and misguided by anyone, no matter his situation in life. Democracy has never been handed on a platter of gold! ... Let us make it clear to those who are hearing us today that, in the view of the Social Democratic Front, the struggle will continue, not only here, but anywhere in the world, as long as there is somebody who is governing and someone who is governed.

It was indeed a memorable day in the annals of Cameroonian history. As the mammoth crowd dispersed after the ceremony, security forces shot and killed six individuals: Fidelis Chosi Mankam (Corn Mill Operator), Tifuh Mathias Teboh (Student), Asanji Christopher Fombi (Student), Nfon Edwin Jatop (Tailor), Juliette Sikod (Student), Toje Evaristus Chatum (Student).

Within a couple of years of its birth which had been "watered" with the blood of these "six martyrs of democracy," the SDF had become the most popular party in Cameroon, and its motto "Power to the People," the rallying cry of the oppressed masses of Cameroon. By the time the SDF and its charismatic chairman challenged President Paul Biya in the October 1992 presidential elections under the banner of the "Union for Change" coalition, the party was already being considered as the most viable alternative to the Biya regime – Fru Ndi's controversial loss to Paul Biya in these elections (generally considered to have been rigged) only made the SDF appeal much stronger.

Fast forward to May 26, 2006.

The SDF, which was launched in blood and tears, is currently going through its most disruptive internal crisis. Two rival factions (one led by Fru Ndi and another by Prof. Clement Ngwasiri) are on the warpath. Both factions planned to hold rival party conventions today in Bamenda and Yaounde respectively. Events that occurred in Yaounde today have transformed May 26 from a day of commemoration and celebration into one that will live in infamy. According to a *Reuters* news report (confirmed by the Cameroonian media):

> Machete-wielding attackers beat a Cameroon opposition faction leader to death, gouged his eyes out and left his body in the street on Friday as an opposition power struggle spilled over into violence, witnesses said.
> The attack came as rival conventions of the main opposition Social Democratic Front (SDF) were due to start, demonstrating a deep rift in a party that presents the biggest challenge to President Paul Biya, one of Africa's longest serving leaders.
> The dead man was Gregoire Diboule, the party's provincial administrative secretary in the capital Yaounde, who had backed a challenge to longstanding SDF leader John Fru Ndi by senior party figure Clement Ngwasiri.
> Ngwasiri, chairman of the party's national advisory council, had organised a breakaway party convention to start in Yaounde on Friday – the same day the main party convention was due to start 280 km (175 miles) away in Bamenda.

All those who once believed in the SDF vision and in the dream of a democratic SDF-led alternative to the Biya regime are shocked and appalled by the turn of events. Many now wonder whether the deaths of May 26 1990 were worth it after all. Even an editorial in the Government Daily, *Cameroon Tribune*, shed a tear at the *gachis democtratique* or the democratic waste that the SDF had become.

On the eve of the 1992 presidential elections, I profiled the three leading candidates (Paul Biya, John Fru Ndi and Bello Bouba Maigari) in *Cameroon Life Magazine* (Vol. II, No. 7, October 1992). In my profile of Fru Ndi, I wrote the following:

> The key to the SDF's success lies in what has been described as its 'charismatic and grassroots leadership' incarnated by Ni John Fru Ndi...
> His detractors also maintain that he is more of a crusading evangelist than a politician; one who never gives room for compromise. His supporters on their part describe his as a progressive social democrat with a great vision; one who is intransigent (and rightly so) when it comes defending the interests of the masses who are the backbone of the SDF.
> SDF militants, who are fanatically devoted to their chairman, tell anyone who cares to listen that John Fru Ndi is a modern-day Moses about to take them to the Promised Land.

As I read those lines today, I cannot help but come to the conclusion that the key to the SDF's success is also the key to its troubles: The reason for the SDF's success over the years and its pre-eminent position on the Cameroonian political scene are intricately tied to the rugged determination of one man – John Fru Ndi. In the same vein, it is obvious that the chairman's personality partly explains the outcome of many of the crises that have rocked the party over the years.

In the conclusion of my *Cameroon Life* piece, I had opined that:

> Whichever way the tables turn on October 11 1992, Fru Ndi will come out head high. For, even if he does not make it to Etoudi (something his supporters consider impossible), he will be remembered by all – both friend and foe – as they who for 25 months running yelled so loudly for the marginalized and oppressed masses of Cameroon that he unleashed an earthquake of unimaginable proportions that shook Cameroon's monolithic political structures to their roots; and led to a slow but irreversible trend towards authentic democracy.

Sixteen years later, there are no grounds for such sweeping statements. It is all but certain that whatever the outcome of ongoing events in Bamenda and Yaounde, the SDF has taken a big hit, and would need all its available resources to put its house in order. No one is going to walk out of the current crisis unscathed as in previous cases – not the Chairman and definitely not Ngwasiri.

What the SDF desperately needs today is a brand new vision and leadership that clearly demarcates itself from the CPDM; it needs a new language of tolerance that encourages open dissent and dialogue within the party; a clear policy of reconciliation that stretches a hand of fellowship to die-hard militants who have been caught up in the ongoing wrangling in spite of themselves; and a far more transparent management style which will quash persistent claims of corruption and cronyism at the top. For these changes to become reality, the SDF needs to elect new and vibrant leaders during this convention – with or without Fru Ndi at the helm – in place of the rear guard and corrupt elements who, like their CPDM counterparts, have played a frontline role in stalling Cameroon's democratization process.

Part Seven

Profiles of Courage

30

A Dream Deferred: Emmanuel Njela Nfor

February 15, 2006: As I surfed the web for Cameroon-related news this morning, I came across an article from the Korea-based citizen journalism site *OhmyNews International* with the ominous title *Remembering Our Cameroon Citizen Reporter*. What followed was a heart-wrenching obituary for OhmyNews' Cameroon and Africa citizen reporter, 28-year old Emmanuel Njela Nfor. The newspaper's editor was full of praise for Njela's talents and dedication:

> From the moment he registered in early July 2005 to cover his native Cameroon – and pan-African news and international sport – I could tell he was going to make an important contribution to citizen journalism. He was the kind of citizen reporter who never refused an assignment. I had no idea how busy he actually was — he never complained — but for every suggested story there would be a finished article waiting for publication in less than 24 hours. His command of English and his overall journalism style was so good that I rarely had to touch them up. Like I said, an editor's dream...
>
> Though very well educated – he had a Masters degree in linguistics from the University of Buea – he could only pick up odd jobs. For a time he was a receptionist at a cyber cafe – a job he took just for fun – and he also sold publishing advertisements in the commercial sector. A part time mobile phone salesman, he quit that job when he started sending regular dispatches to us in Seoul.

This is one of those stories that make you lament about the waste of Africa's rich human potential due to a shameful inability or unwillingness to use these resources as a foundation of its development. We educate them and then cast them off. I can only wistfully think of what could have been...

Njela was definitely an embodiment of his generation; a generation with immense talents and creativity, determination to succeed against all odds, and a love for country. Unfortunately, all over Africa, the dreams and aspirations of Njela's generation are being curbed by stifling conformity, the lack of opportunity, a disregard for talent and merit, and by policies of exclusion. Njela, in life as in death, was a reflection of this paradox: In spite of all his talent, drive and education, he never got a break in his native Cameroon – until hope beckoned from the Korean peninsular of all places! And we learned of his death not from the Cameroonian media but from heartbroken colleagues in far away Asia. Truly, a prophet is never recognized in his home!

> His dreams were to be a great reporter and to always give accurate and relevant information to the people of the world. He also wanted to have a

respectful, honest, understanding and open-hearted wife. Giving good education to his future children.

According to a friend, Njela wanted to dedicate himself to improving journalism in Cameroon. Njela stayed in Cameroon to brave the odds and make his dreams come true rather than embark on that treacherous journey across the Sahara in search of greener pastures in Europe. Alas! He died in his prime, with all the dreams for himself and his country largely unfulfilled.

The tragedy here is that there are thousands of Njelas roaming the streets of Cameroon; highly talented, educated and dedicated individuals who are either undervalued or simply exploited by the system. The story of his generation is that of stolen innocence and of dreams deferred; of lights that do not indicate the end of the tunnel but rather, an endless journey towards a mirage.

Farewell brother – we barely knew you but you will be sorely missed.

31

Isaac Menyoli: Living Up to the Olympic Creed

February 27, 2006: I just watched bits and pieces of the closing ceremony of the 2006 Winter Olympics on TV. From an organizational stand point, the Italians have everything to be proud of. But these games lacked the passion and drama of the 2002 Salt Lake City games. In fact, the most memorable event of the 2006 games was the doping scandal involving the Austrian team. Here in the United States, Bryant Gumbel's putdown of the Winter Olympics on HBO generated more passion than the performance of any athlete in Turin, and virtually started a mini race war.

In fact, the Olympic ideal of creating "a way of life based on the joy found in effort, the educational value of good example and respect for universal fundamental ethical principles" was seriously tested during these games. As the *Tallahassee Democrat* put it, the games were characterized by "spoiled, selfish athletes turning in subpar performances; a panoply of fake 'sports' inserted into the schedule..."

As I watched the closing ceremonies, I could not help but think about the different atmosphere that prevailed four years ago during the Winter Olympics in Salt Lake City. The Salt Lake games were much different – at least from the perspective of someone with only a passing interest in Winter games. Those games had a handful of participants who symbolized the best of the Olympic ideal; athletes from the tropics whose presence in Salt Lake defied convention and logic. These were athletes from countries such as India, Venezuela, Kenya, Ethiopia, Nepal and Costa Rica whose dreams of an Olympic medal were, to quote one report, "as farfetched as space travel did a hundred years ago."

The most famous of Salt Lake's improbable participants was none other than Isaac "'the Ice King' Menyoli,' Cameroon's first and most probably last cross-country skier, or Winter Olympian." Menyoli, an architect resident in Milwaukee, USA, had never seen snow before he came to the United States in 1993, and his Olympic dreams began when he watched Kenya's Phillip Boit take part in the 1998 Winter Olympics in Nagano, Japan.

Unlike his American and European counterparts, Menyoli did not have big name sponsors and had to train on dry land for two hours each day after work. He was not only determined to take part in, and successfully complete, the 10km classical cross-country, he also wanted to use his "15 minutes of fame" to bring attention to the problem of AIDS in his native Cameroon: "When I acquired the talent in the United States for this sport, I wanted to use it to open new doors, to help my people."

People around the world watched as Menyoli proudly marched with the Cameroonian flag into the opening ceremonies. And the world media was at hand again to cover his memorable performance in the 10km classical cross-country at Soldier Hollow. Menyoli finished last, exactly 19 minutes 33 seconds behind winner

Johann Muehlegg of Spain. As he glided through finish line, an ecstatic Menyoli raised his arms in triumph.

According to the Olympic creed which is attributed to Baron Pierre de Coubertin,

> The most important thing in the Olympic Games is not to win but to take part, just as the most important thing in life is not the triumph but the struggle. The essential thing is not to have conquered but to have fought well.

Menyoli, more than any other athlete present in Salt Lake, gave meaning to that creed. In this respect, he was a winner even though he did not go home with a medal. His victory was that of the spirit, of rugged determination and of perseverance. He won the hearts of millions by giving his best – something that some celebrity athletes like Bodie Miller failed to do in Turin.

Although Menyoli was not present in Italy, the fallout of his performance in Salt Lake four year earlier was very evident; there was a record 12 participants from Africa in Torino. That these athletes were not treated as oddities, and not given the kind of media coverage that Menyoli had in 2002 showed how far Menyoli's participation had changed the perception of the games as a purely Euro-American affair.

For his achievement, the Ice King from the slopes of Mount Fako in Cameroon will forever be an Olympic pioneer and legend.

32

Sita Bella: The Final Journey of a Renaissance Woman

March 19, 2006: This weekend, a woman who was a pioneer in many fields was buried at the Mvolye cemetery in Yaounde amidst national soul-searching. Her name was Therese Bella Mbida, popularly known as Sita Bella. It is no surprise that although she died at the ripe age of 73, most Cameroonians never heard of her until her death a couple of weeks ago.

Sita Bella was Cameroon's first female journalist who started plying her trade on the eve of independence. She was also one of the first African female filmmakers, her most popular work being a short 1963 documentary titled « Tam-tam à Paris ». But that was not all; she was Cameroon's first female pilot, a writer, guitarist and model. A woman ahead of her times, she made her mark in a male-dominated system that considered her as an oddity, and blazed the trail for many women of her generation. As she once declared: "Camerawomen in the 1970's? At that time we were very few. There were few West Indians, a woman from Senegal called Safi Faye and I. But you know cinema is not a woman's business."

That Cameroonians did not know or did not care about such an amazing icon and role model in their midst is no surprise, given how that country treats its heroes. So she died in total anonymity. However, this is not the saddest aspect about the life and death of this avant-garde feminist who confidently bestrode a male-dominated world like a colossus at a time when the African woman was largely invisible and confined to the kitchen or the farm. What is revolting is how this national icon spent her last days in a country where she should logically have been celebrated as the role model that she was. According to news reports, Sita Bella died "in the greatest destitution, abandoned and alone, after being thrown out of the flat she lived in the Messa district." She ended up in an old people's home run by catholic nuns (I didn't even know we had those in Cameroon...).

As in the case of Messi Martin, the creator of modern Bikutsi who died penniless and bitter in August 2005, Sita Bella's death was followed by national soul searching and guilt. Did she have to die in such misery and neglect? Should it be the responsibility of the State to provide a "security net" for national icons when they could no longer take care of themselves? What is the responsibility of society as a whole in this tragedy? Must we only wait for the death of our icons, heroes and martyrs to adorn their corpses with meaningless posthumous medals as was the case with Eboua Lottin, Messi Martin and other cultural ambassadors who died in abject poverty and total misery? This is a sample of the questions that have been at the center of debate on many Cameroonian Internet forums. This debate will not go away any time soon, and will definitely resurface when the next hero dies in poverty and anonymity.

So rather than join that debate at this time, we will simply pay our last respects to a great renaissance woman who was a million years ahead of her time. May her soul rest in perfect peace. And, to borrow from an article in the catholic bi-weekly, *L'effort Camerounais*, "May the lights of our heroes and national martyrs shine on despite the futile attempts to always throw a blanket over them."

33

Joe la Conscience: Cameroon's Forgotten Prisoner of Conscience

April 25, 2008: In the past couple of weeks, there have been numerous stories in the national and international media about the arrest of prominent Cameroonian protest singer Lapiro de Mbanga. However, the arrest, summary trial and sentencing of the less known protest singer, Joe La Conscience, has not received as much attention.

Unlike Lapiro who is accused of being the mastermind behind the February riots, particularly in his native town of Mbanga (although eyewitness accounts and initial reports from local officials indicated that he had helped calm down angry rioters…) Joe La Conscience is not accused of any violence. His only crime is that he organized a one-man nonviolent protest against recent moves to scrap presidential term limits in Cameroon.

In this regard, his detention is even more significant than Lapiro's because it is a clear indicator of Cameroon's new authoritarian political landscape where all sources of dissent – real, imagined and symbolic – are systematically silenced. Today it is not only vandals and "apprentice sorcerers" who get caught up in the Biya regime's repressive maelstrom…

Joe La Conscience or the Road to Kondengui

Shortly after regime officials began agitating for an amendment of Article 6.2 late last year, Joe La Conscience (whose real name is Kameni Joe de Vinci) wrote a memorandum titled "50 good reasons not to change the Cameroon constitution" to protest against plans to scrap presidential term limits in Cameroon. He also composed a song condemning the planned constitutional amendment titled "Emmerdement constitutionnel" (constitutional hassle).

After adding 1000 signatures to his anti-amendment memo, Joe La Conscience decided to embark on a 320-kilometre (200-mile) solo trek from his native town of Loum to Yaounde, Cameroon's capital, to hand the said memo to the President. On February 17, Joe began what he called the "Long March for Peace." However, the march ended prematurely after he was arrested on the outskirts of Loum by security forces on grounds that he had violated an order by the governor of littoral banning public rallies and demonstrations in the province.

On February 26, three days after troops sealed Equinoxe Radio and TV, Joe La Conscience began a hunger strike outside the gates of the US embassy in Yaounde to protest the government's crackdown on the media. The next day, troops stormed his residence in Loum, shot his 11-year old son, Aya Kameni Patrick Lionel, to death, and ransacked his workshop. In a letter addressed to President Biya, Joe's wife, Sidonie, describes how Lionel was shot "before my eyes and that of my other children." Unable to travel to Loum due to the rioting, Joe continued his peaceful protest outside the embassy. Two days later, on February 29, about 30 heavily armed gendarmes stormed the US embassy gates and whisked Joe off to a cell at the Secretariat of State of the National Gendarmerie where, according to his wife, he was tortured. He was then transferred to the Kondengui Maximum security prison on March 6.

On March 19, Kondengui became Joe La Conscience's permanent home when the Mfoundi Court of First Instance handed him a six-moth jail sentence for organizing "illegal meetings and demonstrations" after an expeditious trial widely condemned by legal experts. Even non-violent protest *à la Mahatma Gandhi* does not pay in Cameroon. Only the silence of the slave – or of the grave – does…

Joe La Conscience or The Authoritarian Impulse of the Biya Regime

At first glance, the story of Joe La Conscience is just another personal tragedy in good old Cameroon; the tale of an individual and his family paying a heavy price for his political activism. But deep down, this is a story about Cameroon, its government, its people and its future. It is a very telling snapshot of the reigning political climate in Cameroon and a good indicator of what the Biya regime's so-called *troisième mandat* will look like. Nearly two decades ago an observer argued that:

> Under the *ancien regime*, power was mostly exercised in a bullying and overbearing manner to limit people's freedoms and ensure the survival of political leaders, but during the New Deal era it was usually employed in far less brutal ways mainly to feather the nests of our leaders.

We have come a long way since then, as the Biya regime has now merged the brutality of the Ahidjo regime with its own homegrown Kleptocracy. Today, just as during the Ahidjo regime, survival is the name of the game. Recent events have shown that in its bid to hang on to power at all cost, the Biya regime is, more than ever before, driven by an *élan autoritaire* or a dark authoritarian impulse which does not bode well for the country.

Extremists who for years have been itching for a head-on confrontation with "the forces of change" have finally gained a solid footing within the regime and are creating a deleterious political climate reminiscent of that which prevailed in the last years of the Abacha regime in next door Nigeria; a climate characterized by the emasculation of the civil society and organized political opposition, the muzzling of the press and persecution of journalists, the militarization of political life and the increasing use of martial language in regular political discourse, the isolation of potential catalysts for popular mobilization and political reawakening particularly artists, an increasing appeal to ethnicity, etc.

In 1994, Milton Krieger posited that Cameroon's democratization experiment had taken off on the wrong footing because "Biya [was] more likely captive than capo" to obscure political lobbies which had "moved beyond conventional patrimonial politics to… 'ethno-clientelism'." Today, these lobbies, which were largely responsible for the political turmoil during the early multiparty years – and which conceived the infamous "Operation Mygale" in 1991 which bore an eerie similarity to the blueprint for the Rwandan genocide a few years later – are once again coming out of the shadows.

These lobbies have found solace in the motley collection of ethno-regional, political and personal interests which crystallized around the President during the campaign to modify the constitution – a constitutional amendment which was less about support for the Prince or the City and more about a political class desperately clinging to its privileges which would most likely disappear in the event of a regime change in 2011. In such a context, it is no surprise that individuals such as Joe la Conscience or Lapiro de Mbanga with even the slightest potential to mobilize the public against these corporate, ethnic and personal interests are mercilessly crushed.

Joe la Conscience or the Demobilization of the Cameroonian Masses

With no viable organized political force to stand up to Biya, it is now left to artists and other "lone wolfs' to pick up the mantle for political change in Cameroon, usually with dire consequences as we have seen in the cases of Joe and Lapiro. Unfortunately unlike the 1990s where regime attempts to silence its most vocal critics (Yondo Black, Celestin Monga, Pius Njawe, Senfo Tonkam, etc.) was met with resistance and mass mobilization, today there is instead a general feeling of resignation – the all-out militarization of national life has created a state of fear, or at least apprehension, which, although not as palpable or obvious as in some other African countries, is present nonetheless. This "demobilization", argues Cameroonian writer Patrice Nganang who has commented extensively on the Joe La Conscience case, does not augur well for the republic:

> Never before have the arts forewarned us so clearly about the future of Cameroon; but never before have artists been so alone!... That Joe has been abandoned to the care of his wife… and a handful of friends is the most dangerous sign from the Cameroonian political scene… To abandon Joe la Conscience in the hell hole that is his cell, to abandon Lapiro de Mbanga… is to tell anyone who intends to rise up to assert his citizenship that he is alone. To forget these damned individuals… in the miasma of their loneliness, is to plant the seeds of discouragement in the heart of every citizen who, tomorrow, will wish to rise up to push back the darkness that has enveloped us. [my translation].

So are Cameroonians going to abandon Joe La Conscience, Lapiro the Mbanga and others to their fate, thereby giving the Biya regime a free hand to do as it pleases in Cameroon? Or are they going to join them to fully reassert their confiscated citizenship and freedoms?

34

Jean-Marc Ela – Remembering Africa's "Liberation Theologian"

December 17, 2008: The death has been announced of Father Jean Marc Ela, one of Cameroon's leading scholars, who has variously been described as "the nearest Africa has come to a liberation theologian in a Latin American sense, " the "Champion of a theology under the trees," "Africa's first liberation theologian of note outside South Africa," and as "one of the best known and most read African theologians not only in Africa but also elsewhere." He died recently in Canada where he had been on exile since 1995.

Born in 1936 in Ebolowa, Cameroon, Jean-Marc Ela was ordained priest in 1964. He subsequently earned doctorate degrees in Theology from the University of Strasbourg, France (1969) and Sociology from the Sorbonne in Paris (1978).

A very prolific writer, Jean-Marc Ela published dozens books, the most popular being *Ma foi d'Africain* (My faith as an African) "which gave him world notoriety and African renown in particular", *Le cri de l'homme* (African Cry) "which attracted attention the world over", and Voici *le temps des Heìritiers eìglises d'Afrique et voies nouvelles* (co-authored with Christiane Ngendakuriyo; Vincent Cosmao; Reneì Luneau but in which his contributions were so significant that he is generally referred to as the sole author). These three books have been described by many as his "essential contributions to African theology."

Jean-Marc Ela's theology was largely shaped by his 14-year stay among the non-Muslim Kirdi population of Northern Cameroon whose life was characterized by misery, marginalization and exploitation by the state. As a result, according to Sundkler, "no one else expressed the 'cry of the African' with as much prophetic pathos as Fr. Jean-Marc Ela". As Fr. Ela stressed in one of his writings:

> How can the African human being attain a condition that will enable him and her escape misery and inequality, silence and oppression? If Christianity seeks to be anything more than an effort to swindle a mass of mystified blacks, the churches of Africa must all join to come to terms with this question.

But Ela's theology was more than just about liberation. As Benezet Buju points out, "Jean Marc's theology cannot be reduced to theology of liberation as opposed to the so-called theology of inculturation." In this regard, Fr. Ela called for:

> an African theology that incorporates oral culture, myths, symbols, etc. into its method and into the proclamation of the Gospel. For our theologian it is evident that his inculturating effort cannot be undertaken without taking into account liberation in a holistic sense, i.e. one that takes into account cultural identity and the political and socio-economic dimensions... For Jean-

Marc Ela, liberation and inculturation do not oppose each other. They ought to be placed in a relation of 'perichoresis' for an African theology that takes into account each and every person.

Outcast

Jean Marc Ela was a vocal critic of both the Catholic Church in Cameroon, which shunned him, and the Biya regime, which forced him into exile in 1995. According to Paul Gifford,

> For all his *réclame* in the West, it must be noted that Ela has been totally marginalised ('pas bien integré' is the standard euphemism) in the Catholic Church in Cameroon. In the early 1990s he used to celebrate mass every Saturday evening in a parish near the University of Yaounde, to which students would flock in hundreds. This mass was quite an event, being marked both by liturgical inculturation and radical, socially aware sermons. Ela taught at the University of Yaounde and at the *Faculté Protestante*, but not at Yaounde's Catholic University. He was in Rome at the time of the 1994 Synod of bishops for Africa, not as part of the official Cameroon delegation, but invited by an alternative group. When one inquired why he was so marginalised, different answers were given: that he is just writing for the West and what he writes has no bearing on the life of people in the villages, or that he is a sociologist, not a theologian.

But even more significant than his marginalization by the Catholic Church, was his persecution by the Biya regime for his critical stances on a variety of issues, particularly the regime's refusal to give in to the democratization clamor of the early 1990s. On August 6, 1995, Fr. Jean Marc Ela left Cameroon for good after being "alerted to probable attempts on his own life" (Gifford, 271). According to a 1995 memorandum by the *Forum of African Intellectuals in the Diaspora* whose members included Achille Mbembe and Celestin Monga,

> The **general reasons** for this forced departure include the countless bullying, humiliations and harassments, in short, the multiple forms of persecution and the systematic violence that the Cameroonian state has unleashed against scholars, intellectuals, artists and creators whom it suspects of dissidence.
>
> The **immediate cause** of Jean Marc Ela's exile the repeated death threats made against him since the assassination of Fr. Engelbert Mveng...

According to the memorandum, during the "smoldering years" of 1990-1992, members of the ruling elite who belonged to the Head of State's Bulu ethnic group (which was also Fr. Ela's) considered his stance on key issues to be detrimental to their interests. He was reproached for publishing articles critical of the Biya regime in "Bamileke newspapers" that were hostile to the regime, and for refusing to associate himself with the ruling CPDM. In the subsequent years, these threats became more specific and were even extended to members of his family. Fr. Ela was asked to either reaffirm his loyalty to the tribe or be branded a traitor. The threats began to take a more concrete form after the assassination of Fr. Mveng (his collaborator and another priest who was tagged a "troublemaker") on April 24, 1995. On August 6, 1995, he left Cameroon for good.

Jean-Marc Ela's international renown did not translate into national recognition in his native Cameroon where he was not very well known beyond intellectual and religious circles - although his articles in "opposition" newspapers in the early 1990s gave him a certain following among a younger generation who came to know him only as a pro-democracy activist and not as the great scholar that he was. Ela's 13-year exile ensured that the post 1990 generation of Cameroonians was completely unaware of the existence of one of the leading theologians of our times and one of the country's leading scholars of all time. As the 1995 memorandum rightly pointed out, through his life and works, Fr. Jean-Marc Ela was "part of the intellectual patrimony of Africa, its moral conscience and the historic struggles of Africans trying to live full lives in spite of destiny, calamities and numerous challenges."

In their seminal work on African theology in the 21st century, Benezet Bujo and Juvenal Muya offer what is probably the best epitaph for the fallen priest:

> Jean-Marc Ela will be one day remembered by the future African generations as a benefactor and advocate who defended the identity and dignity of black peoples with a real Christian and priestly commitment.

May his soul rest in peace.

References

Bujo, B., & Ilunga Muya, J. (2003). *African theology in the 21st century: The contribution of the pioneers*. Nairobi, Kenya: Paulines Publications Africa.

Gifford, P. (1998). *African Christianity: Its public role*. Bloomington: Indiana University Press.

Sundkler, B., & Steed, C. (2000). *A history of the church in Africa*. Studia missionalia Upsaliensia, 74. Cambridge, UK: Cambridge University Press.

*Although Jean-Marc Ela's death was initially announced on December 13, he actually died a couple of weeks later on December 26, 2008.

Part Eight

Law, Justice & Corruption

35

Trail of Death: Maintaining Law and Order in Cameroon

Freedom of assembly and the right to demonstrate and to protest are widely accepted as basic civil rights and as such are embodied within all international charters of human rights – *Democratic Dialogue*

November 23, 2007: *September 2007* – Three people, two of them teenagers, are shot dead in the town of Abong-bang during a demonstration by secondary school students protesting against frequent electricity cuts on campus which were affecting their studies. According to eyewitness reports, the Divisional Officer of the area, Sylvestre Essama, fired the first shot into the crowd of students, which incidentally killed his own nephew, Marcel Bertrand Mvogo Awono.

October 2007: Police in Bamenda shoot dead two motorcycle taxi-drivers during a protest against police abuses. According to the BBC, "Drivers had invaded the centre of the town of Bamenda to protest at the alleged severe beating of a colleague detained at a police checkpoint. When police tried to clear away the demonstrators' barricades, stones were thrown and police replied with gunfire."

November 2007: Police in the town of Kumba shoot dead two students during another protest triggered by persistent power blackouts at school. According to *Reuters*, "The police officers opened fire as they were pelted with stones and Molotov cocktails during the demonstration on Saturday, hitting two students in the head and killing them instantly. Another five were injured, one of them seriously." An eyewitness quoted by *The Post* newspaper explains how the shooting began:

> the Commissioner [Ela Menye Fils] came to the scene while the students and police were locked in a teargas-and-stone battle... the Commissioner, who was a victim of the students' stones, got enraged and ordered his subordinates to shoot, but they hesitated... the Commissioner pulled his gun and fired at the students.

A common thread in these and similar events elsewhere in Cameroon is the propensity of security forces to use lethal force as a first, instead of a last resort. This disproportionate, violent and often fatal method of maintaining "law and order" is the byproduct of an outdated interpretation of "public order" going back to the Ahidjo era when Cameroon was governed by a series of "emergency laws" – officially instituted to combat terrorism but most often used to silence political dissent. As Abel Eyinga described the situation in Ahidjo's Cameroon,

> The notion of public order does not have in Cameroon the same meaning as elsewhere, even in France. In French public law, public order refers to the

minimum conditions considered necessary for the maintenance of a normal social life, i.e., security of persons and property, sanitation, peace and tranquility, etc. In Cameroon however, "public order" has been transformed and now comprises two fundamental principles: the maintenance of the political status quo and implicit in the first, the retention in power of El Hadj Ahmadou Ahidjo, the privileged intermediary of colonialists. All acts, all proposals, and even all abstentions, capable of being interpreted by the regime as bringing into question one or another of these fundamental principles, are treated as consisting of grave threats to public order and consequently, as instances of subversion subject to prosecution.

Under this system, peaceful demonstrations by unarmed citizens are considered to be criminal or subversive acts, which must be "crushed" at all cost, irrespective of the legitimacy of the complaint.

Although Cameroon theoretically operates under a more liberal socio-political climate today, the Ahidjoist notion of public order is still very much around, even if it is not explicitly articulated as in the days of the one-party system. Maintaining law and order in Cameroon today is not about maintaining communal peace and security. In fact, most "law and order" operations actually result in communal chaos and violence. It is about ensuring "respect for constituted authority." Peaceful demonstrations or protest marches by unarmed civilians in Cameroon are therefore not considered as mere exercises of basic human rights, but as acts of defiance or rebellion against "constituted authority." In this context, even a peaceful march by unarmed 14-year old kids is automatically seen as an attempt to embarrass local authorities and test their resolve. And, since the state must be "strong" at all times and must never appear "weak" to its citizens, it must therefore restore its "authority" as forcefully as possible. With this authoritarian mindset, whenever there is a demonstration, says *Le Messager*, the first reaction of local authorities is to:

> send in the police and the constabulary armed to the teeth, and sometimes the army. Not to manage the demonstration in question nor to prevent destruction, but to instead "break" the demonstrators, arrest them for "disturbing public order," or to beat them up irrespective of their social status.

Proponents of an *état fort* – and there are surprisingly many of them among the masses – will argue that these demonstrations were illegal because they were not authorized by the administration. True, but is violence the only way to deal with this particular "illegality"? Isn't it the duty of the local political and military authorities to create an environment where demonstrations – even illegal ones! – can be managed and controlled peacefully? And are the "legalists" among us even aware that the use of bullets to quell demonstrations is specifically proscribed by law in Cameroon except in clearly defined "exceptional circumstances" which none of the recent events amount to?

Law 90-54 of 19 December 1990 on Maintenance of Law and Order

In 1990, Parliament passed Law 90-54 of 19 December 1990 on maintenance of law and order as part of the "liberty laws" that ushered in the current multiparty era. This particular law was, at least on paper, supposed to mark the legal and political shift from a security apparatus whose primary goal was to protect the regime against its real and imagined enemies, to one whose primary responsibility was to give citizens ample protection in a pluralist political system where dissent was a daily reality thanks to political parties and civil society organizations whose policies were not necessarily aligned to that of the regime in power.

It is worth noting that this law specifically forbids security forces from using weapons in routine law and order operations such as public demonstrations. In fact, the law expressly forbids security forces from using rubber bullets on demonstrators and from even firing warning shots in the air. It however authorizes the use of tear gas, truncheons and other non-lethal weapons for crowd control purposes. The 1990 law allows the exceptional use of lethal weapons only if (a) firearms are used against the forces of law and order, or (2) where the situation has degenerated to such a point that forces of law and order can defend themselves only by using deadly force. Without even looking at the details of the 1990 law, common sense tells us that the throwing of stones by demonstrators does not amount to "exceptional circumstances" requiring the use of live bullets. In fact, to a police force that is well-trained in crowd management, controlling stone-throwing demonstrators is a routine law and order operation.

Even more than training, what needs to change is the current authoritarian mindset which sees every act of public dissent as a "threat to national stability." *Le Messager* sums it best when it argues that:

> those responsible for law and order must accept that a demonstration is neither a crime nor an act of rebellion. In a state governed by the rule of law, and Cameroon claims to be one, it is the citizen's legitimate right to demonstrate… Local administrators and their bosses must learn how to manage demonstrations without giving in to blind, violent and bloody repression because maintaining law and order or social peace is not synonymous to repression.

Reference

Eyinga, A. "Government by State of Emergency." In Richard Joseph (ed) Joseph, R. (2002). *Gaullist Africa: Cameroon under Ahmadu Ahidjo*. Nigeria: Fourth Dimension Publ.

36

Can Cameroon's New Criminal Procedure Code Deliver "Justice with a Human Face"?

January 01, 2007: Cameroon's much heralded new criminal procedure code went into effect today, January 1, 2007. Adopted by Parliament in July 2005, the new code is a hybrid system, which merges key features of the French Civil law and English Common law systems, along with customary law. Before the adoption of the new code, criminal procedure was governed in Francophone Cameroon by the French *code d'instruction criminelle* of February 14, 1838 and its subsequent amendments, while in Anglophone Cameroon it was governed by a variety of common law texts, primarily the Nigerian *Criminal Procedure Ordinance* of 1958. Attempts to "cameroonize" the anachronistic systems began in the mid 1970s but the process stalled after Francophone jurists and legal practitioners balked at the preponderance of common law practices in the draft documents that resulted from those initial attempts.

Nonetheless, the criminal procedure code adopted in 2005 still draws extensively from common law practices, the most significant being the adoption of the *Habeas Corpus* and the accusatory system of justice in place of the more widespread French / civil law inquisitorial system. [In very simplistic terms, the accusatory system is based on the presumption of innocence with the burden of proof on the accuser, while in the inquisitorial system there is a presumption of guilt with burden of proof on the accused].

According to Section 8 of the new code:

(1) Any person suspected of having committed an offence shall be presumed innocent until his guilt has been legally established in the course of a trial where he shall be given all necessary guarantees for his defence. (2) The presumption of innocence shall apply to every suspect, defendant and accused.

And in section 584, the code states that:

(1) The President of the High Court of the place of arrest or detention of a person or any other judge of the said court shall be competent to hear applications for immediate release based on grounds of illegality of arrest or detention or failure to observe the formalities as provided by law.

In a bid to address the common practice of arbitrary arrests and secret detentions, the criminal procedure code lays down clear guidelines for arresting individuals. According to Section 31,

Except in the case of a felony or misdemeanour committed flagrante delicto, the person effecting the arrest shall disclose his identity and inform the person to be arrested of the reason for the said arrest, and where necessary, allow a third person to accompany the person arrested in order to ascertain the place to which he is being detained.

Furthermore, Section 23 states that "The judicial police officer charged with the execution of a warrant of arrest may not enter any place of abode before 6 a.m. or after 6 p.m. for the purpose of executing the warrant."

Protection of the Individual in Custody

Some of the revolutionary changes (particularly for those trained in the Cameroonian civil law system) center around the treatment of individuals in police custody.

No Torture

According to Section 30 (4) "No bodily or psychological harm shall be caused to the person arrested. However reasonable force may be used where necessary." Section 122 (2) adds that:

> The suspect shall not be subjected to any physical or mental constraints, or to torture, violence, threats or any pressure whatsoever, or to deceit, insidious manoeuvres, false proposals, prolonged questioning, hypnosis, the administration of drugs or to any other method which is likely to compromise or limit his freedom of action or decision, or his memory or sense of judgment.

Right to Visitation and Medical Treatment

The right of a defendant to visits, legal counsel and medical treatment is no longer a privilege but a right enshrined in the new law. According to Section 37:

> Any person arrested shall be given reasonable facilities in particular to be in contact with his family, obtain legal advice, make arrangements for his defence, consult a doctor and receive medical treatment and take necessary steps to obtain his release on bail.

Section 122(3) clarifies that:

> The person on remand may at anytime within the period of detention and during working hours, be visited by his counsel, members of his family, and by any other person following up his treatment while in detention.

The Right to Client / Attorney Confidentiality

According to section 239 a remanded defendant has the right to unrestricted correspondence with third parties subject to the said correspondent being read by the Superintendent of Prison. However, Section 242 specifically protects client / attorney confidentiality by stating that:

1) The provisions of section 239 (2) are not applicable to correspondences between the defendant and his counsel or those between the defendant and the judicial authorities. (2) Any information got in violation of subsection (1) above cannot be used against the defendant.

Search & Seizures

One of the areas where police abuse is most rampant is that of search and seizures. The new code tries to provide a legal framework for search and seizures more in line with international norms. According to Section 93(2),

> Any search or seizure shall be carried out in the presence of the occupant of the place and the person in possession of the objects to be seized, or in case of their absence, their representatives, as well as two witnesses chosen from among the persons or neighbours present.

And in a clause that caused outrage and consternation particularly among security officers, individuals now have the right to search the police before they begin their search. According to Section 93(3),

> The occupant of the place and the person in possession of the objects to be seized, or in case of their absence, their representatives shall have the right to search the judicial police officer before the latter commences his search. He shall be informed of the said right and mention of it shall be made in the report of the fulfillment of this formality.

This is ostensibly to prevent against planting evidence.

In cases where the police do not have a search warrant, searches may take place only with the explicit consent of the person being searched. In this regard, Section 94 states that:

(1) In the absence of a search warrant, searches, and seizures of exhibits may be carried out only with the consent of the occupant or of the person in possession of the objects to be seized.

(2) The consent shall be a written declaration signed by the person concerned, and if he cannot sign he shall make a thumb-print at the bottom of the declaration.

(3) The consent of the person concerned shall be valid only if he had been informed before hand by the judicial police officer of his right to object to the search.

A Step Forward

Although the new criminal code has numerous flaws, some of which were identified even before the code became law (see for example, International Bar Association. (2003). *Cameroon Draft Criminal Procedure Code Must be Improved Says IBA*), it is still a landmark legislation which, at least on paper, seeks to promote what the official media has described as "justice with a human face." As Buba Ndifiembeu has pointed out in *A handbook on the criminal procedure code of the Republic of Cameroon*, the new code "paves the way for a much more.... improved human rights practices and provides the possibility for a more humane treatment of accused persons in Cameroon."

But Old Habits Die Hard...

The million-dollar question is whether there is an enabling environment to facilitate and promote the effective implementation of these new laws. In this regard, it should be noted that the criminal procedure code was initially supposed to go into effect on August 1, 2006, but this was postponed to January 1, 2007 apparently because of resistance from some of those charged with implementing it. Many groups were uncomfortable with the "restrictions" placed on judicial and security forces and with the "liberties" given suspected criminals. It is also worth pointing out that even before the adoption of the new code, Cameroon had one of the most stringent laws against torture. However, it is still commonplace to see tortured suspects paraded on national TV, or to read about confessions obtained through torture in the official media.

So, can "justice with a human face" become a reality in an environment where the violation of rules is a national hobby; where the judiciary is still tethered to the executive branch; where police abuse generally goes unpunished; and where the entire penal culture is based on punishment of the accused? Only time will tell...

37

The Untouchables (Politically Mediated Loans and Political Impunity in Cameroon)

July 28, 2006: In his 1993 study on accumulation and the cultural politics of identity in the Grassfields, Michael Rowlands observed that in Cameroon, there was a "natural affinity between the stream of power and the stream of money or credit." He argued that the country was plagued by "an ethos of ostentatious consumption" and by "unproductive patterns of investment and reliance on the state patronage for accumulation." The surest path to the accumulation of wealth in Cameroon was through politics. An analysis of the link between money and power in the early years of the Biya regime confirms Rowlands' observation: Between 1983 and 1987, for example, the Biya regime used its political influence to obtain colossal bank credits for high ranking officials in the regime on very liberal bases. According to Van De Walle, by the mid-1980s, a quarter of the total portfolio of the state-controlled banking sector— amounting to 120 billion FCFA francs (roughly $240 million US) — consisted of unrecoverable loans, most of them being politically mediated loans to elites. The story of Cameroon's unrecoverable politically mediated loans is a key theme that runs throughout the Biya regime. This theme partly explains the economic crisis of the 1980s and 1990s, and the collapse of Cameroon's banking system during that same period.

We were recently reminded of that ethos of ostentatious consumption by the headline of last Thursday's issue of *Le Messager* (July 27, 2007): «IMPUNITE: Voici les barons qui ont pillé nos banques » (Impunity: Here are the barons who plundered our banks). The headline was reminiscent of the early nineties when the nation's pulse beat to the rhythm of endless revelations about the politico-financial shenanigans of the ruling class. It was also a throwback to *Jeune Afrique Economie*'s famous "Ces fripouilles qui nous gouvernent" (These scoundrels who govern us) of 1992, which listed the names of some of the country's most rapacious public officials. Many of the scoundrels of the 1990s are still very much among us and remain still part of the untouchable class.

Yet Another List...

Unlike the lists that made headlines earlier this year (list of alleged homosexuals, list of richest government officials, etc.) which were dreamed up in the editorial offices of the local newspapers concerned, the list published by *Le Messager* is from the files of the Cameroon Collection Corporation which goes by the name *Société de recouvrement du Cameroun* (SRC). The Corporation is charged with liquidating the banks which collapsed in the eighties and nineties, and with tracking down and recovering their outstanding loans. The SRC's list of *mauvais payeurs* (bad debtors) reads like a Who's Who of Cameroon's political jet set. And the amounts borrowed by high ranking officials are simply mind boggling and obscene. For example, the whopping 4.5 billion FCFA loaned to Eyebe Lebogo Paul, a former Member of Parliament turned businessman, who was arrested on March 27 this year as part of the *Operation Epervier*.

While some of the loans were for credible investment ventures, most of them were used to shore up the opulent and ostentatious lifestyles of the rich and mighty, particularly to build the huge castles and mansions (coyly described as "retirement homes" by their owners) in their villages or in posh residential areas such as Santa Barbara and Odja in Yaounde. This is the case, for example, of President Biya's one time personal doctor and former cabinet Minister, the jailed Titus Edzoa, or Mengue Mvondo Marie, the President's younger sister – individuals who definitely did not have the resources to repay the colossal amounts which were given to them without collateral. *Le Messager* does not tell us how Edzoa and Mengue used their loans, but those with good memories will recall that these two names popped up during the infamous Messi Messi affair of 1992.

In his famous interview with *Jeune Afrique Economie* (No. 155 - Mai 1992), Messi Messi, the disgraced General Manager of the *Societe camerounaise de banque*, revealed that he was pressured to grant an unsecured loan of close to 70 Million FCFA to the President's sister for the construction of a mansion in Yaounde: *« le financement de la construction de deux villas de standing à Yaoundé, pour le compte de Marie Mengue, la sœur cadette de Paul Biya. Cela a coûté à peu près 70 millions de F CFA. »* SRC records published by *Le Messager* reveal that Mengue Mvondo Marie actually owes the defunct SCB 53 619 392 Fcfa and has never made any attempt to begin repaying this money.

The same issue of *Jeune Afrique Economie*, also revealed that Titus Edzoa was the beneficiary of an unseciary of an unsecured loan of 120 million FCFA from the SCB to construct a villa in Yaounde. He promised to rent out the villa upon completion, and use the proceeds to repay his loan. He never did. Once his chateau, which became the talk of the town at the time, was completed, Edzoa reneged on his promise and instead moved in with his family. He did not end there. According to *Jeune Afrique Economie*, he conspired with an SCB employee to erase all traces of his loan from SCB files. The only reason why Edzoa did not succeed in his attempt was because prior to the "disappearance" of his file, the SBC had refinanced the loan with the Central Bank, so there was an existing paper trail. To date Edzoa has never paid a dime. He was jailed in 1997 after he fell out with his mentor Paul Biya. This is what *Jeune Afrique Economie* wrote back in 1992:

> *Le docteur Titus Edzoa, médecin personnel du président Paul Biya, est ministre de l'Enseignement supérieur depuis le 9 avril. Il y a quelques années, il avait sollicité auprès de la SCB un crédit de 120 millions de F CFA pour bâtir une villa sur un terrain situé dans un luxueux quartier de Yaoundé. Robert Messi Messi affirme avoir d'autant plus facilement marqué son accord pour le déblocage des fonds que le docteur Edzoa lui a promis de mettre la maison en location et de rembourser son crédit par virement bancaire.*
>
> *La construction achevée, le conseiller spécial du Président aurait changé d'avis, pour habiter lui-même ce que d'aucuns considèrent comme un château. Il aurait non seulement tiré un trait sur sa dette mais fait disparaître toute trace de ce dossier des coffres de la*

banque commerciale, avec la complicité d'une employée de la SCB. Malheureusement pour lui, la SCB avait demandé et obtenu le refinancement de ce concours auprès de la Banque centrale à Yaoundé. Celle-ci ouvrant elle-même des dossiers de réescompte, il était alors facile à la SCB de retrouver et reconstituer cette opération.

Today, the SRC confirms that Edzoa owes SBC 135 865 905 Fcfa – a revealing tale of how high ranking officials use their influence to swindle and re-swindle the state...

A third name which appears on the SRC list and which also appeared in JAE back in 1992 is that of General Asso'o Emane Benoit. According to JAE, the General was also the beneficiary of an unsecured loan of around 200 to 300 million FCFA, which he intended to use to construct a "high class hotel" in Ebolowa. Whether that hotel was ever built is a mystery, but it is certain that the General never bothered to repay his loan. According to the SRC, the exact amount that the garrulous General owes the defunct SBC is 303 411 464 Fcfa... Again, from the pages of *Jeune Afrique Economie* of May 1992:

> *Le général de brigade Benoît Asso'o Emane, commandant du quartier général militaire à Yaoundé, comme le docteur Titus Edzoa, est très proche du chef de l'Etat. Sans aller jusqu'à donner les chiffres, Robert Messi Messi avoue avoir prêté au général Asso'o de quoi financer un « Hôtel de référence » que ce dernier a construit à Ebolowa. Le coût de la construction est estimé entre 200 et 300 millions de F CFA, financés par la Société camerounaise de banque, sans garanties.*

Without doubt, Robert Messi Messi, whom the Government described in 1992 as a delusional and pathological liar must be having a good laugh as the chickens come to roost – even if it is only symbolically...

When the story of the Biya regime is finally written, it will ultimately be about "the rampant [and] ostentatious colonization of the state" by an "arrogant ... elite with little mastery of monetary issues and more inclined towards the ethos of lavishness than production" (Mbembe). An ethos of lavishness, avarice, and unaccountability which explains how a public functionary can walk into a bank totally broke, and then walk out with 50 million FCFA in his pocket, with only his verbal promise to repay....

Le Cameroun c'est le Cameroun indeed!

38

100 Ways to Pilfer a Public Corporation: Notes from the Trial of Gerard Ondo Ndong

January 30, 2007: As the trial of disgraced former Director General of FEICOM, Ondo Ndong, continues this week, the facts that have so far emerged illustrate how Cameroon's public corporations, or parastatals as they are commonly known, have become milking cows for the ruling elite and their cronies. Ondo Ndong, along with 30 of his collaborators, is charged with embezzlement, corruption, forgery and use of forgeries. Ondo Ndong is specifically accused of embezzling 29 Billion Francs CFA – i.e., about 56 million US Dollars – from FEICOM coffers between 2001 and 2005.

Prebendary practices, which were hitherto the subject of rumor and conjecture have now been confirmed in open court. The FEICOM case has also exposed the complete absence of credible oversight mechanisms to either oversee the management of these corporations or to monitor compliance to their statutory missions. As a result, these corporations are run like private estates with their budgets simply serving as piggy banks for officials who spend every living moment planning the next big swindle.

A rundown of the charges that have so far been tackled by the Yaounde High Court point to a systematic plunder of FEICOM coffers and a brazen misuse of the corporation's funds for purposes totally at odds with the corporation's mission which, according to Ambe Njoh is

> to provide credit and loans to municipal governments such as local government councils [who] can in turn, use these funds to finance local infrastructure development projects such as the construction of potable water systems, sanitation facilities, and sites-and-services and slum upgrading projects.

Undue Benefits to Board of Directors

The first charge that came before the court last December was the illegal benefits given to FEICOM board members. According to FEICOM regulations, board members are not entitled to remuneration. Nonetheless, in July 2001, Ferdinand Koungou Edima, the Board Chairman and Minister of Interior at the time, signed an order granting each board member a monthly allowance of 375,000 Fcfa (in a country where the average monthly salary of a civil servant is about 85,000 Fcfa...), along with one million FCFA bonus for each board meeting. It is striking that Ondo Ndong is not being charged for being a party to this flagrant violation of FEICOM rules, but for retroactively disbursing 156 million FCFA of these illegal benefits to Board members some two months before the Board Chair's order went into effect.

In addition, the court also called on Ondo Ndong to explain why he gave two board members a 12 million FCFA "special bonus" in 2002. Ondo Ndong explained, straight-faced, that this was FEICOM's contribution to the "merrymaking" which followed the appointment of these individuals to cabinet positions in the Biya government...

Payments for Non-existent Advertisement Supplements

According to State Prosecutor Christian Ndanga, the court had documents certifying that 328 million FCFA was withdrawn from FEICOM coffers to pay for advertising supplements in major national and international news outlets, but that only the *New York Times* and a handful of other media outlets effective published ads totaling 160 million FCFA. The rest of the money, that is 168 million FCFA, simply disappeared into thin air. In total, 21 national and international news organs were listed as having received payment for adverts that never saw the light of day. Some of the international media houses which supposedly received payments for FEICOM ads include *Le Monde* (France) for 17 millions Fcfa, The Gideppe group (France), 62 millions Fcfa, *Jeune Afrique Economie* (France), 27 millions Fcfa, and of course, the *New York Times* (26 million FCFA).

Ondo Ndong could not confirm in court if any of these newspapers, other than the *New York Times* actually published the ads in question. As he insisted in court, he "could not abandon his administrative duties to deal with minor details concerning the publication or non publication of the ads." He stressed, however, that instructions to buy ad space in newspapers came directly from the Presidency in a bid to highlight the government's actions and policies in the field of local government. He had no comment about the unaccounted 168 million FCFA....

It is worth noting that while the *New York Times* did in fact publish a 12-page special advertising supplement on Cameroon in its November 30, 2001 issue (with the section on FEICOM barely filling up half a page), the paper declared in a statement to the Cameroonian news portal *cameroon-info.net* that "All of the paper's dealings on the Ad were through a New York advertising agency, *Summit Communications*, not with any individual or entity in Cameroon." So who exactly paid for the *New York Times* ad? Were FEICOM funds used to pay for a supplement that also focused on every major corporation in the country? Or did Ondo Ndong simply seize the opportunity to swindle another 26 Million FCFA from the corporation?

The Mvomeka'a Stadium

Another accusation which shows how far FEICOM had strayed from its primary mission of assisting local councils in dire straits was Ondo Ndong's unilateral decision to partially fund the construction of a football stadium for the Meyomessala rural council in Mvomeka'a, President Biya's home town. According to a timeline presented in court, on November 4, 2005, Martin Bile Bidjang, a CPDM Member of Parliament from the Dja et Lobo division, sought FEICOM's assistance for the project. Six days later, Ondo Ndong signed an order authorizing the disbursement of 361 million FCFA (361 729 000 FCFA) to *Ets. Kinepolis*, the company in charge of the project. That same day the FEICOM cashier, Charles Ketchami, withdrew 120 million FCFA from BEAC. However, that money did not make it to Ets. Kinepolis. Mr. Ketchami revealed in court that after he withdrew the funds, the corporation's accountant asked him to hand over 90 million FCFA directly to Ondo Ndong, which he did at the latter's residence. Ondo Ndong was fired a day later before he could move in on the rest of the money...

Fictitious Missions

According to the prosecutor, Ondo Ndong and his accomplices also embezzled a whopping 6.5 Billion FCFA under the guise of field missions which never took place. About 3.8 billion FCFA was disbursed for these missions in 2004, and another 2.5 billion in 2005. When he took the stand, Ondo said he was stunned by the accusations because every mission that he had taken part in was approved by the Board of Directors. However the evidence and testimony of his accomplices told a different story. According to FEICOM records, 540 million FCFA was disbursed ostensibly to pay for missions across the country to explain new procedures for collecting Feicom funds. However, evidence presented in court showed that none of these missions ever took place.

Also, the co-accused who took to the stand sang a different tune from Ondo Ndong's. For example, Moïse Mbella revealed that all the missions related to the monitoring of road tarring projects were fictitious. In the same vein, FEICOM cashier, Charles Ketchami, told the court that he signed off on fictitious missions to a tune of six million FCFA, although he never received a penny for his hard work. He exposed the practice at FEICOM whereby officials withdrew funds for nonexistent missions and passed on the money to the Director General who then distributed the loot as he saw fit. Another co-conspirator, Nkouendjin Yotnda, confirmed this practice but claimed that she took part in the swindle out of "reverential fear" for Ondo Ndong. However, the bombshell came from Ondo Ndong's own nephew, Nguéma Ondo, who was FECOM's Financial Director. According to Mr. Ondo,

> regarding fictitious missions, there was a follow-up commission set up to monitor roads financed by FEICOM. I was a member of this commission. Within the framework of the activities of this inactive structure, some FEICOM officials received millions for missions that never took place. I admit that on numerous occasions, I received millions for fictitious missions. But it was the Director General who organized it all.

According to court documents, close to one billion FCFA was embezzled in this manner within an eight-month period.

Financial Aid

The highlight of the trial came when the court tackled the issue of financial aid dished out with reckless abandon by the General Manager to a dizzying array of corporate entities and individual using a budgetary line item titled « solidarity budgetary line." State Inspector Dieudonné Tchana who put together the report read out loud the names of corporate entities and individuals who received FEICOM aid amounting to 900 million FCFA. The list included items such as 2.6 million FCFA for the defense of a university thesis on... Ondo Ndong; 100,000 FCFA to the Beti language Committee; 500,000 FCFA to a section of the ruling CPDM party; five million FCFA to the Tonerre handball club, etc. The amount read out in court fell short of the 1.5 Billion FCFA listed in the indictment because Mr. Tchana claimed that he could not find original receipts in FEICOM archives for the remaining 600 million FCFA.

Ridiculing the "solidarity budgetary line" inserted in the FEICOM budget, Prosecutor Ebanga Ewodo, insisted that "Ondo Ndong embarked on an operation to alienate public funds under the cover of social action." The prosecutor reminded the court that every cent disbursed under this budgetary line was illegal because it violated the laws governing FEICOM operations, which clearly state that only local councils could receive aid from the corporation

When defense attorney Maitre Nkouendjin took to the floor, he accused the Mr. Tchana for presenting a shoddy report and lambasted his claim that some names were left out of the roll call of infamy due to the absence of receipts. Maitre Nkouendjin caused a huge stir as he revealed that among the names left out were those of the Chantal Biya Foundation, Gervais Mendo Ze, former Director General of CRTV and Lekene Donfack, Minister of State, Minister for Urban Development and Housing. According to Maitre Nkouendjin, on May 30 2001, the Chantal Biya Foundation received 60 million FCFA for a "Filled School Bag" campaign on behalf of marginalized children in the Southwest province. And on September 24, 2001, the foundation received two additional payments of 45.1 million FCFA (medical equipment for the Center and Far North provinces) and 48 million FCFA (another "Filled School Bag" campaign for deprived kids). Similarly, *African Synergy*, the association of African First Ladies whose founding President is none other than First Lady Chantal Biya received 40 million FCFA on August 2002 for its fight against HIV/AIDS.

Defense records also showed that on Nov 27, 2001, Lekéné Donfack – who was one of the recipients of the 12 million FCFA "merrymaking" funds in 2002 – received a two million FCFA "financial aid following a car accident." And in January 21, 2004, Mendo Ze, the CRTV Director General received a 10 million FCFA aid package as FEICOM's contribution to the 2004 African Nations Cup.

These revelations caused an uproar in court as the Prosecutor, Christian Ndanga rushed to defend the First Lady: "The Chantal Biya Foundation is a corporate entity. Let it be known that the First Lady is not a pauper and that she never asked Ondo Ndong for money!" The session was immediately suspended as a clamor of indignation spread throughout the court room.

The solidarity fund was not merely a source of money for the Director General and his friends, but was used to swindle astronomical sums of money. As the Director General's nephew confessed,

> With regard to the [financial] aid, it was the Director General who received the applications and the students [who requested financial aid], and then informed us of the amount to be disbursed so that we could establish the relevant documents. Usually, he [Ondo Ndong] was the one who received the money. When he did, he sometimes gave me two or three million FCFA. I admit these facts.

In a glaring example of the plunder of the solidarity fund, FEICOM records show that 300 million FCFA was disbursed allegedly to organize holiday football tournaments for kids in each of the 10 provinces of the country. However, not even one of these tournaments ever took place! Public prosecutor, Maitre Ongolo Foe summed it best, when he stated categorically that Ondo Ndong was neither Robin Hood nor a social activist but simply a common thief and embezzler:

> Ondo Ndong did not comply with his mission when he gave 45 million FCA to a Common Initiative Group to plant two or three lots of cassava. Let them not deceive the people by telling us that Ondo Ndong constructed hospitals. He embezzled... He claims that he organized holiday tournaments whereas he used our kids to swindle 300 million FCFA.

Perspective

Here are some figures that will help put the FEICOM swindle in context. In Cameroon's draft budget for the 2006-2007 fiscal year, 105 billion FCFA is allocated to Public Health. The FEICOM team allegedly embezzled over a quarter half of Cameroon's entire annual Health budget! According to statistics obtained from another website, the *Bertoua - Garoua-boulai* highway (248 km) completed in 2002 cost 2.5 billion FCFA to construct. Ondo Ndong's 29 billion FCFA loot is more than enough to construct the Kumba-Mamfe road which has not been completed after three decades supposedly because of a lack of funds...

Officials at the University of Buea estimate that the University needs at least 400 million FCFA to effectively kick off its newly-created Faculty of Medicine. The University is currently looking for private donors for this project because the Government of Cameroon claims it can ill afford the cost at this time... Funds just from Ondo Ndong's fictitious "missions" alone could have constructed the basic infrastructure of at least three medical schools in the country...

And the Band Played On...

Writing about the collapse of some of Cameroon's key public corporations and banks in the late 1980s, Nantang Jua argued in the edited volume, *Pathways to Accumulation in Cameroon*, that these institutions collapsed because bad management was deliberately tolerated and financed by the Biya regime as part of its neopatrimonial control system:

> By enabling members of the development coalition to appropriate funds with impunity, the state staved off even the threat of any momentary political deficiency a la Gramsci, which could unleash a struggle among members or factions of the development coalition for political office and control of the patronage system. In the face of this Cameroonians now claim that managers of parastatals have *"titres fonciers"* (in this case a free hand) over their concerns.

The Ondo Ndong / FEICOM case has so far given new meaning to the "free hand" concept which Jua wrote about in 1993. While cash-strapped local councils and communities across the country were – and are still – unable to take care of the most basic amenities and services, FEICOM was busy serving as the milking cow for the ruling elite...

The band played on while Ondo Ndong, the self-proclaimed "King Of Ntumu" swindled...

39

How Cameroon Auctioned Its Internet Namespace...

It's an odd scene to picture: a domainer's reps in a sit-down with Ephraim Inoni, the prime minister of Cameroon, to discuss the power of type-in typo traffic and pay-per-click ads. *CNN*

May 24, 2007: Early in August 2006, the Internet was awash with reports of a "typo-squatting" scheme involving Cameroon. According to these reports, "Internet authorities in the West African nation that owns the .cm top level domain (TLD) have been accused of authorizing a DNS wildcard that has the effect of redirecting all accidental .cm traffic instead of returning an error." In layman's terms, Cameroon Internet authorities were redirecting all misspelled .com addresses (e.g. www.dibussi.cm instead of www.dibussi.com) to an advert-based website (agoga.com), where they were making millions of dollars in pay-per-click advert revenue (Pay-per-click is an advertising system where advertisers pay an agreed amount for each click delivered to their site). While not technically illegal, since the misspelled domain names are not being registered but simply redirected to another site, these actions raised serious ethical concerns.

To many observers, it was obvious that this was too creative a scheme to have been hatched by Cameroonian authorities alone. Some even believed that the wildcarding of non-registered domains within the .cm Top Level Domain may have been done without the official consent of Cameroonian authorities. For months, therefore, attempts to identify the real faces behind the mask became a veritable whodunit saga. This week, CNN finally revealed the person behind the .cm mystery in an article titled "The man who owns the Internet." According to the article, the brain behind it all is Kevin Ham, described as "the most powerful dotcom mogul you've never heard of." Based in the Canadian city of Vancouver, Ham's empire is worth about 300 million dollars. Even more interesting, the article revealed that Cameroonian authorities were active participants and partners in the typo-squatting scheme, and that a cut from the advert revenue (estimated by some to be at least three million dollars a year) goes to "the government of Cameroon" – yeah right! Here is an excerpt from the CNN story:

> Ham makes money every time someone clicks on an ad – as does his partner in this venture, the West African country of Cameroon. Why Cameroon? It has the unforeseen good fortune of owning .cm as its country code – just as Germany runs all names that end with .de. The difference is that hardly any .cm names are registered, and the letters are just one keyboard slip away from .com, the mother lode of all domains. Ham landed connections to the Cameroon government and flew in his people to reroute the traffic...

Over a series of conversations a few weeks later in Vancouver, Ham shares some details about a deal that, despite his innate reticence, he's clearly proud of. About a year ago, he says, he worked his contacts to gain connections to government officials in Cameroon. Then he flew several confidantes to Yaoundé, the capital, to make their pitch...

It's an odd scene to picture: a domainer's reps in a sit-down with Ephraim Inoni, the prime minister of Cameroon, to discuss the power of type-in typo traffic and pay-per-click ads. And yet, as with most of the angles Ham has played, the Cameroon scheme is ingeniously straightforward.

Ham's people installed a line of software, called a "wildcard," that reroutes traffic addressed to any .cm domain name that isn't registered. In the case of Cameroon, a country of 18 million with just 167,000 computers connected to the Internet that means hundreds of millions of names. Type in "paper.cm" and servers owned by Camtel, the state-owned company that runs Cameroon's domain registry, redirect the query to Ham's Agoga.com servers in Vancouver.

The servers fill the page with ads for paper and office-supply merchants. (Officials at Yahoo confirm that the company serves ads for Ham's .cm play.) It all happens in a flash, and since Ham doesn't own or register the names, he's not technically typo-squatting, according to several lawyers who handle Internet issues...

Ham won't reveal specifics but says Agoga receives "in the ballpark" of 8 million unique visitors per month...

"A Disservice to Cameroon"

Like most deals that African government officials sign with business interests in the West, the typo-squatting deal is not such a sweet one for Cameroon, even though a handful of individuals might be reaping huge benefits. As the *Monetize Traffic* blog pointed out back in February, Cameroon could legally use the .cm error to generate legitimate funds destined for Internet development in the country:

> Setting aside the ethical issue with basically typo-squatting the entire .com domain space, this could be a great way for a poor African nation to raise some money. However, they could easily boost their revenue by building customized landing pages for the most frequently accessed domains. For example, amazon.cm should either redirect to the Amazon.com affiliate links or a page targeted towards ecommerce. I can't even imagine how much money they are leaving on the table. The folks at NameView.com, who appear to be providing the landing pages, are doing them a huge disservice here.

Even more critical has been Enow Ebot Godwill, a Cameroonian performance analyst based in Denmark, whose analysis of the Camtel deal has been widely distributed on the Internet in the past couple of days:

If CAMTEL can make money from people mistyping their domains, I'm all for it. The problem that I have is that the situation has led to a perverse effect with CAMTEL making NO EFFORT to manage the .CM registry and promote a real development of the Internet in Cameroon. The "quick buck" mentality has prevailed once again. Well known Cameroon-centric websites such as Cameroon-info.net, postnewsline.com, camerounlink.net, camfoot.com, and dozens of others who are the real actors of Cameroon's presence on the Internet are priced out of their own country's .CM which costs a whopping $400 to $800/year while one can register a .COM name for less than $10 or even get it free with hosting...

As a result, the .CM domain is virtually absent in cyberspace, just as if Cameroon didn't even exist! The reality is that, with CAMTEL making money from unregistered .CM domains, it has no incentive to increase the number of registered .CM domain names. The majority of emails originating and terminating in Cameroon are hosted on .FR, .COM and other registries because no alternative is being developed in the country. Again, when you redo the math, the cost in bandwidth to the country for email traffic hosted outside far outweighs any gain CAMTEL might have from its .CM shenanigans.

This literally means that the shameless sale of Cameroonian patrimony has extended to cyberspace the same way other Cameroonian assets are being often ILLEGALLY disposed of by those in charge of developing them. In the meantime there is no serious Internet policy in Cameroon more than 15 years after the creation of the world-wide-web.

Definitely another black eye for Cameroon...

Reference

Sloan, P. (May 22 2007). *The man who owns the Internet*. CNN Money. Retrieved March 15, 2009 from: http://money.cnn.com/magazines/business2/business2_archive/2007/06/01/100050989/

Part Nine

Random Notes

40

Gerontocracy in Cameroon – These Old Men Who Govern Us

March 03, 2009: Last February 13, President Paul Biya of Cameroon celebrated his 76th birthday. This septuagenarian who has been Cameroon's president for the last for 27 years is the leader of a gerontocracy, which has ruled the country for half a century – old men and women way past their prime but desperately clinging on to power. The result? Cameroon is increasingly looking like the pre-Gorbachev Soviet Union whose entire leadership was made up of the infirm, senile and "walking dead" of the Politburo.

In June 2008, the French language monthly *La Cité* revealed that 80% of Cameroon's ruling class consisted of individuals who were way past the official retirement age, and that 80% of the 34 new ambassadors appointed that year were also above retirement age. In fact, some were actually pulled out of retirement – this, in a country where life expectancy is about 52 years. *La Cité* also profiled 60 key members of the ruling elite, who by virtue of their age, should have long retired and given way to a much younger generation of leaders. Here is a snapshot of that list:

Armed forces
- General James Tataw, 75
- Major General Pierre Semengue, 73 years old (first indigenous head of the armed forces in 1960)
- General Asso'o Emane Benoit, 71
- General Rene Claude Meka – Army Chief of Staff, 70
- General Mambou Deffo, 70
- General Camille Nkoa Atenga, 70.

Public Corporations
- Felix Sabal Lecco – President, National Council of Communication, 90+ years (joined the Ahidjo government in 1969; Minister of Justice in 1970)
- El Hadj Ousman Mey – Chairman, National Social Insurance Fund, 83+ years (founding member of Ahidjo's *Union Camerounaise* in 1958; Federal Inspector/Governor of North province from 1960-1983)
- Simon Achidi Achu – Chairman, National Investment Corporation (SNI), 76 years (First appointed minister in the Ahidjo regime in 1970; Prime Minister under Biya from 1992 - 1996)
- Adolphe Moudiki – Director General National Hydrocarbons Corporation (SNH), 70 years, (the "young" Moudiki first became a government minister "only" in 1987).

State Institutions
- Cavaye Yegue Djibril – President of the National Assembly, 70 years
- Paul Pondi – President of the Civil Aviation Authority – 80+ years (First Cameroonian head of National Security in 1960)
- Paul Tessa – President of the Anti-corruption commission (CONAC), 70 years (First became a government minister in 1972)
- Jean-Baptiste Beleoken – Director of the Civil Cabinet at the Presidency, 76 years (Was the commercial adviser in the Cameroon embassy in Paris in 1961, and ambassador to the Soviet Union in 1973)
- Martin Belinga Eboutou – Adviser to the President of the Republic, 70 years (former ambassador to the United Nations, his first key position in the foreign service was as the Chargé d'Affaires in Cameroon's Embassy in Brazzaville, Congo in 1970).

Roving Ambassadors
- Jean Keutcha, 85+ years (Secretary of State for Public Works in 1964; Minister of Foreign Affairs in 1971);
- Marcel Medjo Akono, 84+ years (First appointed a provincial governor in 1972)
- Joseph Charles Doumba, 72 (First became a government minister in 1972)

This is merely the tip of the iceberg; septuagenarians and octogenarians still occupy key positions at all levels of the public service, public corporations, the police and armed forces, effectively preventing the much needed and long overdue renewal of state institutions. In the process, an entire generation of young Cameroonians has been permanently sidelined, unlikely to ever manage, govern or lead in their lifetime. As *La Cité* laments,

> *Au Cameroun, des dinosaures de 1960, sont toujours en fonction, pendant que leurs petits-fils sont en quête d'un premier emploi* / In Cameroon, the dinosaurs of 1960 are still in office, while their grand children are still searching for their first employment.

Once a Nation of Young Leaders...

> I want to express, on behalf of all of us, our great pleasure in having the President of the Cameroon visit us, and the members of his Cabinet. The President is the second youngest President in the world... The President here is 36-7 and feels that those older than that should step aside! *President John F. Kennedy, March 13, 1962.*

Cameroon was not always a gerontocracy. In fact, most of the individuals who now control the levers of power in the country started off very young. For example, 80 year-old Ferdinand Oyono, who was still a cabinet minister in 2006 and still wields immense power as an unofficial adviser to the President, was Cameroon's representative at the United Nations in 1960 when he was just 31 years old, i.e., before the current US President Barack Obama was born.

Ahmadou Ahidjo became President of the Republic of Cameroun at 36; Paul Biya was 34 years old when he was appointed Director of the Civil Cabinet at the Presidency in 1967 (with the rank of Minister), 42 years when he became Prime Minister in 1975, and 49 when he succeeded Ahidjo as President of the Republic; General Pierre Semengue, was a very young 25-year old Captain when he became head of Cameroon's armed forces in 1960.

And the list goes on...

Joseph Owona became the Director of the International Relations Institute of Cameroon (IRIC) in 1976, "when he was all of thirty-one years old" (Martin Mayer, *The Diplomats*, p. 162); Bello Bouba Maigari became Paul Biya's Prime Minister in 1982 at 35; Dorothy Njeuma, who until a few weeks ago was still the Rector of the University of Yaounde I, became Vice Minister of Education in 1975 when she was 32 years old; Nzo Ekangaki was 28 years old when he became Deputy Minister of Foreign Affairs in 1962, and 38 when he was elected Secretary General of the Organization of African Unity (OAU); Paul Bamela Engo, currently a judge at the International Tribunal of the Law of the Sea, was 33 years old when he became a Minister Counselor at the Cameroon Embassy in Bonn, Germany in 1964 and 38 when he was elevated to the rank of a Minister Plenipotentiary in 1969, Kamdem Niyim became Minister of Health in 1964 at the age of 23, etc., etc.

Lack of Renewal (Political Sclerosis, Economic Stagnation and Insecurity)

The inability or unwillingness of Cameroon's ruling class to renew and reinvigorate its ranks with young blood has led to a political sclerosis that is evident in an over-centralized political system which is out of step with the exigencies of a modern 21st century state particularly with regards to democracy, basic human rights, the rule of law and good governance. The old methods of the one-party era still hold sway in spite of the much touted "political liberalization."

This is also evident in inward-looking and discredited policies from a different age that have no place in today's global village, and are out of sync with the knowledge economy and technology that drive globalization. To Cameroon's gerontocracy, globalization is not about becoming a credible competitor on the African or global market place but about importing cheap products from China or Europe or giving the Chinese and others sovereignty over Cameroonian waters and fertile lands to use as they see fit.

And, the idea that Information and Communication Technologies (ICTs) can actually be harnessed for purposes of national development is considered a far-fetched one, in spite of regular conferences about the value of *les NTIC* to

Cameroon's development. Thus, no effort is being made to create a technical and legal framework for e-commerce, and the notion of e-government is limited to creating rarely updated websites for ministries and public corporations. Any wonder, therefore, why the government would require that the thousands of individuals who want register for the entrance examination into the National Police Academy travel to Yaounde (sometimes for as long as two days) just to personally drop their applications at the school when these applications could simply have been sent electronically from any internet café in the country?

And no one has yet figured out that ICTs present a way out to the overcrowded and overburdened higher education system…

Even the armed forces apparatus is a victim of an aging leadership which has been completely overwhelmed by today's security and military challenges, from the proliferation of arms and armed gangs in the central African region and the resultant insecurity on Cameroon's borders; the rise of *grand banditisme* within the country, with last year's attack on banks in Limbe being one of the most glaring examples; piracy in the oil-rich Gulf of Guinea and armed insurgency on the Bakassi peninsular, etc. Young officers, many of whom are graduates of top military institutions such as West Point, are sidelined by the old generals who studied at the Saint-Cyr in France (Generals Semengue, Meka, Youmba, Mpay, Tchemo…) or military academies elsewhere in the 1950s and 60s, and who are versed in conventional WWII-type warfare which is of little relevance in dealing with today's challenges. According to one report, even the armed forces handbook, the top secret *doctrine d'emploi des forces camerounaises*, has apparently not been revised since 1980. The results are there for all to see...

End Note

I am in no way claiming that Septuagenarians and even octogenarians cannot contribute to national development or that they are unable to lead simply because of their age. Far from it! I am referring specifically to the Cameroonian case where a gerontocracy, which as been in power since independence, has abdicated its leadership role, lost all interest in innovation and modernization to the extent of becoming an obstacle to development, and is more interested in accumulating wealth and devising creative strategies for hanging onto power at all cost.

In a recent interview with *Eden Newspaper*, Chris Fomunyoh of National Democratic Institute for International Affairs (NDIIA) explained why leadership renewal is critical:

> It is extremely important to frequently renew political leadership in every country so new leaders can bring a fresh perspective to global trends and developments, and help move their countries in ways that may differ from previously long held typical and traditional approaches.

Cameroon has, unfortunately, not learned this lesson. The result, as we have seen, is political sclerosis, economic stagnation and rising insecurity within the country and at its borders. Today, Cameroon's gerontocracy has not just sidelined an entire generation of active Cameroonians willing and able to contribute their quota to national development, but is dragging the country back into the 19th century. Making the leap back into the 21st may soon become a virtually impossible task if nothing is done to rectify the situation.

41

Football and the "Burden of Patriotism" in Africa

January 25, 2006: The African continent, from Cape to Cairo, is awash with Football Fever. All eyes are on Egypt where the African Nations Cup is currently taking place. The competition, with its mixture of unrealistic expectations and unexpected triumphs; of Cinderella stories and mighty falls; of epic David and Goliath battles; of great illusions and shattered ambitions; and of pure flashes of genius rivaled by pedestrian displays, will end on February 10th.

As in previous years, Cameroon is one of the favorites. The Cameroonian national team started the competition on a high note with a 3-1 defeat of World Cup-bound Angola. Samuel Eto'o who plies his trade in Barcelona, Spain scored Cameroon's three goals. Eto'o, who had initially flirted with the idea of skipping the tournament because of persistent administrative and other problems in the national team, was instantly hailed as a "true patriot" who had risen to the occasion to defend the honor and pride of the nation. As I read these glowing tributes couched in ultra nationalistic terms reminiscent of Communist Russia, I could not help but marvel at how African politicians have succeeded in transforming football into a most potent tool for political mobilization around vague notions of national unity.

As I mulled over this fact, I recalled the observation of an American Peace Corps in Cameroon when Marc Vivien Foe collapsed and died in 2003 while playing for the Cameroon national team: "Anyway, the entire country is mourning here. It's quite different. People are calling him a patriot and I keep thinking that he's just a soccer player who left his country to make more money playing in France and England but still plays on his country's national team when they play." I must confess that like any Cameroonian who loves his football, I found this observation a tad sacrilegious, and was initially ticked off by what seemed like a trivialization of Foe's death. However, I eventually started thinking about the real and imagined significance of football in Cameroon and other African countries, and its appropriation by politicians for political gain.

Why is it that when a Cameroonian soldier dies in Bakassi (fighting in what most Cameroonians consider a "Just War") he is never given a hero's burial or lauded as a patriot or a valiant soldier – his death is not even a footnote on the news – but when a Cameroonian footballer excels in his trade like Roger Milla, or "dies in battle" (another military term!) like Foe, he is hailed as a patriot, a true soldier, etc., etc.,? Why label a footballer a soldier and then make the soldier invisible? Why the double standards? Do we have our priorities all wrong?

I shared my thoughts with members of CAMFOOT, the Cameroon football forum, back in December 2004 and all the answers pointed to the fact that "normal" rules do not apply to football because it is simply a different ball game (excuse the pun...). Here is a sample of the responses:

- Football is one of the few things that truly unites Cameroonians. When national team players step on the pitch, nobody asks about their ethnic origins; all the focus is on their performance.
- The Indomitable Lions are a source of national identity and pride. Cameroon today is seen as a football nation, hence Foe's death on live TV while defending our national colours affected us a lot more that those killed in Bakassi.
- Someone once said religion was the opium of the masses. Football is our own opium.
- That football has become a religion for Cameroonians doesn't bother me. What annoys me most is the never-ending irresponsibility of this government, which exploits the fans ... and keeps them uneducated about real issues (job creation, social welfare, politics and war).

The Burden of Patriotism

All of these points are true in one way or the other, but they don't explain why footballers are the only ones required to carry the "burden of patriotism" in Africa. Is Eto'o less patriotic when he fails to score a goal, as was the case in last year's crucial encounter against Egypt, which resulted in Cameroon's elimination from the 2006 World Cup tournament? Did Inter Milan's Pierre Wome commit treason when he missed that vital 95th minute penalty during the game against Egypt, which could have taken Cameroon to Germany? Cameroonians and the Cameroonian Government seem to think so. Wome was initially selected by Cameroon's Portuguese coach Artur Jorge for the ongoing Egyptian campaign (can't just stay from the marshal language, can we...), but he was later dropped from the squad because Cameroonian authorities considered his presence in Egypt as "problematic" – after all, hadn't he betrayed the nation in its time of need?

I can't help but wonder if those punishing Wome for missing a penalty – a very common occurrence in football – have thought of extending this uniquely Cameroonian "performance clause" to all sectors of national life. Why not impose the same standards on teachers in failing schools; on managers of underperforming corporations; on incompetent civil servants and corrupt government officials, etc.? Wouldn't that be the beginning of a real revolution in Africa? Of course, that is just wishful thinking. The prebendal political systems of post-Independent Africa will continue as African governments thank their gods that the masses still view football as something unique with its own set of rules and expectations.

In Africa, "with its density, variety, vivacity, open wounds, illusions, beliefs and battles," once wrote Heidi Hamel of *African football* magazine, "football is the only opium with which one can keep the withdrawal symptoms at bay. This painful dependency reflects an unavoidable need. Africans love their football to the point of desperation. To the point of madness." African regimes have understood this madness and appropriated it so well, which is why football is a potent tool that these unpopular regimes use not only to get a veneer of legitimacy, which they would otherwise not have, but also to stifle opposition. I guess it is a two-way street after all; the people get their "opium" and the politicians get another day to plunder....

When Private and Public Spaces Collide: Power, Sex and Politics in Cameroon

February 08, 2006: Three weeks after the issue erupted on the national scene like a volcano, Cameroonians are still talking about the "outing" of alleged homosexuals in what the international media has variously described as an "anti-gay frenzy" (*Times Online*, UK), a "Gay witch hunt" (BBC News Online) or a "purity" campaign that bears all the hallmarks of 21st century McCarthyism. Expectedly, gay rights activists around the world are up in arms and have been venting their anger in Internet chat groups, forums and blogs. British gay activist Peter Tatchell has even called for protests at the Cameroonian embassy in London and demanded that Western governments halt all aid to Cameroon as long as the country remains a haven for homophobia:

> British and EU governments should warn Cameroon that if these witch hunts are not halted we will suspend our aid and trade agreements. We cannot continue to have normal relations with a regime that condones and colludes with the violation of human rights.

Protests have also come from some members of the African blogger community such as Sokari Ekine of the popular *Black Looks* blog:

> The suffering of LGBT [i.e., Lesbian, Gay, Bisexual, and Transgender] people is occurring all over Africa. Everyone who is a defender of human rights needs to join with together with the LGBT community in a show of progressive African solidarity. The current situation in Nigeria and now this in Cameroon provide an opportunity to everyone to join together in a show of strength. If we do not, we jeopardize our ability to continue our work and our lives in the future and everyone is affected.

Of course, like with most things Cameroonian, there is more to the entire saga than meets the eye. True, the campaign by the tabloids definitely has a McCarthyist feel to it, and some individuals and groups are obviously using it to settle old political and personal scores. Nonetheless, this is less about homosexuality (even though most Cameroonians are unapologetically conservative on this issue) and more about Cameroon politics.

We will get to that later, but first let us try to place the "gay bashing" in Cameroon in its proper context.

Going Beyond the Hysteria

In recent years, the issue of homosexuality has become a major topic of discussion in Cameroon not so much because of homophobia, but mainly because of a widespread belief that social mobility and ascension is generally no longer achieved through hard work and merit, but through membership in numerous esoteric sects that use homosexuality as a rite of passage. This is a topic which until recently was discussed only in private. However, it literally came out of the closet when the Roman Catholic Archbishop of Yaoundé, Victor Tonyé Bakot, lashed out against the politization of homosexuality during his now famous Christmas 2005 homily: "In the name of an employment offer, of a possible promotion; in the name of admission into a Professional School, they want to impose homosexuality on young people as a path to success…" This was followed by a similar cry by the Imam of Douala. In one fell swoop, allegations that homosexuality was being used as a tool for socio-political and economic advancement in Cameroon, gained credibility and became legitimate topics of public discussion.

Whether one is pro or anti-gay rights, the situation described by the Archbishop Bakot, which is backed by anecdotal evidence, should be a cause for concern. In fact, if this type of alleged institutional sexual coercion happened in the "liberal West," there would be a flurry of sexual harassment lawsuits, accusations of the abuse of power, and even regime collapse. So, with all due respect to the well-intentioned gay-rights activists, the *broader* Cameroonian homosexuality discourse is not about the violation of privacy, but about the imposition and institutionalization of private sexual predilections on the public sphere. As an article in *Le Messager* rightly insists, it is a matter of public concern and debate when individuals engage in same-sex relationships not out of choice, but because they are forced to do so in order to obtain a government contract, an employment, a scholarship, a degree, or a promotion. It becomes a State affair because homosexuality ceases to be a private act between two-consenting individuals and instead becomes a method of managing the public space.

From this perspective, the ongoing discourse on homosexuality – no matter how poorly defined, or how crassly exploited by certain segments of the country's elite – is about a fight for the soul of Cameroon, not so much in the moral sense, but in a socio-political sense: Will Cameroon become a true democracy and meritocracy where all citizens will have an equal shot at jobs, promotions, and admission into the prestigious Professional Schools which guarantee lifetime employment in the public service and direct access to state resources? Will the esoteric sects that control the state apparatus continue to determine the destiny of Cameroonians to the exclusion of all others? Or, will Cameroon become a Sextocracy, where political and other decisions are determined primarily by sexual orientation? That is the subtext of the ongoing brouhaha.

That said, there is no doubt that legitimate public interest in the alleged widespread use of sex as a method of governance is currently being exploited for political purposes, and that the many, if not the majority, of individuals on the said lists have no connection whatsoever with homosexuality. In this regard, many analysts argue that the timing and inquisitional nature of these lists have little to do with morality and everything to do with politics.

The War of "Clans"

In the September 1997 issue of *Le Monde Diplomatique* (English edition), Claude Wauthier wrote an article titled *Africa's Freemasons: A strange inheritance* in which he analyzed the foray of freemasons into African politics. He pointed out that in many countries, including Cameroon, the rise of the freemasons as a political force had led to power struggles among its members and with similar sects:

> These excursions into politics naturally cause serious divisions, not only between rival chapters but also between the masons and other organizations more or less closely associated with them, at least in the minds of the public. This was the case in Cameroon, where the masons and the Rosicrucians apparently became embroiled in a struggle for power.

Today, many observers believe that the "anti-gay frenzy" in Cameroon is merely another chapter in age-old struggles for political supremacy between and within the different "networks" of the Biya regime, which are apparently positioning themselves either for the next cabinet shake-up, or even for the post-Biya era. *La Nouvelle Expression* backs this theory by pointing out that many of the individuals on the infamous lists are well-known freemasons, and that most of them had featured earlier on another less famous list of alleged corrupt Government officials. It theorizes that the Cameroonian ruling class may be copying the French example where high-level scandals implicating freemasons resulted in a purge within their ranks, and the emergence of a new leadership which was able to access hitherto inaccessible spheres of influence and power.

Yes, there is a witch-hunt alright, but it is a political one. Ekane Anicet, president of MANIDEM sums it best in an interview in *Le Messager*:

> these lists are a manifestation of the unraveling of a system which is destroying itself from within... whether we like it or not, this affair – or non affair – has a strong political coloration ... Future generations will be told that in the last moments of the Biyaism, the Republic was seized by a violent spasm caused by the question of homosexuality.

End Note: The Private Press on Trial

Rather than creating a platform for a rational, legitimate, informed and long overdue debate about homosexuality in Cameroon, and the real or imagined influence of esoteric sects on national life, the tabloids have created a feeding frenzy where the key issues have been obscured by collective hysteria. This once again raises serious ethical issues about the Cameroonian private press, which has always promised more than it has delivered in terms of professionalism, independence and objectivity. "Our pens," as Cameroonian columnist Shanda Tomne has written, "must be at the service of the truth, of courage and honor, and not of defamation, blackmail and cowardice." But that is another topic for another day...

43

Political Rumor in Cameroon: The "Weapon of Mass Destruction" of the Masses

February 20, 2006: In June 2004, Cameroon came to a virtual standstill for close to a week following a rumor that President Paul Biya had died in Switzerland. This was just another in a long series of rumors that appear with mathematical regularity on the Cameroonian socio-political scene. Without doubt, rumor, popularly referred to as *Radio trottoir* (sidewalk radio), is part and parcel of Cameroonian life. And, it is driven by the absence of trustworthy information from the official channels of communications and the need of the masses to be informed about key events and personalities.

Today, as Cameroonians ponder over the social, legal and ethical dimensions of the publication of the names of alleged "homosexuals of the Republic" and "billionaire civil servants," it is necessary to take a closer look at the role and place of political rumor in Cameroon. Why does it have such a powerful force in the country? Why are Cameroonians so readily inclined to believe rumors about those in high places – or to propagate them even when they are not certain about their veracity?

I will try to respond to these questions by drawing from a chapter in Francis Nyamnjoh's groundbreaking publication on the media in Cameroon titled *Africa's Media, Democracy and the Politics of Belonging* – a must-read for anyone interested in the interplay between the media (private and public), the public and the political elite in Africa.

In a chapter titled "Creative appropriation of ICTs, rumour, press cartoons and politics" (pp. 204-230), Nyamnjoh states that in Cameroon, rumor is "is arguably the most popular source of information both for the private press and for the information-starved public." He argues that rumor has become an ubiquitous and legitimate source of information because of "the rigid control of information and communication by the power elite":

> Thus rumour, far from being something essentially negative and false – to be rejected as unaccountable and unconfirmed and not to be romanticised, is like the voice of the voiceless seeking to challenge passivity and the oppressive discourses of officialdom. Rumour, Bourgault observes, 'is underground news, an alternative to the official press, which is tedious, censored, uninformative, and often unintelligible', and as such, is a 'free and uncontrolled "medium"', to which 'everyone is a potential contributor'.

Purpose of Political Rumor

Rumor, according to Nyamnjoh, serves many purposes in Africa. It is a method of interpreting and understanding events and issues, a tool for promoting alternative truths to government dogma, a counter-power to government oppression, and, finally, a weapon for the derision and mockery of the power elite. Because all official channels of communications offer information, which the public rarely finds credible, rumor is used to discuss and propagate alternative narratives of events and issues. Hence, "Rumour, far from being falsehood because not confirmed or accounted for, is the undoctored counter-truth of citizens questioning life at the margins of state power and skewed indicators of newsworthiness." In this context, rumor should not be viewed "as falsehood but as the emergence and circulation of information that is either not yet confirmed publicly or refuted by official sources; rumour as a sort of 'black market for information', seeking to provide understanding of important events on which the official sources are silent."

In the West, the media is commonly referred to as the fourth estate whose duty is to protect democracy and defend the public interest. In Cameroon, the private media serves as the 4th estate only to the extent that it has the ability to frame national discourse on key issues, especially those that the government would rather ignore or avoid. Political rumor in Cameroon like in most of Africa, plays a similar role, serving as a 5th estate working in tandem with the 4th to prove, by all means necessary, that the King and all the King's men have no clothes on. The current national debates on corruption and homosexuality stem from this symbiosis. Whether the rumors are true or not is largely irrelevant in this context. As Nyamnjoh points out:

> *radio trottoir* has proved effective not only as a vehicle for popular and informal discussion of power and current affairs by urbanites in particular but also as a counter-power: the 'poor person's bomb' or the 'weapons of the powerless' in the face of government's arbitrariness, water cannons, tear gas and guns. Usually in the form of 'anecdotical gossip', radio trottoir serves the poor as 'a phenomenon of revenge and a rebuttal of censorship' against 'the totalitarian discourse of the Party-State', often through the display of 'an extraordinary verbal creativity' rich in humour, parody, and irony.

Finally, rumor in its most potent form is used as a tool to ridicule, demystify and cut the ruling class down to size. As Nyamnjoh states:

> Wherever it has been studied, radio trottoir (epitomised by rumour and political derision) has proved itself the perfect medium of communicating dissent and discussing the powerful in unflattering terms... Through ridicule... ordinary people can tame, shut up and render powerless state power. The autocrat thus stripped of his aura or magic, becomes domesticated - a mere idol, a familiar friend or a member of the family as much for the ruled as for the rulers.

The powerless majority, whom the French refer to as *"le petit peuple,"* thrive on rumor because of its ability to humiliate and demonize their oppressors. From this perspective, the recent "gay outing" of the Cameroonian jet set was a veritable "weapon of mass destruction" particularly in an environment where popular imagery views homosexuality as an act of "submission and enslavement" to occult forces rather than a natural predisposition. In this context, the list published by *l'anecdote* becomes "a list of shame" as one analyst puts it – shame that stems from the supposed humiliating moral and sexual compromises that the elite have allegedly made in order to be rich and powerful. As far as the silent majority is concerned, the price that the elite have allegedly paid in order to be part of that exclusive club is simply too humiliating and morally repugnant. In such circumstances, they cannot help but feel morally superior to, and more dignified than, the "pitiful sex slaves" who lord over them.

The Role of the Press

So how do we explain the role of the press in what Francis Kasoma has described as "muckraking journalistic exploits, libeling, invading privacy… and …'vendetta journalism'"? Without justifying (in fact condemning) the excesses of the private press in Cameroon and Africa, Nyamnjoh nonetheless puts its actions – "which may appear bizarre and highly implausible to Western reporters and readers" – in context:

> That the press often readily sacrifices its cannons of rigorous investigation, objectivity and proof (*à l'occidentale*) is also indicative, I would argue, of a journalism under constant pressure to be grounded in the popular epistemologies of African societies, where reality is not simply a question of appearances and truth not always what is legitimated by 'official' or 'confirmed' sources.

44

Mystery and Intrigue in a Tropical Paradise – Revisiting the Speedboat Attack on Limbe

<u>**October 10, 2008**</u>: With its wide beaches laden with purpleblack volcanic sands, its magnificient botanic gardens, its historic seafront, its proximity to Mount Fako, the tallest mountain in West Africa ,and to Debundscha the second wettest place on the planet, etc., Limbe is a tourist's paradise. The Down Beach area, which now serves as the town's banking district, was once the nucleus of the "historic" Victoria – that strip of land, some twelve miles long along the Atlantic coast and five miles into the interior – settled in 1858 by Alfred Saker and freed Jamaican slaves from Sierra Leone and the neighboring island of Fernando Po. Today, Down Beach, with its century-old administrative buildings and churches reminds a traveler of a British outpost in the Caribbean – the kind of place that inspires romance novels and definitely not the setting for a James Bond thriller.

In spite of developments in the past quarter of a century, which have largely stripped Limbe of its erstwhile colonial feel, this is still a quintessential colonial town where vestiges of British – and German – colonial rule abound. In many respects, it is a town that time left behind – or a town that is "stuck in a gentle lethargy" as one observer puts it – caught between the 19th and 21st centuries. Today it lags behind other port cities on the West African coast, which it was on par back in the 1950s and 1960s.

Victoria is strategically located on the Gulf of Guinea along an important maritime route and shares a boundary with the oil-rich Bakassi peninsular, which has been a hotspot for years. It is also barely a couple of hours drive from Douala, Cameroon's economic capital and home to SONARA, Cameroon's lone oil refinery. Thanks to its location, Limbe has a natural maritime defense system which was put to use as far back as the 18th and 19th centuries by the British whose *Men O' War* patrolled the area protecting maritime trade routes or tracking down rogue merchant ships involved in the Transatlantic slave trade – Man O' War Bay, located on the outskirts of Limbe is named after these famous navy ships. In addition to its natural defenses, Limbe is today a town ringed by a series of military installations which make it (at least on paper) one of the most secure cities on the West African coast.

Straight out of a Crime thriller

Given the preceding background, what happened in the scenic Down Beach in the night of September 27-28 was totally at odds with Limbe's reputation as a laid back (some say sleepy) town with excellent security. According to news reports, about 20-50 gunmen arrived in speedboats under cover of darkness and attacked four prominent banks. On paper, this brazen attack was a foolhardy one because this is precisely the kind of *grand banditisme* that the Government of Cameroon has been preparing for in the past decade with the creation of special task forces such as

- The GSO (*Groupement Special d'Operation* or Special Operations Task Force) for the police;
- The GPIGN (*Groupement Polyvalent d'Intervention de la Gendarmerie Nationale* or National Gendarmerie Multi-dimensional Intervention Task Force) for the Gendarmerie;
- The BIR (*Bataillon d'Intervention Rapide* or Rapid Intervention Battalion) for the Army

According to newspaper reports, at the time of the attack, members from these task forces had fanned out across the Southwest province (including Limbe), deployed to quell demonstrations and other activities by the SCNC in the run-up to October 1.

In addition, there were no less than six different military units/installations around Limbe whose reach extended as far as Douala to the West and Bakassi to the East:

- The Man O War Bay military base located some seven kilometers away from the crime scene;
- The Rapid Intervention Battalion (BIR) temporarily based at the Man O War Bay military;
- The Special Battalion for the Protection of SONARA (CSPS), about one nautical mile from the crime scene;
- The Bakassi Operation Delta Command with headquarters in Bota, also located barely a few miles from the crime scene;
- The Isongo Naval Base;
- Tiko Special Amphibious Battalion;
- To this we can add the Douala naval base from where forces could easily be deployed by sea to Limbe in a couple of hours.

Thus, the speedboat attack on the Limbe seafront which, according to eyewitness accounts, lasted about three hours, should in theory have been easily crushed with the disproportionate firepower and skills of the Special Forces in the area, some of whom have been specifically trained to tackle criminal activity involving the use of "small arms and light weapons." However things turned out differently. According to one news report:

> Residents were awakened... by sustained heavy gunfire... followed by sporadic firing into the air ...Using explosives, they blasted their way into four banks in central Limbe, seizing large sums of money. They barricaded roads leading into the town, repelled a group of Cameroonian soldiers and shot at the office of the local prefect.

By the time the assailants boarded their speedboat and fled into the night – unscathed – they had killed one civilian and wounded five, and made away with about 240 million FCFA (about half a million dollars) from one of the four banks.

Who Dunnit?

Initial reports suggested that the attacks may have been carried out by rebels from Bakassi or even from the Delta region in Nigeria, or by SCNC militants. Others surmised that this was an "internal job" carried out by members of the Cameroonian military, which would not only explain the surgical precision of the attacks but also the failure of military and security forces in the area to put up robust riposte. Other conspiracy theorists have linked the attack to US attempts to set up the United States Africa Command (AFRICOM), arguing that increased insecurity on the West African coast will force African regimes more receptive to the idea of setting up the AFRICOM headquarters and even bases in the region. Cameroon's Minister of Defense, on his part, tried to downplay the incident, arguing that the attack was not the work of a sophisticated group, but of neighborhood thugs: "In our opinion, these were not big thieves who came from afar. They must have been people who know the place well; people who live among us."

Wholesale Incompetence

Whichever version catches your fancy, one fact is irrefutable. Cameroonian military and security forces failed woefully. Even if this were the work of elements from within the military, it is unlikely, if not impossible, that they were able to involve all the military branches and special units in and around Limbe, including the local police and gendarmerie. So the incompetence argument still stands – Those shiny new navy speedboats never showed up; troops did not pour in from SONARA, Isongo, Man O' War Bay or elsewhere; the Special Forces who had infiltrated the province in anticipation of the October 1 showdown with Southern Cameroons "separatists" were a no-show, along with the local police and gendarmerie; the Rapid Intervention Battalion, which became a household name after the bloody February 2008 riots, intervened at a snails pace and when it finally made it to the scene it failed to neutralize the bandits. Of what use is a "rapid intervention battalion" which cannot be mobilized in less than 15-30 minutes? Worse, some BIR elements allegedly got lost on their way to Down Beach. According to *Eden Newspaper*, "At about 4:15 am, a special military intervention unit ran into Eden and others at Half Mile, Limbe and surprisingly inquired where the bandits were. On being told, they had sailed away. They expressed regret"...

Conspiracy or not, internal military plot or not, what happened in Limbe was a manifestation of a complete breakdown or the absence of communication and coordination between the different military and security branches in and around Limbe. The slow, clumsy and uncoordinated response demonstrated, if need be, the absence of a viable defense strategy for Limbe and other key port cities on the Cameroonian coast – a shortcoming which is criminal considering that these attacks did not just occur out of the blue:

- On December 5, 2007 a similar commando-style attack took place in Bata in neighboring Equatorial Guinea when "heavily armed gunmen attacked two banks simultaneously grabbing bags of cash and shooting passers-by before making off in speedboats into the Atlantic Ocean."
- Four months later on April 1, 2008, bandits launched a similar brazen daylight attack on two banks in Cotonou, Benin, carted away huge sums of money then fled off in speedboats.

And according to the French language daily, *Quotidien Mutations*, Cameroonian authorities were specifically warned months ago that banking institutions in Limbe and elsewhere on the Cameroonian cost were being targeted. This position is shared by *The Post* newspaper which clarifies that

> Limbe security, some time in December 2007, received instructions from Yaounde alerting them of a planned attack... Fako and Limbe administrators, at the time, took measures and security around the banks was stepped up. But as time went on, the measures lapsed.

These reports tie in with the Minister of Defense's declaration that the government knew of the attack in advance. In spite of this glaring security failure, the Minister of Defense nonetheless sought to shift the blame onto the banks, arguing that the they were expected, in fact required, to provide the first line of defense against such attacks with security forces simply coming in as a second line of defense. Thus, by failing to put in place a security system capable of repelling the commandos, the minister argued, the banks had failed in their duty! Please tell; how many banks in the world actually design their internal security in anticipation of an attack by 40-50 commandos armed with AK 47s, grenades and explosives, etc. who are able to hold off elite forces for 3 hours?

This was not a regular bank hold-up but a military attack. Thus, to argue that it was the place of banks to provide the "first line of defense" while security forces took their beauty sleep is a most illogical argument and a major copout – elsewhere, government officials have been fired for less!

Contaminated Evidence

The incompetence in Limbe continued well after the bandits had left. Seasoned investigators where shocked to note that the entire crime scene, from the banks to the streets, was never completely secured or cordoned off from the public. Barely hours after the attack, TV crews, government officials and other hangers-on were let into the banks for a series of "inspection tours", trampling over, touching and compromising potential evidence, even though the preliminary investigations were not yet wrapped up. As a result, it is unlikely that any credible or useful evidence will ever be obtained from the crime scene, that is, if a thorough and professional investigation was ever in the cards…

So should heads roll? Yes, they should! It is under this same military command and political leadership that 21 Cameroonian soldiers were killed in Bakassi November 21, 2007 after another surprise speedboat attack; it was under this same leadership that Divisional Officer for Kombo Abedimo, still in Bakassi, was ambushed and murdered along with four soldiers; and it is under their watch that the Limbe attack occurred. Downplaying the Limbe incident or blaming the banks does not cut it.

Unfortunately, all these events are taking place in a system where officials are never held accountable for their actions or inactions…

End Note

In 1982 the Biya regime decided that the name *Victoria* was too foreign for a Cameroonian town. So it decided to rename the town "Limbe". However, the name *Limbe* is neither indigenous to the area, nor to Cameroon for that matter; it is merely a corruption of *Lindbergh*, the name of the German engineer who in the early 20th century built the bridge across the river which separates the botanical gardens from "old" Victoria. Skeptics argue that the goal of the Biya regime was never to "indigenize" the town's name, and that the name change was merely part of a policy to strip Victoria of its erstwhile "British character." But that is a story for another day…

45

The Government of Cameroon on a PR Offensive in the United States

July 20, 2008: The July/August 2008 issue of *Foreign Affairs* (an influential American journal on international relations published by the Council on Foreign Relations) carries a "sponsored country report" on Cameroon titled *Cameroon at Crossroads*. This advertising supplement was produced by the Washington, DC-based lobbying firm, *SML Strategic Media* (SML), in collaboration with *Stratline Communication*, a Public Relations firm with headquarters in Geneva, Switzerland. According to its website, SML "provides strategic communications advice to corporations, organizations and governments around the world... We strongly believe that communications used strategically have the power to change perceptions, alter behaviors and create value."

Stratline Communication, on the other hand, specializes "in improving the image of the African continent". It seems to focus almost exclusively on Cameroon and has placed infomercials on behalf of the government of Cameroon in *Le Monde*, *Le Figaro*, *Fortune Magazine*, *New African*, etc. Its TV spots on Cameroon have also appeared on *France Television* and *TV5 International*. According to the sponsored ad,

> In two years, Cameroon will celebrate the 50th anniversary of its independence. The journey of the country from difficult beginnings to its present condition as a united entity with considerable positive prospects has been remarkable. This report gives an insight into the country's challenges as it grows into a hub for central African trade and interests. Cameroon is at the crossroads of development, and shows all the signs of having chosen the most fortuitous path.

It stresses that:

> As part of its policy to promote good governance, Cameroon is committed to the war on corruption, which has seen some major casualties from the highly competitive political elite. Although the anti-corruption moves come partly from donor pressure, it responds to a popular mood, often expressed in Cameroon's quasi-independent media.

The ad also makes a case for the Biya presidency by arguing that:

> The main opposition leader John Fru Ndi, head of the Social Democratic Front, who was a serious challenger in the 1992 elections, has become an increasingly isolated figure. Thus, with less influence being exerted by the opposition, **President Paul Biya is said to represent the best advocate of stability in Cameroon**.

Advertising Spree

The advertisement supplement in *Foreign Affairs*, a key player in shaping US foreign policy since World War II, is the second one that has appeared in the US this month. On July 2, another advertising supplement on Cameroon appeared in the *Washington Post*. According to the anti-corruption watch group *Global Integrity*, that supplement highlighted moves by the Biya regime to "consolidate the rule of law and fight corruption" and the increased transparency of public financial management, including "stepped up efforts to improve the quality of public spending" and "progressive measures [...] such as [public disclosure] of a summary of investments."

Intrigued by the advert, *Global Integrity* decided to find out more about it. Using the *Foreign Agents Registration Act*, which requires that all foreign governments lobbying the U.S. government or seeking to influence U.S. public opinion file regular reports about such activities with the U.S. Department of Justice, the group found out that over the years, the government of Cameroon has used PR firms such as Burson-Marsteller and Patton to spruce up its image in the US.

Most interestingly, it unearthed the actual contract of $350,000 a year [about 145 million FCFA] between the Government of Cameroon and *GoodWorks International* (GWI), an Atlanta-based consulting firm (co-chaired by former US ambassador Andrew Young) which placed the ad in the *Washington Post*. According to *Global Integrity*:

> The GWI contract with the Cameroonian Minister of Economy and Finance, signed in July 2007, details a 'strategy for securing a Compact under the Millennium Challenge Account [...] in as little as 12-18 months [by raising] some of the negative indicators that now make the country ineligible.' The contract also stipulates that 'GWI will assist the Cameroonian authorities to devise a communications strategy to show-case Cameroon's reform efforts.' Now, two weeks before the contract is due to expire, with a Compact yet to be achieved, the ad appeared in last week's Post...
>
> At a cost of "only" $350,000 a year – the price of Cameroon's annual retainer with GWI – perhaps we shouldn't be surprised when hundreds of millions of MCC dollars are at stake.

Is It Worth It?

Exactly one year ago, a firestorm erupted when another watch group revealed that the government of Cameroon had paid $250,000 (120 million FCFA back then) for an advertising supplement in *New York Times Magazine*. Back then, the widespread view was that the *New York Times Magazine* ad and others like it rarely led to concrete business leads or investment, and that they generally served no credible purpose other than a fleeting PR exposure for the Biya regime. As one commentator put it,

> ... as far as Cameroonians are concerned, the Biya regime has just "wasted"

about 120 million FCFA of taxpayers' money on a prestige project with no real benefit to Cameroon – no different from paying 250 million FCFA annually to those ineffective lobbyists in Washington, DC. After all, how many new businesses or even business leads resulted from the 2001 supplement [in the *New York Times*] or from the others published in *Le Monde*, *Jeune Afrique*, etc.?

If we assume that each advertising supplement averages about $250,000 (using last year's *New York Times* advert as the standard), it is not a stretch to assume that the Biya regime spends no less than five billion FCFA annually, worldwide, on these ads (that is, apart from the annual retainer paid to lobbyists and PR firms around the world, particularly in the US).

Without doubt, this is money flushed down the drain since very little, if anything, ever comes from these infomercials – i.e., apart from lining the pockets of lobbyists in Washington and elsewhere, the newspapers which carry these infomercials, and high ranking government officials back in Cameroon who negotiate these lucrative deals (a review of the transcripts of the Ondo Ndong trial is instructive in this regard). After about two decades of government-sponsored ads, the generally negative perceptions in the United States about the Biya regime and/or the investment climate in Cameroon have not changed fundamentally. In fact, Cameroon's US lobbyists will be hard-pressed to cite one example of a credible business venture that resulted from these ads.

If Cameroon is serious about changing the negative perceptions in the United States, it should start by transforming its embassy in Washington DC into a proactive and responsive diplomatic mission and establishing a fully functional trade mission staffed with qualified personnel who have a firm understanding of American business practices and are able to express themselves in English. Such a trade mission will also need modern communications tools such as a cutting-edge and regularly updated website with relevant information for potential investors, not stale propaganda pieces. Embassy employees should also step out of their comfort zone and participate regularly in the plethora of trade fairs that take place in the US each year, or organize business forums between Cameroonian and US businesses similar to those organized annually by the US government in Washington, DC and Chicago, etc.

This will be a good start but it will not be enough: The truth is that serious investors and policy makers in the US do not base investment or foreign policy decisions on infomercials. They rely on credible and vetted information from US government agencies or from international donor agencies and political and economic think tanks, which publish peer-reviewed country-by-country surveys and rankings on key political and economic indicators each year. These annual surveys/rankings include the *Corruption Perceptions Index* (Transparency International), *Doing Business* (World Bank), *Economic Freedom of the World Report* (Cato Institute), *Freedom in the World* (Freedom House), *Global Competitiveness Index*; *Travel & Tourism Competitiveness Report* (World Economic Forum), etc. A favorable mention in any of these reports, based on real and observable changes on the ground, is worth more than 10 infomercials in the *Washington Post*.

In the end, therefore, the real impetus for change can only come from within Cameroon. Establishing less cumbersome foreign investment procedures, making it easier for foreigners to do business in Cameroon, cracking down on the endemic and systemic corruption rather than indulging in show arrests and trials that leave the structures of corruption intact, making palpable moves towards more political freedoms etc., will be much more effective than any lobbying campaign by spinmeisters in the US or elsewhere.

Until then, Cameroon's PR campaign in the US will continue to be a catalogue of failures and frustrations that only serve to attract the wrath of watchdog groups such as *Global Integrity* and *Global Justice* which are only too happy to expose the seedy underbelly of Cameroon's lobbying efforts in the United States.

46

The Lake Nyos Disaster 20 Years After: Revisiting the Israeli Connection

August 21, 2006: On August 16, 1984, a gas eruption in Lake Monoun in the Western province of Cameroon killed 37 people. Reports revealed that "victims suffered vomiting, paralysis, and very rapid death; some lost the outer layer of their skin."

Two years later on August 21, 1986, a similar but more deadly incident occurred in Lake Nyos in the Northwest province. Toxic gas emanating from the lake killed some 1834 people along with 3500 livestock within a 12-mile radius.

According to D'Amato & Engel (*International Environmental Law Anthology*),

> The 'Dead Land' is a perfect allegory to describe the affected areas in the aftermath of this incident. The once fertile lands in the Camerounian villages of Sobum, Chah, Koshing, and Nyos lay barren and defoliated, with charred remains of burnt crops and carcasses of rotting animals. Survivors of the disaster who were evacuated complained of heartburn, eye lesions, and neurological problems such as monoplegia, a condition that affects one muscle or group of muscles, one limb or one part of the body, and paraplegia, paralysis of the lower part of the body and limbs.

One survivor, Pa Ful Jeremiah, describes the scene thus:

> We thought the lake had overflowed its banks. Many people were so confused especially women and children. In Panic and fright they ran out of houses to escape from unknown and dropped dead like chickens during a plague. Some of us managed to keep our heads straight and only survived through the will of God. The next day we discovered that hundreds of people had died. They had burns on their bodies. It was only after another day that the first people arrived and decided that we should arrange to bury the dead. (Cited in *Times & Life*, Vol. 1, no. 4. Sept. 1991, p. 7)

From the beginning, scientists were confounded by the disaster. As George Kling, an ecologist at the University of Michigan recalls in *The Guardian* newspaper (UK), "It was one of the most baffling disasters scientists have ever investigated. Lakes just don't rise up and wipe out thousands of people."

In his 2003 award-winning article on the Lake Nyos and Monoun disasters, Kevin Krajick writes that "Conspiracy theories abound in Cameroon, where unexplained events are often attributed to political intrigues." And that was exactly what happened immediately after the Nyos disaster. With the scientists unable to pinpoint the cause of this unprecedented event, the Cameroonian public quickly concluded that this was a man-made disaster. This belief was reinforced by numerous stories of alleged suspicious happenings in the Nyos area in the months preceding the explosion. According to one version which appeared in an article on the *Ambazonia Indymedia* website,

> the most conspicuous incident prior to the explosion was the fact that the traditional ruler of Nyos and the Royal family moved out of the village a few days before the explosion... Did the Traditional ruler of Nyos know of a timed explosion, too? Other reports, even from the Cameroun radio stations, said many months earlier "a strange white man" or 'a geologist' had visited the Lake and warned that people should evacuate the village before a certain date.

The most prevalent theory was that the gas emission was due to the detonation of a neutron bomb in a secret military test. This theory obviously originated from national and international news reports, which constantly compared the effects of the gas emission to that of a neutron bomb. For example, according to an August 26, 1986 article in the *Washington Post*,

> Reporters in the area described it as looking like the aftermath of a neutron bomb, with damage only to living things, and no visible effect on the village huts and other buildings. A few chickens seemed to be the only animals to have survived in the three hardest-hit villages.

This theory got a boost a few months later when the April 14 1987 issue of the *National Examiner*, an American tabloid noted for its questionable and sensationalistic stories, claimed that the gas emission,

> was really a magnetic bomb perfected at secret hollow earth bunkers beneath Las Vegas, Nevada. The so-called underground nuclear tests there were actually strategic bombing of hollow earth forward attack lines using similar magnetic weapons. The nuclear blasts were merely side-effects of the device.

The Prime Suspects

Depending on which version catches your fancy, the neutron bomb was exploded in Lake Nyos either by the Americans, the French, or the Israelis. However, the most notable, most persistent and most widespread theory is that it was the handiwork of the Israelis. 20 years later this theory is still firmly rooted in the Cameroonian psyche as comments on a recent story on the *Postnewsline* website about planned Israeli development projects in the Northwest province indicate.

Proponents of the Israeli theory point to the fact that barely days (some say hours) after the incident, the Israeli Prime Minister arrived in Cameroon with a planeload of medical doctors and scientists. As the *New York Times* reported on August 26, 1986,

When Prime Minister Shimon Peres arrived from Israel for a one-day visit on the restoration of Israeli-Cameroon relations, he brought with him a 17-member medical team along with tons of medical supplies. The Israeli team went straight to the Nios area as soon as it arrived this morning. Other Aid Is Offered.

Conspiracy theorists wonder how the Israelis were able assemble the scientific team and be in Cameroon barely a few hours after, or within 48 hours of the incident, even though news of the incident filtered out to the world some 72 hours after it occurred. They argue that this could not have been possible without any prior knowledge of the event. In an article on his blog, Cameroonian Journalist Ntemfac Ofege writes that:

> The arrival in Cameroon of the then Israeli Prime Minister, Shimon Peres, with a fully-equipped hospital plane, on a so-called State visit less than 48 hours after the Lake Nyos explosion, is very suspicious.
> Actually, the Israelis remain Mr. Biya's guardian angels. They not only train and equip his close guards (the presidential guard) but they also monitor events in Cameroon from their Mont Febe hideout and other locations in Yaounde.

Ofege adds that:

> Mr. Biya has also not reacted to a Denis Sassou Nguessou interview published in a San Francisco newspaper suggesting that the Lake Nyos gas explosion was an Israeli thermonuclear device. Mr. Sassou Nguesso said in that interview that he was approached by the Israeli to test the device in his country and he said no. Mr. Biya apparently accepted the indecent proposition.

Ambazonian activist Justice Mbuh who has written extensively about the Lake Nyos disaster on numerous Cameroonian Internet fora has also pointed to "the very perfect coincidence of the Israeli Prime Minister's visit to Cameroun with the explosion," and insists that the Cameroonian government "accepted monies to test weapons of mass destruction in our country's beautiful lake Nyos…" In his most recent posting on the Nyos disaster, he writes that:

> suspected gas was used to test mass killing in the name of natural disaster at Lake Nyos. It was published in Cameroun newspapers that Paul Biya took Ten Billion Dollars to allow the testing of a neutron Bomb-like weapon. The effects of the devastation are now very similar to what we are seeing from Lebanon. Now it seems Israel has modified it twenty years after, making it a target-specific weapon with same but more deadly effects than did the Nyos mass killings!

Wrong Timeline

Evidently, if the timeline presented by the conspiracy theorists is correct, then the presence of the Israeli team is hard to explain and merits closer scrutiny. But is this timeline correct? In an attempt to answer this key question, I spent some time looking at news reports from 20 years ago about the disaster and the visit of the Israeli Prime Minister to Cameroon.

According to news reports and stories from survivors, the explosion happened on the night of Thursday August 21, 1986, around 9:00 p.m. It wasn't until Saturday August 23rd that the first group of outsiders, led by Reverend Father Tenhorn, arrived on the scene and began burying the victims. And, it would be another 24 hours before the national and international community became aware of what had occurred in Nyos. As soon as news of the disaster broke, the international mobilization began. According to a BBC report at the time,

> Scientists from the United States and France are on their way to investigate the lake. They will bring with them rescue teams and emergency aid to help the survivors. The US has pledged $25,000 in immediate aid, while France, Britain and other Western European countries have promised logistical support. The Israeli Prime Minister, Shimon Peres, has said he will not cancel his state visit to Cameroon, due to start on Monday ... He said he would be bringing a medical team and equipment for treating the victims.

Prime Minister Shimon Peres did arrive in Cameroon on Monday August 25 with the Israeli medical and scientific team as planned exactly four days after the explosion – enough time for the Israelis to put together a complete medical and scientific team. The Medical team was still holed up in Bamenda 24 hours after it arrived in Cameroon. A *Washington Post* report filed from Yaounde on August 26, 1986 was categorical on this point:

> No foreign disaster team has yet reached the lakeside area.
> An Israeli medical team, which arrived here yesterday with Prime Minister Shimon Peres, was waiting this morning in the provincial capital of Bamenda, about 40 miles from the lake. Although the team plans to set a field hospital closer to the site, officials acknowledged that the fatality rate was so high that there was little they could do beyond treating a relatively small number of injured survivors.

Conclusion

So what really happened at Lake Nyos? The scientific community seems to have concluded that it was a natural disaster caused by toxic gases trapped beneath the lake which rose to the surface – a Limnic eruption – hence ongoing attempts to degas the lake. I am in no position to confirm or refute this scientific conclusion. However, I believe there is ample evidence showing that the "perfect coincidence theory" regarding the Israelis is based on a false premise and wrong timeline. While this does not in itself eliminate the military test theory, it definitely knocks down one of the pillars on which the Israeli military test theory hinges, and gives us reason to pause.

So what do you think? Was the Lake Nyos disaster a natural disaster or man-made one? Was the killer a neutron bomb or Carbon-dioxide? And, do you believe the Israelis are responsible?

47

Zimbabwe at 27: When a Fairy Tale Becomes a Gory Nightmare...

April 18, 2007: The year was 1979 and on Radio Cameroon (there was no TV then) Zimbabwe was a permanent if not dominant fixture on the international news. The black government of Bishop Abel Muzorewa – a suspect government, had replaced the racist Ian Smith regime, which, for all intents and purposes, was merely an extension of the racist Smith regime. Zimbabwean nationalists in exile led by Joshua Nkomo and Robert Mugabe fiercely challenged the farce. And the rest of the world agreed. In the end, Muzorewa was dragged kicking and screaming to London for talks at Lancaster House under the auspices of Lord Carrington. One didn't need to be a grown up back then to understand what was at stake; white supremacist rule (hiding behind Muzorewa's black face) vs. black majority rule represented by Joshua Nkomo and Robert Mugabe. How we envied Zimbabwe when the Lancaster talks ended with an agreement for new internationally supervised elections!

This was a time when Cameroon was solidly under the control of a dictator called Ahmadou Ahidjo; an era of rule by terror, which a generation of Cameroonians cannot begin to relate to and even occasionally romanticize – the result of a quarter of a century of misrule by Ahidjo's successor Paul Biya....

And how we again turned green with envy when Zimbabwe became independent on April 18, 1980 after free and fair elections that saw Mugabe besting his old comrade in arms Joshua Nkomo! Racist Rhodesia was finally dead and black-led Zimbabwe born. Even the great Bob Marley, that immortal icon of our generation, showed up for the party to sing his famous tribute to the new nation:

> *Every man gotta right to decide his own destiny,*
> *And in this judgement there is no partiality.*
> *So arm in arms, with arms, we'll fight this little struggle,*
> *'Cause that's the only way we can overcome our little trouble.*
> *...*
> *Natty Dread it in-a (Zimbabwe);*
> *Set it up in (Zimbabwe);*
> *Mash it up-a in-a Zimbabwe (Zimbabwe);*
> *Africans a-liberate (Zimbabwe), yeah.*

But that euphoria did not last long and the honeymoon was soon over. In 1982 the affable Joshua Nkomo was accused of attempting to overthrow Mugabe's regime. Mugabe then unleashed a six-year reign of terror in Nkomo's native Matabeleland where, according to some estimates, the North-Korean trained Fifth Brigade allegedly killed about 40,000 people – nearly twice the number who died during the war of liberation. Mugabe called the campaign "Operation

Gukuruhundi," meaning "the wind that sweeps away the chaff." Zimbabwe had lost its luster. And suddenly, Paul Biya's Cameroon felt a million times safer ... and freer!!!

No more internal power struggle;
We come together to overcome the little trouble.
Soon we'll find out who is the real revolutionary,
'Cause I don't want my people to be contrary.

By the time Mugabe got his way and imposed one-party rule in the late eighties, Zimbabwe was faithfully following that disheartening political blueprint which newly-independent African states used in the 1960s; excessively high hopes at the birth of the nation followed by a short honeymoon; then the imposition of one-man-one-party rule and the jailing of political opponents; the pauperization of the masses and the illicit enrichment of a select few; the institution of a culture of fear and brutal repression; economic stagnation and the collapse of the middle class; the descent into the abyss and the loss of innocence.

To divide and rule could only tear us apart;
In everyman chest, mm - there beats a heart.
So soon we'll find out who is the real revolutionaries;
And I don't want my people to be tricked by mercenaries

But the worse was yet to come with the bungled land distribution campaign and Mugabe's maniacal obsession with hanging to power whatever the cost. Whatever one's take on the historical legitimacy (or lack thereof) of the land distribution campaign, it is now evident that this was a fly-by-night operation whose implementation was driven primarily by cynical political and populist motives. This was not a carefully planned program aimed at rectifying the errors of the past and at jump-starting the Zimbabwean economy. The end result is there for all to see. As Zimbabwean Bishops lament in a recent pastoral letter:

> Following a radical land reform programme seven years ago, many people are today going to bed hungry and wake up to a day without work. Hundreds of companies were forced to close. Over 80 per cent of the people of Zimbabwe are without employment. Scores risk their lives week after week in search of work in neighbouring countries. Inflation has soared to over 1,600 per cent, and continues to rise, daily. It is the highest in the world and has made the life of ordinary Zimbabweans unbearable...

The downhill slide would continue with the mass eviction of "illegal dwellers" across the country in the infamous "operation *Murambatsvina*" (get rid of the filth) of 2005. The operation, which had strong political and partisan undertones, only worsened the socio-economic situation in the country. According a United Nations fact finding mission:

An estimated that some 700,000 people in cities across the country have lost either their homes, their source of livelihood or both. Indirectly, a further 2.4 million people have been affected in varying degrees. Hundreds of thousands of women, men and children were made homeless, without access to food, water and sanitation, or health care. Education for thousands of school age children has been disrupted. Many of the sick, including those with HIV and AIDS, no longer have access to care. The vast majority of those directly and indirectly affected are the poor and disadvantaged segments of the population. They are, today, deeper in poverty, deprivation and destitution, and have been rendered more vulnerable.

In recent months, Mugabe has upped the ante on political repression and recklessness as he uses every bloody trick in the book to hang on to power in perpetuity; the hounding, jailing, torture and even murder of anyone who is rightly or wrongly considered an enemy of the regime is now a national hobby.

Today, Zimbabwe is a shadow of its old self, a fairytale transformed into a gory nightmare right before our eyes. That rainbow nation where black and white were supposed to live happily ever after, where political opponents were supposed to carry on with the business of nation building without fear or repression, is now a distant and even laughable dream. Zimbabwe has gone full circle, right back to the worst days of good old Rhodesia as the Bishops point out in their letter:

> None of the unjust and oppressive security laws of the Rhodesian State have been repealed; in fact, they have been reinforced by even more repressive legislation… in particular. It almost appears as though someone sat down with the Declaration of Human Rights and deliberately scrubbed out each in turn. [S]oon after Independence, the power and wealth of the tiny white Rhodesian elite was appropriated by an equally exclusive black elite, some of whom have governed the country for the past 27 years through political patronage. Black Zimbabweans today fight for the same basic rights they fought for during the liberation struggle. It is the same conflict between those who possess power and wealth in abundance, and those who do not; between those who are determined to maintain their privileges of power and wealth at any cost, even at the cost of bloodshed, and those who demand their democratic rights and a share in the fruits of independence....

Zimbabwe, says one news dispatch,

> …is reaching the end game, witnessing the last, desperate throes of a regime that has destroyed one of Africa's few successful economies, plunged millions of people into grinding poverty and led to the deaths of tens of thousands from malnutrition and lack of medical care.

This view is shared by the Bishops who warn that:

> The confrontation in our Country has now reached a flashpoint. As the suffering population becomes more insistent, generating more and more pressure through boycotts, strikes, demonstrations and uprisings, the State responds with ever harsher oppression through arrests, detentions, banning orders, beatings and torture. In our judgement, the situation is extremely volatile.

The Bishops add that what Zimbabwe desperately needs is "a new people-driven Constitution that will guide a democratic leadership chosen in free and fair elections that will offer a chance for economic recovery under genuinely new policies." For that to happen, African countries, particularly those in the Southern African region led by South Africa, must bring pressure to bear on Mugabe. Unfortunately they have been reluctant to openly take on Mugabe, preferring a failed behind-the-scenes diplomacy that has only emboldened Mugabe.

As we look at the situation unfolding in Zimbabwe we cannot help but be very sad at the lost opportunities, the broken promises and the shattered dreams. When and how will it end? Will Zimbabweans finally get the right to decide their own destiny as Bob Marley urged back in 1979? Will Thabo Mbeki and other African leaders stop pussyfooting and finally live up to their historic responsibility to the Zimbabwean people by calling Mugabe to order? How much longer will this horror movie last?

How much more of this punishment can the people of Zimbabwe endure?

Reference

Bob Marley & the Wailers (1979). "Zimbabwe." [B. Marley] On *Survival* [Record]. Kingston, Jamaica: Tuff Gong/Island records.

Catholic Bishops' Conference. (2007). *God Hears the Cry of the Oppressed.* Pastoral Letter by the Zimbabwe Catholic Bishops' Conference on the Current Crisis of Our Country Holy Thursday, 5 April 2007.

48

Obama and Africa: Change and Changelessness in US Foreign Policy

January 28, 2009: President Obama's admonishment of those leaders "who cling to power through corruption and deceit and the silencing of dissent" during his January 20 inaugural address has been widely interpreted in Africa to mean that, unlike previous US administrations, the Obama administration will go after leaders who oppress their people, violate human rights and prevent the growth of genuine democracy. In fact, in the past week, African newspapers, blogs, and Internet forums have been replete with gleeful commentary announcing the impending discomfiture of those African dictators who refuse to "unclench their fists."

As I watch the unfolding euphoria, I cannot help but think back to an era long gone when another generation of Africans placed so much hope on another American president who embodied **Hope** and **Change** (history really does repeat itself...) That president was Bill Clinton. That generation of Africans who witnessed the end of the cold war and the coming of the "East wind" believed that the Clinton administration would be unrelenting in promoting the establishment of democracy, the rule of law and good governance in Africa. Alas! 16 years later, the democracy, which many hoped for has been a fleeting reality only in a handful of African countries.

Recently, I stumbled across a contribution that I made in a special January 1993 issue of *Cameroon Post* dedicated to the Clinton Inaugural. It is uncanny how the expectations that Africans have of the Obama administration today are exactly the same ones that they had of the Clinton administration in 1993. Here are excerpts of the 1993 article, which we can now read with the benefit of hindsight:

Will US Policy Change After George Bush? *Cameroon Post,* **Special 42nd Inaugural, January 13-20, 1993, p. 15**

On November 3, 1992, the American people put an end to the twelve-year Republican control of the American executive by electing Bill Clinton and Al Gore as President and Vice President respectively... Most Africans, particularly those craving for genuine democracy, expect the new administration to launch an uncompromising campaign against those regimes still holding out against political liberalism on the continent...

Can the forces of change on the continent safely rely on the new team in Washington?

[...]

In a recently published book on US foreign policy, Michael Clough says that "the Bush administration... failed to provide leadership on African issues"... Clough says that while middle level officials involved with Africa had a relatively free hand on the continent, they nonetheless had to respect three State Department injunctions: "Don't spend much money, don't take stands that might create domestic controversies, don't let Africa complicate policy towards other more important parts of the world."

Today, Africans expect a more aggressive policy from Democrats. In fact, their November victory is looked upon with much relish because Democrats are generally credited with a more humane approach to Third World issues, particularly towards human rights issues – one of the most important legacies of the Jimmy Carter era.

Is Drastic Change Possible?

Former Secretary of State Henry Kissinger once pointed out that "one of the most unsettling things for foreigners is the impression that our foreign policy can be changed by any new president on the basis of the president's personal preference". This is the reason behind the widespread belief that the "new Kennedy" whose entire campaign was based on the need for "change" will change things for the better. However, in spite of all the rhetoric about change, American foreign policy has basically been consistent over the years. It has been more of a gardening exercise than an act of bulldozing; a phenomenon described as the "change and changelessness" of US foreign policy. Clinton seems to have espoused this view when in his first post-election statement on foreign affairs he reminded the world that "... America's administrations change, America's fundamental interests do not."

As Desler, Gleb and Lanike have underlined, "serious nations do not redefine their national interests every few years... Foreign accomplishments generally come about because a nation has been able to sustain a course of action over a long period of time"...

Secretary of Sate John Foster Dulles usually argued that "A consistent and dependable national course must have a base broader than the particular beliefs of the those who from time to time hold office", and the young Turks in the White House will definitely adhere tot this cautious policy, particularly in a continent that is more of a liability than an asset on all counts.

The Likely Scenario

[...]

Thanks to the new team in the White House, there will definitely be renewed lingering interest in African affairs in general, but natural areas of American interest like... Kenya, South Africa...will drain most of America's energy and imagination.

In other parts of the continent, particularly in areas within the French sphere of influence, the US, while frowning at the anti-democratic antics of the rulers, will avoid moves what might be interpreted as going against French interests. The radical shift in American policy expected by African masses will rarely take place...

Roger Hilsman in *To Move a Nation* is of the opinion that "Rather than through grand decisions and grand alternatives, (foreign) policy changes seem to come through a series of slight modifications of existing policy with the policy emerging slowly and haltingly by small and usually tentative steps, a process of trial and error in which policy zigs and zags, reverses itself and then moves forward in a series of incremental steps".

This holds true for US policy of the next four years. There will be a lot of high-sounding political rhetoric and grandiose slogans promising new courses of action in Africa, but the changes will affect more the shadow than the substance and will be more symbolic than real. The low cost, low profile, no controversy policy of the Bush years will be maintained, albeit under a new banner.

Fast Forward 2009

A decade after Bill Clinton left office, the predictions in that 1993 article turned out to be generally true. The Biyas, the Bongos, etc., who were around when Clinton became president are still around. And with regards to promoting democracy on the continent, the US promised more than it could deliver. The Clinton administration made the right noises about Africa, but there was no dramatic change in America's Africa policy.

The lesson from all this? It is very difficult, and in some cases virtually impossible, to change American foreign policy significantly, especially in those regions where American interests are marginal. Having an American President with a direct connection to and an apparent heightened interest in Africa will not automatically lead to African strongmen tumbling down like dominoes.

The fact that so many Africans, from all walks of life, are counting heavily on President Obama to "bring" democracy to Africa is a clear signal that we have failed to grasp the real significance of Obama's political story, and are therefore unable to appropriate and adapt the Obama playbook to African realities. The message from Obama's improbable presidential run and his equally improbable victory is a fairly simple but not very obvious one for Africa; change activists on the continent must start working towards creating inclusive and vibrant grassroots political coalitions that will be able, in the long run, to successfully take on the political establishment. As Mufor Atanga noted on the eve of the November 2008 presidential elections:

> the importance and relevance of a likely Obama election as president of the most powerful state in the world lies in the lessons that could be drawn by the new generation of Africans who aspire for leadership positions on the continent. This is largely with respect to how Obama has been able to build a machinery that took on the establishment and, against all odds, emerged victorious... how he's been able to inspire the youth to have an interest in the electoral process.

There are invaluable lessons of organizational and transformational leadership here, and those who aspire to take on the dinosaurs in Africa will do well to study carefully. Obama's greatest contribution to Africa will be, if his campaign succeeds, in catalysing - like in the late 1980s and early 1990s - a new wave of, but this time a more sustained, democratic reawakening on the continent.

Sure, this is a tall order in a continent replete with authoritarian regimes with little or no democratic traditions and which are only too anxious to crush all forms of dissent. But it is not an impossible task. It is time for Africans to fold up their sleeves and go to work, rather than wait for the *miracle solution* from Big Brother Obama. If change is going to come to Africa, it will be primarily, if not solely, due to the efforts of Africans themselves.

References

Clough, M. (1992). *Free at last?: U.S. policy toward Africa and the end of the Cold War.* New York: Council on Foreign Relations Press.

Destler, I. M., Gelb, L. H., & Lake, A. (1984). *Our own worst enemy: The unmaking of American foreign policy.* New York: Simon and Schuster.

Hilsman, R. (1967). *To move a nation: The politics of foreign policy in the administration of John F. Kennedy.* Garden City, N.Y.: Doubleday.

49

In Search of the Elusive "Big Foot": Where are the Cameroonian Bloggers?

<u>July 07, 2006:</u> In March 2006, South Africa organized its second annual *South African Blog Award* to recognize and celebrate the best South African blogs. The vibrancy of the South African blogging community was evident from the wide range of blog categories that were short-listed. On June 1, 2006, Kenyan bloggers celebrated the first ever *Kenyan Bloggers Day* during which Kenyan bloggers around the world wrote about the state of Kenyan society, presented their vision of Kenya, and celebrated the ties that bind the tight-knit Kenyan blogging community. Ethiopia, which has one of the pioneer blogging communities on the continent, caught the attention of the international media in November 2005 when Ethiopian bloggers gave minute-by-minute accounts of post-election political disturbances in that country. Thanks to these bloggers, the world was able to get an alternative narrative of what was happening in the country. As a BBC report later pointed out:

> These eyewitness accounts of Ethiopia's November unrest did not come from the news wires or even on the BBC News website, where thousands of emails were received, but from a small but growing set of citizen journalists - Ethiopia's band of bloggers.

With over 400 blogs, Nigeria has one of the most dynamic African blogging communities. Although Nigerian bloggers do not form a tight-knit community like the Kenyan bloggers, they have the same diversity in the issues that they tackle – personal musings, politics, music, sports, alternative lifestyles, expatriate views, etc. While they are a very small minority relative to the population of the country, the visibility of Nigerian bloggers (many of whom write from within Nigeria) is steadily growing. And it is not far-fetched to imagine that with a little more organization, the Nigerian blogging community will become an influential political force within the next decade.

The Watchdogs

Increasingly, African bloggers in the Diaspora and on the continent are acting as watchdogs of the continent's fledging democracies, and challenging the last vestiges of oppression; covering stories and issues ignored by mainstream media, particularly the West; and presenting a more upbeat and positive image of Africa and Africans. Says a leading a leading Zimbabwean blogger, *The Zimbabwean Pundit* (http://zimpundit.blogspot.com/), in an article on the state of blogging in Africa:

> Far removed from the grotesque images of yet another civil war, or pictures of extreme poverty and hunger from the slums on the continent as is usually the portrayed on mainstream media, Africa's bloggers are telling

the continent's story from a rare and fresh perspective. Unrestrained by neither geographic boundaries, nor the repressive tendencies of corrupt regimes at home, African bloggers are sharp, incisive, and precise in their perspective on the problems that riddle the continent. And as blogs emerge as a credible news source, the African blogosphere is growing every day. African bloggers have seized the opportunity to share the continent's story with the rest of the world.

As in all ventures of that involve any form of critical appraisal of the African socio-political landscape, African blogging has a seamy and dangerous side. In many African countries, bloggers face the same trials and tribulations as print and radio journalists, and they can be jailed for their views. In May 2006, the Zimbabwean Parliament passed the *Interception of Communications Bill* which is meant, among other things, to put a leash on the Zimbabwean blogging community and punish those bloggers who run afoul of the Mugabe regime, particularly those blogging from inside Zimbabwe. The effects of the bill are already being felt. According to *EnoughZimbabwe*;

> The Interception of Communications Bill is having a pronounced toll on the Zimbabwean blogosphere. Posts from domestic bloggers have slowed down noticeably over the last two weeks. Despite this tragic reality, several cyberactivists continue to chronicle the largely unheard Zimbabwean story.

A potential victim of the draconian communications bill is *Zimbabwean Pundit* who worried about his/her fate months before the communications bill was passed:

> The thought of what fate would meet my family and me as well as the other Zimbabwean bloggers if we were discovered sends a chill down my spine and is the impetus behind several protective measures I take. Fortunately for me, I can still relish the opportunity to have this thought. There are several African bloggers who have been killed, imprisoned, and persecuted for their efforts. I'm thankful.

In spite of the daunting technological challenges and the heavy hand of repressive regimes, African bloggers are slowly coming of age against all odds and making their voices heard. In the coming years, many of them will play key roles in the public discussions and debates that will shape future of their respective countries. Also, with the passage of time and the ubiquity of blogging tools, the African blogosphere will become more balanced with more bloggers writing directly from the continent, and focusing on non-political issues (gender, development, culture, economics, etc.,) that are also relevant to continent and its people.

So where does Cameroon fit in the picture of the emerging African blogosphere?

Cameroon Again on the Fringes

There are over 1000 Cameroonian Internet discussion forums – some with thousands of members – that are kept alive thanks to the daily contributions of some of the most prolific writers in the African cyber community. Cameroonian forums such as CamNetwork have an average of about 5000 messages per month. Paradoxically, this robust presence on Internet forums has not translated into a vibrant Cameroonian blogging community. In fact, there are virtually no Cameroonian bloggers out there....

A search of the *Technorati* the blog aggregator which currently tracks 47.1 million sites and 2.7 billion links, and Blogger.com, the largest and most popular blogging platform, pulled up only a handful Cameroon-related blogs, over 95 per cent of which are run by expatriates (American Peace Corps Volunteers, Christian missionaries, etc.) resident in the country. Indigenous Cameroonian presence in the blogosphere is primarily due to *JimbiMedia*, a US-based multimedia company founded by Dibussi Tande and Emil Mondoa which has been creating free blogs for Cameroonian academics, political analysts, writers, and journalists since 2004. In fact, very few Cameroonians have taken up on the offer for free high-end blogs. And, the dozens of *JimbiMedia* blogs are not updated regularly. Most simply serve as repositories for articles published by their owners in scholarly journals, newspapers and magazines, rather than spaces for fresh and off-the-cuff commentary and debates on events in Cameroon. An exception to this rule is *Scribbles from the Den*, arguably the most popular Cameroonian blog, which is updated regularly and keeps pace with socio-political developments in Cameroon.

The leading Cameroonian blog – another *JimbiMedia* creation – is *Postnewsline* (http://www.postnewsline.com) which is run by Cameroon's leading English language newspaper, *The Post*. With over two million hits to date, *Postnewsline* is updated twice a week with articles from the print edition of *The Post*. The blog became a big hit within the Cameroonian community during the violent strike at the University of Buea in April-May 2005. Thanks to an army of citizen journalists armed with cameras, the blog was able to publish minute-by-minute accounts of the student protest and the resulting police crackdown, along with pictures that ultimately became the iconic images of the student uprising. During this period, over of 1000 comments were posted on the blog by Cameroonians in the Diaspora and in Cameroon who could get the true story of events only from the Postnewsline blog. Surprisingly, even though *The Post* became a household name thanks to its aggressive coverage of this uprising, and is arguably the most visited Cameroonian news website today, it has not fully capitalized on the blogging tools at its disposal to do more "citizen reporting" similar to its coverage of the UB crisis.

According to a Cameroonian cyberspace observer, two reasons explain the paucity of Cameroonian blogs. First, most Cameroonians are still very unfamiliar with blogging tools, many of which are free. They do not realize that unlike conventional websites, blogs can be maintained even by the most technologically-challenged individuals. Second, many of the individuals who are very active on Cameroonian Internet forums are wary of the discipline, commitment, and consistency required to maintain a successful blog. They would rather stick to the "free style" of standard (and relatively safe) subscriber-based Internet fora such as those hosted by *Yahoogroups*.

No Excuses!

In June 2004, Cameroon was paralyzed for days following a cyber rumor that President Paul Biya had died in Geneva. For an entire weekend, thousands of Cameroonians invaded the country's cybercafés to read every available information about the President's alleged death. In the Diaspora, Cameroon Internet fora and chat rooms had the highest traffic ever. According to Francis Nyamnjoh,

> The rumour arguably the most widely disseminated ever in the history of the country, benefited from a fascinating combination of the Internet, the cellphone, word of mouth and a popular hunger for democracy to spread far and wide, embarrassing a government unfamiliar with dealing with alternative media.

This incident proved, if need be, that the Internet is the most powerful and most affordable tool for information, sensitization and mobilization, and that it has the potential to shape public opinion and bring pressure to bear on the powers that be. The Biya regime understood this after the 2004 event and even created a committee to monitor internet postings on and about Cameroon.

Thanks to blogs, web publishing is no longer the exclusive domain of computer geeks with mastery of bytes and bits, and of html and other programming codes. It is now the common man's missile which any individual comfortable enough to use hotmail or Yahoo mail can set up and share his or her thoughts with the rest of the world. Says *Zimbabwean Pundit*,

> This miracle of cyberspace—that it allows for cheap communication unfettered by geopolitical boundaries—has made it possible for the African odyssey to share center stage alongside the big issues in the west, thanks in part to Africa's bloggers. The latest news from Africa is available to anyone in the world with access to the internet.

Given the number of free blog hosting sites that now exist, Cameroonians have no excuse for being at the rear of Africa's ongoing blogging revolution. And, if the hundreds of comments posted everyday on the PostNewsline blog and the thousands of write-ups posted daily on various Cameroonian Internet forums are any indication, Cameroonians already have the tools to join the blogging bandwagon.

With municipal and parliamentary elections around the corner, with the perennial "Anglophone Problem" taking dramatic twist and turns every day, with the Biya regime stubbornly trying to pass a new set of "liberty laws" to muzzle the Cameroonian press, and with the Cameroonian Diaspora trying to make its voice heard on issues such as dual citizenship and Diaspora voting rights, the time is just right for a Cameroonian blogging revolution. Of course, not everyone is a political animal. The blogging tent is big enough for those who are more interested in the economy, education, technology, humor, literature, culture, etc.

Let a thousand blogs blossom and a hundred schools of thought contend!!!

Reference

Heavens, A. (20 December 2005). *African bloggers find their voice*. BBC Focus on *Africa magazine*. Retrieved March 15, 2009 from: http://news.bbc.co.uk/2/hi/africa/4512290.stm

www.ingramcontent.com/pod-product-compliance
Lightning Source LLC
Chambersburg PA
CBHW020301010526
44108CB00037B/367